Lecture Notes in Computer Science 14379

Founding Editors

Gerhard Goos
Juris Hartmanis

The series Lecture Notes in Computer Science (LNCS), including its subseries Lecture Notes in Artificial Intelligence (LNAI) and Lecture Notes in Bioinformatics (LNBI), has established itself as a medium for the publication of new developments in computer science and information technology research, teaching, and education.

LNCS enjoys close cooperation with the computer science R & D community, the series counts many renowned academics among its volume editors and paper authors, and collaborates with prestigious societies. Its mission is to serve this international community by providing an invaluable service, mainly focused on the publication of conference and workshop proceedings and postproceedings. LNCS commenced publication in 1973.

Yuan Xue · Chen Chen · Chao Chen ·
Lianrui Zuo · Yihao Liu

Editors

Data Augmentation, Labelling, and Imperfections

Third MICCAI Workshop, DALI 2023
Held in Conjunction with MICCAI 2023
Vancouver, BC, Canada, October 12, 2023
Proceedings

Springer

Editors

Yuan Xue (ID)
Ohio State University
Columbus, OH, USA

Chao Chen (ID)
Stony Brook University
Stony Brook, NY, USA

Yihao Liu (ID)
Johns Hopkins University
Baltimore, MD, USA

Chen Chen (ID)
University of Sheffield
Sheffield, UK

Lianrui Zuo (ID)
Johns Hopkins University
Baltimore, MD, USA

ISSN 0302-9743   ISSN 1611-3349 (electronic)
Lecture Notes in Computer Science
ISBN 978-3-031-58170-0   ISBN 978-3-031-58171-7 (eBook)
https://doi.org/10.1007/978-3-031-58171-7

This Springer imprint is published by the registered company Springer Nature Switzerland AG
The registered company address is: Gewerbestrasse 11, 6330 Cham, Switzerland

Paper in this product is recyclable.

Preface

This volume presents the proceedings of the 3rd International Workshop on Data Augmentation, Labeling, and Imperfections (DALI 2023), held on October 12, 2023, in Vancouver, Canada, in conjunction with the 26th International Conference on Medical Image Computing and Computer Assisted Intervention (MICCAI 2023). Building on the success of DALI 2021 and DALI 2022, the workshop continued to foster a collaborative environment for addressing the critical challenges associated with medical data, particularly focusing on data, labeling, and dealing with data imperfections in the context of medical image analysis.

The increasing demand for large volumes of labeled data in medical image analysis is challenged by the heterogeneity of the data and the high cost and variability of expert annotations. These challenges are even more pronounced for rare conditions, underscoring the importance of the workshop's goal to unite the MICCAI community in rigorously investigating these issues, promoting novel research, and sharing methodologies to overcome these hurdles.

This year's workshop attracted 25 submissions globally, with 23 undergoing a rigorous double-blind review process after an initial screening for formatting issues, resulting in 16 high-quality papers being accepted for publication. The program featured 6 oral presentations and poster presentations for all accepted papers, showcasing the depth and breadth of research in this field. We were honored to have distinguished keynote speakers at DALI 2023 who are leaders in their respective fields: Dimitris N. Metaxas from Rutgers University, Lena Maier-Hein from the German Cancer Research Center, and Paul M. Thompson from the University of Southern California. Their insights and perspectives significantly enriched the workshop's discussions.

We owe much of DALI 2023's success to the 29 peer reviewers, whose dedication ensured the high quality of our scientific program. Their time and expertise, along with the valuable contributions of all authors, were instrumental in the workshop's achievements. We also extend our gratitude to our sponsors, SenseTime and InferVision, for their generous support, which was instrumental in the success of the workshop.

In closing, we hope that DALI 2023's proceedings will serve as a valuable resource for the medical image computing community, spurring further research and innovation in addressing the challenges of data augmentation, labeling, and imperfections. We look forward to continuing these discussions in future workshops, building upon the foundation laid by this year's successful event.

October 2023

Yuan Xue
Chen Chen
Chao Chen

Organization

Program Chairs

Yuan Xue   Ohio State University, USA
Chen Chen   University of Sheffield, UK
Chao Chen   Stony Brook University, USA

Editorial Chairs

Lianrui Zuo   Johns Hopkins University, USA
Yihao Liu   Johns Hopkins University, USA

Advisory Board

Ehsan Adeli   Stanford University, USA
Nicholas Heller   University of Minnesota, USA
Sharon X. Huang   Pennsylvania State University, USA
Dimitris N. Metaxas   Rutgers University, USA
Hien V. Nguyen   University of Houston, USA
Jerry Prince   Johns Hopkins University, USA
Daniel Rückert   Technische Universität München, Germany
Stephen Wong   Houston Methodist Hospital, USA

Program Committee

Amogh S. Adishesha   Pennsylvania State University, USA
Zhangxing Bian   Johns Hopkins University, USA
Weidong Cai   University of Sydney, Australia
Kexin Ding   University of North Carolina at Charlotte, USA
Peiyu Duan   Yale University, USA
Nicha Dvornek   Yale University, USA
Yubo Fan   Vanderbilt University, USA
Christoph M. Friedrich   University of Applied Sciences and Arts
     Dortmund, Germany
Michael Götz   University Hospital Ulm, Germany

Saumya Gupta	Stony Brook University, USA
Nicholas Heller	University of Minnesota, USA
Sharon X. Huang	Pennsylvania State University, USA
Peng Jin	Pennsylvania State University, USA
Edward Kim	Drexel University, USA
Zeju Li	Imperial College London, UK
Gilbert Lim	SingHealth, Singapore
Jiachen Liu	Pennsylvania State University, USA
Luyang Luo	Chinese University of Hong Kong, China
Weimin Lyu	Stony Brook University, USA
Haomiao Ni	Pennsylvania State University, USA
Cheng Ouyang	Imperial College London, UK
Samuel Remedios	Johns Hopkins University, USA
Ruochen Wang	AbleTo, Inc., USA
Fan Wang	Stony Brook University, USA
Yuli Wang	Johns Hopkins University, USA
Zuhui Wang	Stony Brook University, USA
Muchao Ye	Pennsylvania State University, USA
Chenyu You	Yale University, USA
Samira Zare	University of Houston, USA

Contents

URL: Combating Label Noise for Lung Nodule Malignancy Grading

Xianze Ai[1,2], Zehui Liao[1,2], and Yong Xia[1,2(✉)]

[1] Ningbo Institute of Northwestern Polytechnical University, Ningbo 315048, China
[2] National Engineering Laboratory for Integrated Aero-Space-Ground-Ocean Big
Data Application Technology, School of Computer Science and Engineering,
Northwestern Polytechnical University, Xi'an 710072, China
yxia@nwpu.edu.cn

Abstract. Due to the complexity of annotation and inter-annotator variability, most lung nodule malignancy grading datasets contain label noise, which inevitably degrades the performance and generalizability of models. Although researchers adopt the label-noise-robust methods to handle label noise for lung nodule malignancy grading, they do not consider the inherent ordinal relation among classes of this task. To model the ordinal relation among classes to facilitate tackling label noise in this task, we propose a Unimodal-Regularized Label-noise-tolerant (URL) framework. Our URL contains two stages, the Supervised Contrastive Learning (SCL) stage and the Memory pseudo-labels generation and Unimodal regularization (MU) stage. In the SCL stage, we select reliable samples and adopt supervised contrastive learning to learn better representations. In the MU stage, we split samples with multiple annotations into multiple samples with a single annotation and shuffle them into different batches. To handle label noise, pseudo-labels are generated using the similarity between each sample and the central feature of each class, and temporal ensembling is used to obtain memory pseudo-labels that supervise the model training. To model the ordinal relation, we introduce unimodal regularization to keep the ordinal relation among classes in the predictions. Moreover, each lung nodule is characterized by three orthographic views. Experiments conducted on the LIDC-IDRI dataset indicate the superiority of our URL over other competing methods. Code is available at https://github.com/axz520/URL.

Keywords: Lung nodule malignancy grading · Label noise · Ordinal relation · Multiple annotators

1 Introduction

Deep convolutional neural networks (DCNNs) have achieved impressive performance in lung nodule malignancy grading [2,5,21] using chest computed tomography (CT). Their success depends on a large amount of reliably-labeled training data. Medical professionals perform the annotation of chest CT scans on a

---

X. Ai and Z. Liao—Equal contribution.

Y. Xue et al. (Eds.): DALI 2023, LNCS 14379, pp. 1–11, 2024.
https://doi.org/10.1007/978-3-031-58171-7_1

slice-by-slice basis, which always requires a high degree of expertise and concentration and is labor-expensive and time-consuming [8]. Due to the complexity of annotation and inter-annotator variability, the collected training data often contain label noise [19], which inevitably impair the performance and generalizability of the model trained with them. Therefore, improving the robustness of the model against label noise is a crucial task for accurate and reliable lung nodule malignancy grading. In the broad area of pattern recognition, increasing research efforts have been denoted to the label noise issue, resulting in several innovative solutions. Among them, some aim to identify noisy samples and reduce their impact by using semi-supervised algorithms, sample reweighting, or assigning them pseudo labels [10,15,26], while others aim to resist the label noise via designing a noise-robust loss function or estimating the noise transition matrix [22,23,25]. Despite their success in natural image processing, these solutions rarely consider the cases where each sample has several inconsistent annotations provided by different annotators, which is common in clinical diagnosis [9,18–20].

Recently, a few methods have been proposed to deal with the label noise issue in medical image classification tasks, where each sample may have one unreliable or more inconsistent annotations [9,14,19]. An intuitive solution is to generate proxy labels, such as using the average/median/max voting of multiple annotations [14,28,29]. Besides, Jensen et al. [7] introduced a label sampling strategy that randomly selects the proxy label from the multiple annotations of each sample. Ju et al. [9] proposed an uncertainty estimation-based framework that selects reliable samples using uncertainty scores and proceeds with course learning. Liao et al. [19] proposed a 'divide-and-rule' model which reduces the impact of samples with inconsistent and unreliable labels by introducing the attention mechanism. Although these methods can tackle the label noise in the scenario of multiple annotations, they do not take into account the inherent ordinal relation among classes in grading tasks. The probabilities of neighboring labels should decrease with the increase of distance away from the ground truth. For instance, a lung nodule with a ground-truth malignancy of 2 is more likely to be misclassified into the categories of malignancy 1 and 3, instead of the categories of malignancy 4 and 5. In other words, the distribution of class transition probabilities is unimodal. It should be noted that, although the ordinal relation among classes has been studied using the random forest, meta-learning, and ordinal regression in previous research on lung nodule malignancy grading [14,28], such research ignores the label noise issue.

In this paper, we propose a **U**nimodal-**R**egularized **L**abel-noise-tolerant (URL) framework for lung nodule malignancy grading using chest CT. Under the URL framework, a nodule malignancy grading model can be trained in two steps, including warming up on reliable samples and fine-tuning on noisy samples. In the warming-up step, reliable samples are first selected by adopting the negative learning strategy [12] and then employed to warm up the grading model using contrastive learning. In the fine-tuning step, two tricks are designed to alleviate the impact of noisy labels. First, the memory pseudo-label generation (MPLG) module is constructed to generate pseudo-labels according to the feature similarity between each sample and the mean feature of each class and to improve those pseudo-labels by applying the temporal ensembling technique to them. Second, considering the fact that the ordinal relation among classes means that the probability of each class label follows a unimodal distribution, we apply a unimodal regularization to the predicted probabilistic labels of each sample, forcing the distribution to have a single mode. We have evaluated our URL framework against six competing methods on the LIDC-IDRI dataset [1] and achieved state-of-the-art performance.

The main contributions of this work are as follows. (1) We identify the importance of the inherent ordinal relation among classes in the task lung nodule malignancy grading with noisy labels and thus propose the URL framework to tackle this issue. (2) Based on the ordinal relation among classes, we design a unimodal regularization to constrain the predicted probabilistic class label, leading to improve grading performance. (3) Experimental results indicate that our RUL framework outperforms than six competing methods in combating label noises for the lung nodule malignancy grading.

2   Method

2.1   Problem Definition and Overview

We define the dataset $D = \{(x_i, y_i^1, y_i^2, ..., y_i^{s_i})\}_{i=1}^N$ for noisy C class classification problem, where x_i is the i-th image, s_i is the number of annotations of x_i, y_i^j is the j-th annotation of x_i, and N is the number of samples in dataset D. Note that $y_i^j \in \{0, 1\}^C$ is the one-hot label over C classes and it might be incorrect. Our goal is to train a robust classification model using noisy training set D for the lung nodule malignancy grading task.

The proposed framework is shown in Fig. 1. There are two stages in our URL framework. In the SCL stage, we first select reliable samples through negative learning and then train a feature extractor f_θ using these selected samples via supervised contrastive learning. In the MU stage, pseudo-labels are generated to handle label noise using the MPLG module, and unimodal regularization is introduced to model the inter-class ordinal relation.

Note that taking into account balancing performance and memory consumption, we suggest using multi-view 2D slices instead of 3D images. Specifically, given an input image x_i, we extract three 2D slices on the axial, sagittal, and coronal planes (*i.e.*, $x_i^{v1}, x_i^{v2}, x_i^{v3}$), and concatenate them at the channel-wise as the input. We now delve into the details of our framework.

2.2   SCL Stage

Negative Learning for Reliable Sample Selection. There is inconsistency in multiple annotations, but their complementary labels are more reliable. Take $C = 5$ for example, if three annotators individually conclude that a nodule malignancy is 3, 4, and 5, then we consider that the nodule is highly unlikely

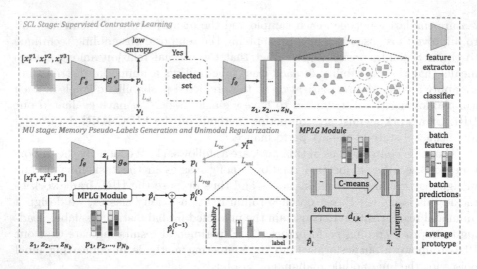

Fig. 1. The overview of our proposed URL framework. $[x_i^{v1}, x_i^{v2}, x_i^{v3}]$ means that three 2D views of the i-th image are concatenated at channel level, z_i is the feature of x_i and $y_i = y_i^1 \vee y_i^2 \vee ... \vee y_i^{s_i}$. N_b is the batch size. $z_1, z_2, ... z_{N_b}$ is batch features and $p_1, p_2, ... p_{N_b}$ is batch predictions. $\hat{p}_i^{(t)}$ is the memory pseudo-label of x_i at the t-th epoch. y_i^{sa} is one of the candidate labels of x_i.

to be classified as 1 or 2. Hence, negative learning which uses complementary labels can ensure the reliability of annotations. The adopted backbone contains an encoder f'_θ and fully-connected layers g'_ϕ followed by a softmax layer S. Given an input image x_i, its prediction is calculated as follows

$$p_i = S(g'_\phi(f'_\theta(concat(x_i^{v1}, x_i^{v2}, x_i^{v3})))), \tag{1}$$

where p_i is the predicted probabilistic vector. The negative learning loss is calculated by

$$\mathcal{L}_{nl} = -(1 - y_i)\log(1 - p_i), \tag{2}$$

where $y_i = y_i^1 \vee y_i^2 \vee ... \vee y_i^{s_i}$ and $\mathbf{1}$ is all-one vector. We select the first $\frac{M}{C}$ low-entropy samples in each class as a reliable set $D_r = \{x_i, y'_i\}_{i=1}^M$, where y'_i is the predicted label of the backbone.

Supervised Contrastive Learning. Supervised contrastive learning [11] is powerful in representation learning, but it is degraded when there are noisy labels [17]. Therefore, we perform supervised contrastive learning using D_r to learn better representations. It can maximize the feature similarities of the different classes. The feature of x_i is calculated as $z_i = f_\theta(concat(x_i^{v1}, x_i^{v2}, x_i^{v3}))$, where f_θ is the other encoder. In a mini-batch, we select samples with the same label as x_i as positive examples and select samples with different labels from x_i as negative examples. The supervised contrastive loss is calculated as follows:

$$\mathcal{L}_{con} = -\sum_{i \in I} \frac{1}{|U(i)|} \sum_{u \in U(i)} \log \frac{\exp(z_i \cdot z_u / \tau)}{\sum\limits_{a \in A(i)} \exp(z_i \cdot z_a / \tau)}. \tag{3}$$

Here, $i \in I = \{1, 2, ..., N_b\}$ is the index of batch samples and $A(i) = I \setminus \{i\}$. $U(i) = \{u \in A(i) : y'_u = y'_i\}$ is the set of indices of positive examples and $|U(i)|$ is its cardinality, and τ is a temperature parameter.

2.3 MU Stage

Based on the encoder f_θ trained by supervised contrastive learning, we conduct a lung nodule malignancy grading model which contains an encoder f_θ, fully-connected layers g_ϕ followed by a softmax layer S, and the MPLG module. We split training samples with multiple annotations into multiple samples with a single annotation and the reorganized training set is denoted as $D_a = \{x_i, y_i^{sa}\}_{i=1}^{N_{sa}}$. Given an input image x_i, the prediction is calculated as $p_i = S(g_\phi(f_\theta(concat(x_i^{v1}, x_i^{v2}, x_i^{v3}))))$ which is supervised by its label y_i^{sa} using following cross-entropy Loss:

$$L_{ce} = -y_i^{sa} \log p_i. \tag{4}$$

Memory Pseudo-Labels Generation. To handle label noise, we first generate pseudo-labels using MPLG Module. In a mini-batch, we calculate the central feature $\bar{z}_k$ of k-th class as follows

$$\bar{z}_k = \frac{1}{N_k} \sum_{i=1}^{N_b} \mathbb{1}[\hat{y}_i = k] z_i, \tag{5}$$

where $k \in \{1, 2, ..., C\}$, $\hat{y}_i = argmax(p_i)$ and N_k is the number of samples that satisfy $\hat{y}_i = k$. $\mathbb{1}[A]$ means the indicator of the event A. We calculate the feature similarity between the feature z_i and k-th central feature $\bar{z}_k$ by the cosine distance as $d_{i,k} = \frac{z_i \bar{z}_k^T}{\|z_i\| \|\bar{z}_k\|}$. Then we calculate pseudo-label $\hat{p}$ shown as follows:

$$\hat{p}_{i,k} = \frac{\exp(d_{i,k}/\tau)}{\sum_{j=1}^{C} \exp(d_{i,j}/\tau)}. \tag{6}$$

Inspired by early learning and memorization phenomena [22], we initialize the memory pseudo-label $\hat{p}_i^{(0)}$ with zeros and use temporal ensembling to update it as follows

$$\hat{p}_i^{(t)} = \beta \hat{p}_i^{(t-1)} + (1 - \beta)\hat{p}_i. \tag{7}$$

We maximize the inner product between the model output and the memory pseudo-label shown as follows:

$$\mathcal{L}_{reg} = -\log(1 - \langle \hat{p}_i^{(t)}, p_i \rangle). \tag{8}$$

Table 1. Malignancy distribution in the training/test set of the LIDR-IDRI dataset.

Datasets	Malignancy					Number
	1	2	3	4	5	
training set	400	1140	1476	708	370	2174
test set	149	63	143	10	29	394

Unimodal Regularization. In order to tackle label noise in the grading task according to its characteristics, we model the inter-class ordinal relation for facilitating label-noise-robust learning. Hence, we introduce a unimodal regularization to constrain the class ordinal relation of the prediction p_i as follows:

$$\mathcal{L}_{uni} = \sum_{k=1}^{\hat{y}} max(0, p_{i,k} - p_{i,k+1}) + \sum_{k=\hat{y}}^{C} max(0, p_{i,k+1} - p_{i,k}). \qquad (9)$$

Finally, the objective loss function of the MU stage is denoted as follows:

$$\mathcal{L} = L_{ce} + \alpha_1 L_{reg} + \alpha_2 L_{uni}, \qquad (10)$$

where α_1 and α_2 are hyper-parameters.

3   Experiments and Results

3.1   Dataset and Experimental Setup

Dataset. We use the largest public lung nodule dataset LIDC-IDRI [1] for this study. It contains 2568 lung nodules from 1018 chest CT scans. Each nodule is individually annotated by up to four annotators. The malignancy of each nodule is assessed using a rating scale ranging from 1 to 5, denoting an ascending malignancy. We split the dataset as shown in Table 1. In the test set, all samples are annotated by multiple annotators and the annotations are consistent. 20% of the training data is split as the validation set. We can approach the optimal model by approximately maximizing the accuracy on noisy distribution [3]. For each 3D image, we first sample each scan to a cubic voxel size of $1.0 \times 1.0 \times 1.0 \, m^3$ and crop a $64 \times 64 \times 64$ cube which contains a lung nodule in its center. Before multi-view concatenation, all patches are resized to 224×224. For data augmentation, we employ random horizontal flipping and vertical flipping.

Implementation Details. We use EfficientNet-B0 [24] as the backbone that is pre-trained on the ImageNet dataset [4]. Adam [13] optimizer with a batch size of 32 is used to optimize the model. All competing methods are trained for 30 epochs with an initial learning rate of 0.0001 and we use the exponential decay strategy with a decay rate of 0.95. The best checkpoint used for reliable sample selection is obtained using the early stop strategy on the validation set during negative learning. In the SCL stage, the encoder is pre-trained for 10 epochs. The experiments were performed on the PyTorch framework using a

Table 2. Performance (mean ± standard deviation) of our URL framework and other competitors in the lung nodule malignancy grading task (**5-class classification**). The best and second-best results are highlighted in **bold**/*underlined*, respectively.

Method	Results (%)		
	Accuracy	AUC	F1-score
AVE	58.21 ± 0.56	78.55 ± 0.57	46.55 ± 0.52
LS [7]	65.39 ± 0.40	83.35 ± 0.35	51.16 ± 0.34
UCL [16]	65.73 ± 0.39	84.35 ± 0.66	54.09 ± 0.22
DU [9]	67.08 ± 0.26	82.56 ± 0.17	*55.14* ± 0.69
SCE [27]	69.28 ± 0.56	83.37 ± 0.35	54.01 ± 0.41
ELR [22]	70.16 ± 0.27	83.18 ± 0.13	53.95 ± 0.30
NCR [6]	*71.23* ± 0.18	*85.17* ± 0.38	54.95 ± 0.42
Ours	**73.18** ± 0.18	**85.82** ± 0.43	**57.25** ± 0.40

Table 3. Performance (mean ± standard deviation) of our URL framework and other competitors in the lung nodule malignancy grading task (**3-class classification**). The best and second-best results are highlighted in **bold**/*underlined*, respectively.

Method	Results (%)		
	Accuracy	AUC	F1-score
AVE	67.25 ± 0.70	85.77 ± 0.43	68.56 ± 0.48
LS [7]	68.28 ± 0.28	88.75 ± 0.27	68.42 ± 0.60
UCL [10]	72.01 ± 0.24	88.87 ± 0.43	71.84 ± 0.15
DU [9]	72.55 ± 0.14	87.54 ± 0.02	72.54 ± 0.75
SCE [27]	72.67 ± 0.40	87.93 ± 0.54	70.60 ± 0.41
ELR [22]	74.02 ± 0.27	89.70 ± 0.10	72.06 ± 0.61
NCR [6]	*76.30* ± 0.10	*91.22* ± 0.02	*76.70* ± 0.37
Ours	**77.15** ± 0.17	**91.58** ± 0.21	**77.41** ± 0.38

workstation with one NVIDIA GTX 1080Ti GPU. The experimental results were reported over three random runs. Hyper-parameters are set as $M = 200$, $\beta = 0.9, \tau = 0.1, \alpha_1 = 0.8$ and $\alpha_2 = 3$.

Evaluation Metrics. We evaluate the performance of the 5-class classification problem (from 1 to 5) and the 3-class classification problem (benign, unsure, and malignant) in the lung nodule malignancy grading tasks. And accuracy, F1-score, and area under the ROC curve (AUC) are used as the metrics.

3.2 Comparative Experiments

We compared our URL framework with seven methods, including (1) two baseline methods: Average (AVE) uses the average proxy label, while Label Sampling

Table 4. Performance (mean ± standard deviation) of our URL framework and its four variants in the lung nodule malignancy grading task (**5-class classification**). The best results are highlighted in **bold**. 'SV' and 'MV' mean single-view and multi-view, respectively.

method	Results (%)		
	Accuracy	AUC	F1-score
Ours	**73.18** ± 0.18	**85.82** ± 0.43	**57.25** ± 0.40
MV+Baseline+L_{con}+L_{reg}	71.40 ± 0.02	85.40 ± 0.31	56.04 ± 0.19
MV+Baseline+L_{con}	68.02 ± 0.55	83.70 ± 0.13	53.32 ± 0.02
MV+Baseline	65.93 ± 0.69	83.32 ± 0.39	52.59 ± 0.52
SV+Baseline	61.57 ± 0.67	81.30 ± 0.82	48.33 ± 0.31

Table 5. Performance (mean ± standard deviation) of our URL framework and its four variants in the lung nodule malignancy grading (**3-class classification**). The best results are highlighted in **bold**. 'SV' and 'MV' mean single-view and multi-view, respectively.

method	Results (%)		
	Accuracy	AUC	F1-score
Ours	**77.15** ± 0.17	**91.58** ± 0.21	**77.41** ± 0.38
MV+Baseline+L_{con}+L_{reg}	75.63 ± 0.55	91.24 ± 0.17	75.88 ± 0.23
MV+Baseline+L_{con}	71.73 ± 0.53	90.32 ± 0.70	72.57 ± 0.32
MV+Baseline	68.74 ± 0.49	88.65 ± 0.50	68.63 ± 0.44
SV+Baseline	66.41 ± 0.22	85.77 ± 0.48	64.92 ± 0.78

(LS) [7] randomly selects one proxy label from multiple annotations; (2) one method for modeling ordinal relation: Unimodal-Concentrated Loss (UCL) [16] combines concentrated loss and unimodal loss for ordinal classification; (3) three methods for tackling noisy data with single annotation: SCE [27], ELR [22], and NCR [6]; (4) and one method for handling noisy data with several annotations: Dual Uncertainty (DU) [9] evaluates the uncertainty of each sample and then adopts sample reweighting and curriculum training. Multi-view concatenation is adopted for all competing methods. Table 2 shows the results of the 5-class classification task and Table 3 shows the results of the 3-class classification task. Experimental results demonstrate that our URL framework achieves the highest accuracy, AUC, and F1 score.

3.3 Ablation Analysis

We conducted ablation studies on the LIDC-IDRI dataset to investigate the effectiveness of each component of our URL, respectively. Table 4 shows the results of the 5-class classification task and Table 5 shows the results of the 3-class classification task. Compared to taking a single view as input, taking multiple views as input provides more information and performs better. And then we investigate the contribution of L_{uni}, L_{reg}, and L_{con}. Experimental results reveal that the performance of our URL framework is degraded more or less when L_{uni}, L_{reg}, or L_{con} is removed.

4 Conclusion

In this paper, we propose to model the inter-class ordinal relation for facilitating the label-noise-robust learning for the lung nodule malignancy grading task. To achieve this, we propose the URL framework. We generate memory pseudo labels by calculating feature similarity to handle label noise and introduce unimodal regularization to model the inter-class ordinal relation. Moreover, supervised contrastive learning is used to learn better representations. We conducted experiments on the LIDC-IDRI dataset and the results show that our URL framework performs better than other competing methods significantly. Ablation studies demonstrate the contribution of modeling the class ordinal relation to label noise learning.

Acknowledgement. This work was supported in part by the Ningbo Clinical Research Center for Medical Imaging under Grant 2021L003 (Open Project 2022LYK-FZD06), in part by the Natural Science Foundation of Ningbo City, China, under Grant 2021J052, in part by the National Natural Science Foundation of China under Grant 62171377, in part by the Key Technologies Research and Development Program under Grant 2022YFC2009903 / 2022YFC2009900, and in part by the Innovation Foundation for Doctor Dissertation of Northwestern Polytechnical University under Grant CX2022056.

References

1. Armato, S.G., III., et al.: The lung image database consortium (LIDC) and image database resource initiative (IDRI): a completed reference database of lung nodules on ct scans. Med. Phys. **38**(2), 915–931 (2011)
2. Chen, L., et al.: An artificial-intelligence lung imaging analysis system (alias) for population-based nodule computing in ct scans. Comput. Med. Imaging Graph. **89**, 101899 (2021)
3. Chen, P., Ye, J., Chen, G., Zhao, J., Heng, P.A.: Robustness of accuracy metric and its inspirations in learning with noisy labels. In: Proceedings of the AAAI Conference on Artificial Intelligence, vol. 35, pp. 11451–11461 (2021)
4. Deng, J., Dong, W., Socher, R., Li, L.J., Li, K., Fei-Fei, L.: Imagenet: a large-scale hierarchical image database. In: 2009 IEEE Conference on Computer Vision and Pattern Recognition, pp. 248–255. IEEE (2009)
5. Gu, D., Liu, G., Xue, Z.: On the performance of lung nodule detection, segmentation and classification. Comput. Med. Imaging Graph. **89**, 101886 (2021)
6. Iscen, A., Valmadre, J., Arnab, A., Schmid, C.: Learning with neighbor consistency for noisy labels. In: Proceedings of the IEEE/CVF Conference on Computer Vision and Pattern Recognition, pp. 4672–4681 (2022)

7. Jensen, M.H., Jørgensen, D.R., Jalaboi, R., Hansen, M.E., Olsen, M.A.: Improving uncertainty estimation in convolutional neural networks using inter-rater agreement. In: Shen, D., et al. (eds.) MICCAI 2019, vol. 11767, pp. 540–548. Springer, Heidelberg (2019). https://doi.org/10.1007/978-3-030-32251-9_59

8. Joskowicz, L., Cohen, D., Caplan, N., Sosna, J.: Inter-observer variability of manual contour delineation of structures in ct. Eur. Radiol. **29**, 1391–1399 (2019)

9. Ju, L., et al.: Improving medical images classification with label noise using dual-uncertainty estimation. IEEE Trans. Med. Imaging **41**(6), 1533–1546 (2022)

10. Karim, N., Khalid, U., Esmaeili, A., Rahnavard, N.: CNLL: a semi-supervised approach for continual noisy label learning. In: Proceedings of the IEEE/CVF Conference on Computer Vision and Pattern Recognition, pp. 3878–3888 (2022)

11. Khosla, P., et al.: Supervised contrastive learning. Adv. Neural. Inf. Process. Syst. **33**, 18661–18673 (2020)

12. Kim, Y., Yim, J., Yun, J., Kim, J.: NLNL: negative learning for noisy labels. In: Proceedings of the IEEE/CVF International Conference on Computer Vision, pp. 101–110 (2019)

13. Kingma, D.P., Ba, J.: Adam: a method for stochastic optimization. arXiv preprint arXiv:1412.6980 (2014)

14. Lei, Y., Zhu, H., Zhang, J., Shan, H.: Meta ordinal regression forest for medical image classification with ordinal labels. IEEE/CAA J. Automatica Sinica **9**(7), 1233–1247 (2022)

15. Li, J., Socher, R., Hoi, S.C.: Dividemix: learning with noisy labels as semi-supervised learning. arXiv preprint arXiv:2002.07394 (2020)

16. Li, Q., et al.: Unimodal-concentrated loss: fully adaptive label distribution learning for ordinal regression. In: Proceedings of the IEEE/CVF Conference on Computer Vision and Pattern Recognition, pp. 20513–20522 (2022)

17. Li, S., Xia, X., Ge, S., Liu, T.: Selective-supervised contrastive learning with noisy labels. In: Proceedings of the IEEE/CVF Conference on Computer Vision and Pattern Recognition, pp. 316–325 (2022)

18. Liao, Z., Hu, S., Xie, Y., Xia, Y.: Modeling annotator preference and stochastic annotation error for medical image segmentation. arXiv e-prints, pp. arXiv–2111 (2021)

19. Liao, Z., Xie, Y., Hu, S., Xia, Y.: Learning from ambiguous labels for lung nodule malignancy prediction. IEEE Trans. Med. Imaging **41**(7), 1874–1884 (2022)

20. Liao, Z., Xie, Y., Hu, S., Xia, Y.: Transformer-based annotation bias-aware medical image segmentation. In: Greenspan, H., et al. (eds.) MICCAI 2023, vol. 14223, pp. 24–34. Springer, Heidelberg (2023). https://doi.org/10.1007/978-3-031-43901-8_3

21. Liu, L., Dou, Q., Chen, H., Qin, J., Heng, P.A.: Multi-task deep model with margin ranking loss for lung nodule analysis. IEEE Trans. Med. Imaging **39**(3), 718–728 (2019)

22. Liu, S., Niles-Weed, J., Razavian, N., Fernandez-Granda, C.: Early-learning regularization prevents memorization of noisy labels. Adv. Neural. Inf. Process. Syst. **33**, 20331–20342 (2020)

23. Sun, Z., et al.: PNP: robust learning from noisy labels by probabilistic noise prediction. In: Proceedings of the IEEE/CVF Conference on Computer Vision and Pattern Recognition, pp. 5311–5320 (2022)

24. Tan, M., Le, Q.: Efficientnet: rethinking model scaling for convolutional neural networks. In: International Conference on Machine Learning, pp. 6105–6114. PMLR (2019)

25. Wang, D.B., Wen, Y., Pan, L., Zhang, M.L.: Learning from noisy labels with complementary loss functions. In: Proceedings of the AAAI Conference on Artificial Intelligence, vol. 35, pp. 10111–10119 (2021)
26. Wang, X., Hua, Y., Kodirov, E., Clifton, D.A., Robertson, N.M.: Proselflc: progressive self label correction for training robust deep neural networks. In: Proceedings of the IEEE/CVF Conference on Computer Vision and Pattern Recognition, pp. 752–761 (2021)
27. Wang, Y., Ma, X., Chen, Z., Luo, Y., Yi, J., Bailey, J.: Symmetric cross entropy for robust learning with noisy labels. In: Proceedings of the IEEE/CVF International Conference on Computer Vision, pp. 322–330 (2019)
28. Wu, B., Sun, X., Hu, L., Wang, Y.: Learning with unsure data for medical image diagnosis. In: Proceedings of the IEEE/CVF International Conference on Computer Vision, pp. 10590–10599 (2019)
29. Xu, X., et al.: Mscs-deepln: evaluating lung nodule malignancy using multi-scale cost-sensitive neural networks. Med. Image Anal. **65**, 101772 (2020)

Zero-Shot Learning of Individualized Task Contrast Prediction from Resting-State Functional Connectomes

Minh Nguyen[1](✉), Gia H. Ngo[1], and Mert R. Sabuncu[1,2]

[1] School of Electrical and Computer Engineering, Cornell University, Ithaca, USA
bn244@cornell.edu
[2] Radiology, Weill Cornell Medicine, New York, USA

Abstract. Given sufficient pairs of resting-state and task-evoked fMRI scans from subjects, it is possible to train ML models to predict subject-specific task-evoked activity using resting-state functional MRI (rsfMRI) scans. However, while rsfMRI scans are relatively easy to collect, obtaining sufficient task fMRI scans is much harder as it involves more complex experimental designs and procedures. Thus, the reliance on scarce paired data limits the application of current techniques to only tasks seen during training. We show that this reliance can be reduced by leveraging group-average contrasts, enabling zero-shot predictions for novel tasks. Our approach, named OPIC (short for Omni-Task Prediction of Individual Contrasts), takes as input a subject's rsfMRI-derived connectome and a group-average contrast, to produce a prediction of the subject-specific contrast. Similar to zero-shot learning in large language models using special inputs to obtain answers for novel natural language processing tasks, inputting group-average contrasts guides the OPIC model to generalize to novel tasks unseen in training. Experimental results show that OPIC's predictions for novel tasks are not only better than simple group-averages, but are also competitive with a state-of-the-art model's in-domain predictions that was trained using in-domain tasks' data.

Keywords: out-of-domain · zero-shot · functional connectivity · task-induced fingerprint

1 Introduction

Functional connectomes derived from resting-state functional MRI (rsfMRI) scans contain subject-specific characteristics that could be used as "fingerprints" of individual cognitive functions [4,18]. Such fingerprints have many uses [19], for example predicting individual developmental trajectories [12], behavioral

---

M. Nguyen and G. H. Ngo—indicates equal contribution.

Supplementary Information The online version contains supplementary material available at https://doi.org/10.1007/978-3-031-58171-7_2.

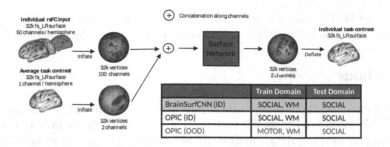

Fig. 1. OPIC predicts individualized task-evoked contrast using group-average contrast and subject's rsFC. OPIC is based on BrainSurfCNN which is a surface-based CNN with spherical convolutional kernels. However, OPIC can predict both ID (e.g. trained and tested on SOCIAL contrasts) and OOD individualized contrasts (e.g. trained on WM and MOTOR but tested on SOCIAL contrasts as shown in red) while BrainSur-fCNN is not capable of OOD prediction. ID: in-domain, OOD: out-of-domain. (Color figure online)

traits [16,28], or individualized task-evoked activities [9,24,36,39]. The last one is useful in pre-surgical planning or studying of neurological disorders [3,7,11,34] and has been tackled using various methods, e.g. GLM [36], ensembles [39], or neural networks [24,25]. For each task-evoked activity, existing methods need paired task fMRI-rsfMRI scans as training data. Thus, they cannot predict for activities unseen in training data (out-of-domain generalization). Besides, paired training data is hard to collect because it is hard to reliably collect high quality task fMRI scans [13] (due to poor task performance and measurement noise). The lack of out-of-domain generalization and the scarcity of paired training data limit the potential utility of these methods. Meta-learning or few-shot learning [1,14,31] can improve generalization given some paired data from out-of-domain activities. However, when no additional paired data is available, generalizing to unseen task-evoked activities requires zero-shot learning [21,22,32,38].

We propose OPIC (short for Omni-Task Prediction of Individual Contrasts), an approach that relaxes the need for paired training data and enables zero-shot predictions for novel tasks. OPIC takes as input a subject's rsfMRI-derived connectome and a group-average contrast, and predicts the subject-specific task-evoked activity (contrast). The group-average controls the task identity while the rsfMRI input determines subject-specific patterns in the contrast. OPIC can make individualized predictions from rsfMRI connectomes for both in-domain and out-of-domain contrasts. Although zero-shot learning using additional model's input in a multitask setting [6] has been widely used in natural language processing [5,30], as far as we know, we are the first to examine its utility in our application domain. Our experiments with the HCP dataset [17] show that the proposed OPIC's out-of-domain prediction is better than a simple group-average and competitive with a state-of-the-art (SOTA) model's in-domain prediction that requires paired training data. OPIC's out-of-domain prediction also matches the SOTA model's in-domain prediction in subject identification, an important requisite for creating individualized task-evoked fingerprints.

2   Methods

Figure 1 shows the OPIC model. Its input and output are multi-channel icosa-hedral fs_LR meshes with 32,492 vertices per brain hemisphere [37]. fs_LR is an atlas based on imaging data (anatomical/structural, resting-state, myelination) from a large pool of subjects to achieve better inter-subject correspondence [37]. The output is a subject-specific task-evoked contrast. OPIC's surface network is similar to the publicly-available BrainSurfCNN [24], a U-Net-based [23,33] surface-based CNN with spherical convolutional kernels [8] (see [24] for the network specifics). However, OPIC differs from BrainSurfCNN in two key ways.

First, while BrainSurfCNN designates 2 specific output channels for each task, OPIC uses the same 2 output channels for all tasks (parameter-sharing). Although BrainSurfCNN can predict for multiple tasks, it cannot predict for a new task because each task uses different output channels and the number of output channels is fixed. In contrast, through parameter-sharing, OPIC can use the same output channels to predict for previously unseen (out-of-domain) tasks.

Second, in addition to the rsfMRI derived functional connectome (rsFC) input, OPIC also has a group-average contrast input. The rsFC consists of functional connectivity features, each of which is the Pearson's correlation between the timeseries of a vertex on the icosahedral mesh and the averaged timeseries of an ROI. In our experiments, the group-average contrast is the average of all the task contrast maps across (training) subjects for a specific task. Since the group-average provides a rough estimate of subject-specific task-evoked contrast, this setup encourages OPIC to learn to map differences in rsFC to individual differences in task-evoked contrasts. Thus, for an out-of-domain activity, OPIC can refine the group-average input using information from rsFC to produce the individualized task-evoked contrast. Since this is possible without having to fine-tune using new paired data, this setup reduces the burden of collecting paired data.

3   Experimental Setup

3.1   Data

Our experiments used 3-Tesla resting-state fMRI (rsfMRI) and task fMRI (tfMRI) data of subjects from the Human Connectome Project (HCP) [17]. Data acquisition and pre-processing details are described in [2,17,35]. Each HCP subject has up to four 15-minute runs of rsfMRI data and tfMRI data from 86 tasks belonging to 7 task groups. The 7 task groups are EMOTION, GAMBLING, LANGUAGE, MOTOR, RELATIONAL, SOCIAL, and WM (working memory) [2]. For each contrast, there is one corresponding group-average contrast. Following [24,36], we excluded redundant negative tfMRI contrasts (47 tasks remained). We also excluded subjects with fewer than 4 rsfMRI runs. Of the remaining subjects, 39 subjects are held out for testing, 774 subjects are used for training and 19 are used for validation. All test subjects have second visits (retest data). No family members are split across test and training or validation sets. The 50-component ICA timeseries data included in HCP are used to compute subjects' functional connectomes. Each element in a subject's connectome corresponds to the Pearson's correlation between the rsfMRI timeseries at a vertex and the timeseries of an ICA-component. The group-average map is scaled so that its absolute maximum value is 1, matching the magnitude of the functional connectomes.

Table 1. Comparing OPIC's in-domain (ID) and out-of-domain (OOD) performance against the baselines' in term of average AUC. OPIC is significantly better than linear regression (Lin. Regr.) and group-average (Grp. Avg.) prediction. OPIC's in-domain performance is on-par with BrainSurfCNN (BSC) for all contrasts. While it is an unfair comparison for OPIC, OPIC's out-of-domain performance is on-par with BrainSurfCNN's in-domain performance in some contrasts (e.g. "GAMBLING REWARD" contrast). OPIC is also on-par with the retest session (Retest).

Contrast	OPIC		BSC	Grp. Avg.	Lin. Regr	Retest
	ID	OOD				
GAMBLING PUNISH	0.287	0.284	0.287	0.272*†	0.259*†	0.274*
GAMBLING REWARD	0.296	0.293	0.295	0.279*†	0.266*†	0.281*
LANGUAGE MATH-STORY	0.287	0.284	0.288	0.272*†	0.269*†	0.286
MOTOR CUE	0.257	0.253	0.255	0.240*†	0.218*†	0.243*
MOTOR CUE-AVG	0.254	0.250	0.252	0.241*†	0.222*†	0.248
RELATIONAL MATCH	0.311	0.307	0.310	0.294*†	0.279*†	0.305
RELATIONAL REL	0.317	0.312	0.316	0.299*†	0.284*†	0.310
SOCIAL RANDOM	0.302	0.300	0.299*	0.289*†	0.259*†	0.302
SOCIAL TOM	0.308	0.306	0.308	0.292*†	0.266*†	0.312
WM 0BK	0.296	0.291	0.295	0.280*†	0.266*†	0.281*
WM 2BK	0.305	0.299	0.304	0.285*†	0.271*†	0.297
WM FACE	0.282	0.277	0.281	0.266*†	0.249*†	0.268*

*: ID OPIC beats baseline, †: OOD OPIC beats baseline (paired 2-tail t-test at $p<1e-4$)

3.2 OPIC's Training

To test both in-domain and out-of-domain generalization, OPIC was trained in a leave-one-group-out manner. Specifically, we trained OPIC seven times and each time the model was trained from scratch with one task group excluded from the training data. For out-of-domain evaluation, the model was tested on the excluded task group. For in-domain evaluation, the model was tested on the task groups seen during training, but on independent test subjects. Since

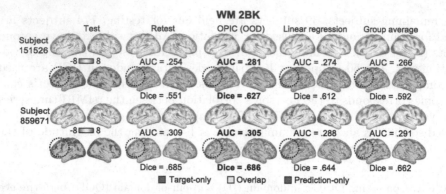

Fig. 2. Surface visualization for a representative task contrast ("WM 2BK") of 2 subjects. OPIC prediction is out-of-domain (Sect. 4.2) while linear regression was trained with the target contrast on the training subjects (in-domain). For each subject, the top row shows the unthresholded prediction or reference, and the bottom row show the overlap between the prediction or reference and the target. The right-most column shows the group-average contrasts for comparison.

there are six different predictions for a subject's task contrast, we averaged the predictions. The OPIC model was trained to minimize the l^2 loss using the Adam optimizer [20]. It was trained for 20 epochs with batch size 10 and learning rate 3E-3. Training the OPIC model took 1 day using a NVIDIA Titan Xp GPU. The iteration with the lowest validation error was chosen for evaluation.

3.3   Baselines

We compared the OPIC model against 4 baselines: the state-of-the-art Brain-SurfCNN model, a linear regression model, the group-average, and the retest scan. The BrainSurfCNN model's training follows [24] whereby the model was first trained with l^2 loss and then finetuned using the R-C loss. The R-C loss [24] minimizes the error reconstructing an individual task contrast from their functional connectome and maximizes the difference with other subjects' contrasts. The linear regression is set up similar to [24,36] whereby there is one regressor for each parcel (parcellation was derived from group-level ICA; Sect. 3.1). For each parcel and task, subject-specific regressors were fitted and the weights of fitted regressors of subjects from the training and validation set were averaged to create an average regressor used for prediction. The group-average map is a naive baseline that ignores inter-subject variability. This baseline would be inadequate for tasks with high inter-subject variability and thus is considered a lower-bound on performance. On the other hand, outputting the retest (repeat) scan as the prediction would be an effective upper-bound on performance since there should be high consistency between two scans of the same subject [24].

3.4   Metrics

We computed Dice scores [10] at different thresholds, where the overlap between the top X-percent (where X is varied between 5 and 50) of vertices in the predicted and target (tfMRI-derived, observed) contrast maps was quantified. This strategy allows us to assess the quality of the prediction at different levels of detail [24]. The area under the Dice curve (AUC) across all thresholds is used to measure how similar the models' predictions are to the target contrast.

In quantifying OPIC's prediction accuracy, we consider three different scenarios. First, we examine the relatively easy problem of in-domain prediction, where the test-time task was seen in training. Second, we consider the more difficult problem of out-of-domain prediction, where the performance is assessed for tasks that were not part of the groups seen in training. Finally, in the third scenario, we consider test-time tasks that are part of a group that was previously seen but the specific task was not included in the training.

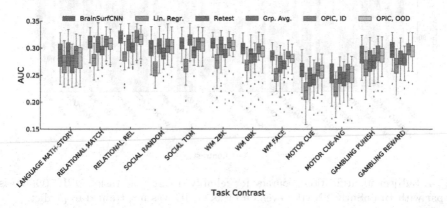

Fig. 3. Average AUC for reliably predictable tasks. OPIC's in-domain prediction (OPIC, ID) is on-par with BrainSurfCNN's in-domain prediction. Both OPIC's in-domain prediction (OPIC, ID) and out-of-domain prediction (OPIC, OOD) are consistently better than in-domain prediction from linear regression (Lin. Regr.) and group-average (Grp. Avg.) prediction. OPIC's performance is on-par with the retest session (Retest). See Table 1 for more details.

In addition to AUC, we used "subject identification accuracy" that measures how specific the predicted contrasts are to individual subjects [24,36]. In this analysis, for each subject, the AUC between the subject's predicted and observed contrasts of all subjects is first computed. This results in a square identification matrix with a dimension equal to the number of test subjects. Subject identification accuracy is in turn computed as the fraction of subjects whereby the subject's prediction accurately identifies the subject, i.e., accuracy is the average row-wise sorted rank order of the diagonal elements. Following [24,36], the identification matrices were normalized before computing accuracy.

4   Results

4.1   In-Domain Prediction Quality

Figure 3 and Table 1 show the comparison between OPIC's in-domain performance against the baselines for reliably predictable tasks. Following [24], a predictable task is defined as one in which a subject's tfMRI test scan is more
similar to their retest scan (on average, measured by AUC), compared to the
group-average map. The results for *all* tasks are included in the Supplementary
Material. The results show that OPIC's performance matches BrainSurfCNN,
and is on par with test-retest reliability. OPIC consistently outperforms the
group-average baseline and the linear regression baseline.

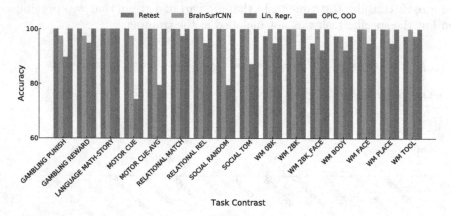

Fig. 4. Subject identification accuracy for reliably predictable tasks. OPIC (OOD) is
on-par with BrainSurfCNN (ID) even on tasks OPIC was not trained to predict.

4.2   Out-of-Domain Prediction Quality

Figure 3 and Table 1 also show the comparison between OPIC's out-of-domain
(OOD) prediction and the baselines' performance. While OPIC was tested on
tasks from a group unseen in training, the linear regression baseline and the
BrainSurfCNN baseline can only make predictions for tasks seen in training.

Figure 2 shows the prediction of a representative task contrast, "WM 2BK",
(which has median average target-retest Dice AU), for 2 test subjects with the
10th and 90th percentile target-group average Dice AUCs. Note that OPIC prediction is from a model trained with the OOD setup, i.e. it was not trained on
any "WM" task in the HCP dataset, while linear regression model was estimated
from training subjects on the target "WM 2BK" task. Despite the handicap,
OPIC outperforms the linear regression baseline and group-average reference in
Dice score for the top 25% most activated vertices, and the overall Dice AUC

score of the unthresholded maps. Focusing on the prefrontal cortex (circled), although the group-average contrast coarsely overlaps with the subjects' activation, OPIC prediction significantly matches the subject-specific minute variation. This suggests that OPIC does not merely copy the group-average contrast of the training subjects, but indeed makes subject-specific prediction.

The quantitative results also show that OPIC consistently outperforms the group-average baseline. Thus, OPIC is able to combine the group-average contrast input with the subject-specific rsFC input to accurately predict a subject-specific contrast map. In addition, OPIC is consistently better than the linear regression's in-domain prediction and is on-par with the retest AUC. These results demonstrate OPIC's ability to generalize well to new tasks from previously unseen groups. Comparing OPIC's OOD prediction with BrainSurfCNN in-domain prediction is not exactly fair for OPIC because OPIC only knows about a prediction task (via the group-average contrast) during test time while BrainSurfCNN was trained to perform the task. Yet, we observe that OPIC manages to reach BrainSurfCNN's level of performance in some contrasts such as "GAMBLING REWARD" or "SOCIAL TOM" (Table 1).

Table 2. OPIC generalizes well to OOD contrasts, almost matching that of in-domain predictions. AUC values are listed. P-values are for paired 2-tail t-test comparison.

Task	In-domain	OOD, seen group	OOD, new group
WM PLACE-AVG	0.209 (p = 7e–2)	0.208	0.206 (p = 3e–3)
WM TOOL-AVG	0.178 (p = 3e–3)	0.177	0.177 (p = 8e–1)

Figure 4 shows the subject identification accuracy of predictions for reliably predictable task contrasts. The OPIC model prediction is out-of-domain (unseen tasks) while the BrainSurfCNN's and linear regression's prediction is in-domain (tasks seen during training). OPIC matches BrainSurfCNN in subject identifiability even on contrasts OPIC was not trained to predict. Thus, OPIC seems to produce accurate predictions of individualized task contrast maps.

4.3   New Task Contrast from a Seen Task Group

In practice, a model is more likely to encounter an unseen task from a seen group than a completely new group. We compared OPIC's performance in this scenario against its in-domain prediction results. Specifically, we trained an OPIC model on all the available contrasts except two, "WM PLACE-AVG" and "WM TOOL-AVG". Table 2 shows that OPIC's performance on a new task from a seen group is better than a new task from an unseen group, but slightly worse than the scenario where the task was seen during training (in-domain).

5 Conclusion

Accurate prediction of individual differences in task-evoked brain activities [9, 25,36,39] using cognitive fingerprints extracted from rsfMRI [15,16] has several potential clinical applications [3,7,11,34]. Alas, prior approaches needs paired rsfMRI-task-fMRI scans for model fitting but paired data are scarce because of measurement noise and subjects' poor task performance. Predicting individualized task-evoked activities for novel (out-of-domain) tasks that have no paired data would require zero-shot generalization. In this paper, we proposed an approach to make individualized prediction for both in-domain and out-of-domain tasks by additionally leveraging group-average contrasts. Our OPIC model not only is on-par with competitive baselines in in-domain setting, but also can predict out-of-domain activities, something that prior approaches cannot do.

Although having presented a wide range of experimental settings, there are many unexplored areas left for future work. First, this work shows out-of-domain tasks in the same dataset. Can OPIC predict out-of-domain tasks across different datasets or different populations (e.g. different age groups, patients vs. controls)? Verifying OPIC's reliability when applying to populations with some cognitive or mental health issues would be important before clinical adoption. Second, can OPIC predict using imperfect group-average contrasts, for example group-average contrasts from meta-analyses [26,27,29]? Third, we did not use the contrastive R-C loss in training, as this loss function was originally designed for a model that predicts multiple contrasts from the same input concurrently. However, it would be interesting to study if some form of contrastive objective further improves predictive performance while retaining inter-subject variability.

References

1. Andrychowicz, M., et al.: Learning to learn by gradient descent by gradient descent. NIPS **29**, 1–9 (2016)
2. Barch, D., et al.: Function in the human connectome: task-fMRI and individual differences in behavior. NeuroImage **80**, 169–189 (2013)
3. Bernstein-Eliav, M., Tavor, I.: The prediction of brain activity from connectivity: advances and applications. Neuroscientist (2022)
4. Biswal, B., et al.: Toward discovery science of human brain function. PNAS **107**(10), 4734–4739 (2010)
5. Brown, T., et al.: Language models are few-shot learners. In: NeurIPS (2020)
6. Caruana, R.: Multitask learning. Mach. Learn. **28**(1), 47–75 (1997)
7. Castellano, A., Cirillo, S., Bello, L., Riva, M., Falini, A.: Functional MRI for surgery of gliomas. Curr. Treat. Opt. Neurol. **19**(10), 1–23 (2017)
8. Chiyu, M., Huang, J., Kashinath, K., Prabhat, M., Niessner, M.: Spherical cnns on unstructured grids. In: ICLR (2019)
9. Cole, M., Ito, T., Bassett, D., Schultz, D.: Activity flow over resting-state networks shapes cognitive task activations. Nat. Neurosci. **19**(12), 1718–1726 (2016)
10. Dice, L.: Measures of the amount of ecologic association between species. Ecology **26**(3), 297–302 (1945)

11. Dimou, S., Battisti, R., Hermens, D.F., Lagopoulos, J.: A systematic review of functional MRI and DTI modalities used in presurgical planning of brain tumour resection. Neurosurg. Rev. **36**(2), 205–214 (2013)
12. Dosenbach, N., et al.: Prediction of individual brain maturity using fMRI. Science **329**(5997), 1358–1361 (2010)
13. Elliott, M., et al.: What is the test-retest reliability of common task-functional MRI measures? new empirical evidence and a meta-analysis. Psychol. Sci. **31**(7), 792–806 (2020)
14. Finn, C., Abbeel, P., Levine, S.: Model-agnostic meta-learning for fast adaptation of deep networks. In: ICML. PMLR (2017)
15. Finn, E., Rosenberg, M.: Beyond fingerprinting: choosing predictive connectomes over reliable connectomes. NeuroImage **239**, 118254 (2021)
16. Finn, E., et al.: Functional connectome fingerprinting: identifying individuals using patterns of brain connectivity. Nat. Neurosci. **18**(11), 1664–1671 (2015)
17. Glasser, M., et al.: The minimal preprocessing pipelines for the human connectome project. NeuroImage **80**, 105–124 (2013)
18. Kelly, C., Biswal, B., Craddock, C., Castellanos, X., Milham, M.: Characterizing variation in the functional connectome: promise and pitfalls. Trends Cogn. Sci. **16**(3), 181–188 (2012)
19. Khosla, M., Jamison, K., Ngo, G., Kuceyeski, A., Sabuncu, M.: Machine learning in resting-state fMRI analysis. Magn. Reson. Imaging **64**, 101–121 (2019)
20. Kingma, D., Ba, J.: Adam: a method for stochastic optimization. In: ICLR (2014)
21. Lampert, C., Nickisch, H., Harmeling, S.: Attribute-based classification for zero-shot visual object categorization. IEEE TPAMI **36**(3), 453–465 (2013)
22. Larochelle, H., Erhan, D., Bengio, Y.: Zero-data learning of new tasks. In: AAAI, vol. 1 (2008)
23. Milletari, F., Navab, N., Ahmadi, S.A.: V-net: fully convolutional neural networks for volumetric medical image segmentation. In: International Conference on 3D Vision. IEEE (2016)
24. Ngo, G., Khosla, M., Jamison, K., Kuceyeski, A., Sabuncu, M.: From connectomic to task-evoked fingerprints: individualized prediction of task contrasts from resting-state functional connectivity. In: Martel, A.L., et al. (eds.) MICCAI 2020, vol. 12267, pp. 62–71. Springer, Heidelberg (2020). https://doi.org/10.1007/978-3-030-59728-3_7
25. Ngo, G., Khosla, M., Jamison, K., Kuceyeski, A., Sabuncu, M.: Predicting individual task contrasts from resting-state functional connectivity using a surface-based convolutional network. NeuroImage **248**, 118849 (2022)
26. Ngo, G., Nguyen, M., Chen, N., Sabuncu, M.: Text2brain: synthesis of brain activation maps from free-form text query. In: de Bruijne, M., et al. (eds.) MICCAI 2021, vol. 12907, pp. 605–614. Springer, Heidelberg (2021). https://doi.org/10.1007/978-3-030-87234-2_57
27. Ngo, G., Nguyen, M., Chen, N., Sabuncu, M.: A transformer-based neural language model that synthesizes brain activation maps from free-form text queries. Med. Image Anal. **81**, 102540 (2022)
28. Pang, L., Li, H., Liu, Q., Luo, Y.J., Mobbs, D., Wu, H.: Resting-state functional connectivity of social brain regions predicts motivated dishonesty. NeuroImage **256**, 119253 (2022)
29. Poldrack, R., Yarkoni, T.: From brain maps to cognitive ontologies: informatics and the search for mental structure. Ann. Rev. Psychol. **67**, 587–612 (2016)
30. Raffel, C., et al.: Exploring the limits of transfer learning with a unified text-to-text transformer. JMLR **21**, 1–67 (2020)

31. Ravi, S., Larochelle, H.: Optimization as a model for few-shot learning. In: ICLR (2017)
32. Rohrbach, M., Stark, M., Schiele, B.: Evaluating knowledge transfer and zero-shot learning in a large-scale setting. In: CVPR. IEEE (2011)
33. Ronneberger, O., Fischer, P., Brox, T.: U-net: convolutional networks for biomedical image segmentation. In: Navab, N., Hornegger, J., Wells, W., Frangi, A. (eds.) MICCAI 2015, vol. 9351, pp. 234–241. Springer, Heidelberg (2015). https://doi.org/10.1007/978-3-319-24574-4_28
34. Salama, G., Heier, L., Patel, P., Ramakrishna, R., Magge, R., Tsiouris, A.: Diffusion weighted/tensor imaging, functional mri and perfusion weighted imaging in glioblastoma-foundations and future. Front. Neurol. **8**, 305877 (2018)
35. Smith, S., et al.: Resting-state fMRI in the human connectome project. NeuroImage **80**, 144–168 (2013)
36. Tavor, I., Jones, P., Mars, R., Smith, S., Behrens, T., Jbabdi, S.: Task-free MRI predicts individual differences in brain activity during task performance. Science **352**(6282), 216–220 (2016)
37. Van Essen, D., Glasser, M., Dierker, D., Harwell, J., Coalson, T.: Parcellations and hemispheric asymmetries of human cerebral cortex analyzed on surface-based atlases. Cerebral Cortex **22**(10), 2241–2262 (2012)
38. Yu, X., Aloimonos, Y.: Attribute-based transfer learning for object categorization with zero/one training example. In: Daniilidis, K., Maragos, P., Paragios, N. (eds.) ECCV 2010, vol. 6315, pp. 127–140. Springer, Heidelberg (2010). https://doi.org/10.1007/978-3-642-15555-0_10
39. Zheng, Y.Q., Farahibozorg, S.R., Gong, W., Rafipoor, H., Jbabdi, S., Smith, S.: Accurate predictions of individual differences in task-evoked brain activity from resting-state fmri using a sparse ensemble learner. Neuroimage **259**, 119418 (2022)

Microscopy Image Segmentation via Point and Shape Regularized Data Synthesis

Shijie Li[1]($\boxtimes$), Mengwei Ren[1], Thomas Ach[2], and Guido Gerig[1]

[1] Computer Science and Engineering, New York University, Brooklyn, NY, USA
{shijie.li,mengwei.ren,gerig}@nyu.edu
[2] Ophthalmology, University Hospital Bonn, Bonn, Germany

Abstract. Current deep learning-based approaches for the segmentation of microscopy images heavily rely on large amount of training data with dense annotation, which is highly costly and laborious in practice. Compared to full annotation where the complete contour of objects is depicted, point annotations, specifically object centroids, are much easier to acquire and still provide crucial information about the objects for subsequent segmentation. In this paper, we assume access to point annotations only during training and develop a unified pipeline for microscopy image segmentation using synthetically generated training data. Our framework includes three stages: (1) it takes point annotations and samples a pseudo dense segmentation mask constrained with shape priors; (2) with an image generative model trained in an unpaired manner, it translates the mask to a realistic microscopy image regularized by object level consistency; (3) the pseudo masks along with the synthetic images then constitute a pairwise dataset for training an ad-hoc segmentation model. On the public MoNuSeg dataset, our synthesis pipeline produces more diverse and realistic images than baseline models while maintaining high coherence between input masks and generated images. When using the identical segmentation backbones, the models trained on our synthetic dataset significantly outperform those trained with pseudo-labels or baseline-generated images. Moreover, our framework achieves comparable results to models trained on authentic microscopy images with dense labels, demonstrating its potential as a reliable and highly efficient alternative to labor-intensive manual pixel-wise annotations in microscopy image segmentation. The code can be accessed through https://github.com/CJLee94/Points2Image.

1 Introduction

Instance segmentation is vital in medical imaging as it accurately segments individual objects of interest, allowing clinicians to explore the statistical pattern of

---

S. Li and M. Ren—These authors contributed equally to this work.

Supplementary Information The online version contains supplementary material available at https://doi.org/10.1007/978-3-031-58171-7_3.

Y. Xue et al. (Eds.): DALI 2023, LNCS 14379, pp. 23–32, 2024.
https://doi.org/10.1007/978-3-031-58171-7_3

diseases. Although learning-based methods have excelled, the lack of large-scale datasets with dense annotations is a significant challenge. Manually outlining each object in closely clustered 2D microscopy images is time-consuming and laborious, requiring extensive domain expertise. This problem is even more pronounced in 3D acquisitions. To address this limitation, various approaches have been adopted based on unsupervised pretraining coupled with one/few-shot finetuning [7] which have shown promise in reducing the number of required annotations. However, acquiring accurately annotated samples for the finetuning is still extremely challenging. Another microscopy image labeling strategy that reduces costs is to perform sparse annotation such as bounding boxes, scribbles [26], or center points. These sparse annotations can be utilized to generate a pseudo mask or probability map [5,18,20,29] to train the segmentation model. However, compared to fully supervised methods, they may compromise accuracy and fail on objects with fuzzy boundaries or overlapping structures.

Alternatively, training on synthesized data is another option to compensate for insufficient training datasets by artificially generating large numbers of image and segmentation pairs. For instance, [1] samples brain MRI scans with randomized contrast and resolution from an input label map, greatly benefiting brain segmentation. [12,13] generate microscopy patches by separately synthesizing foreground/background textures. Yet, they require color-based super segmentation, thus limiting their generalization ability to other image modalities. Conditional GANs [15,32] have been employed for semantic image synthesis, which generate realistic images conditioned on an input semantic label [24,25,28]. Accordingly, variants of these semantic synthesis models have then been developed for mask-to-microscopy image translation [3,4,9,21,30] to enhance the microscopy image analysis. Nevertheless, they still rely on pairwise dense label and image during the training stage. Conversely, unpaired image-to-image translation methods [14,32] do not rely on pairwise data, and are repurposed for microscopy images synthesis [10,19,22]. However, [22] requires a joint training using both synthetic and real pairs which is infeasible in our setup as we only have access to point annotations. The most relevant works [10,19] apply CycleGAN to 3D grayscale microscopy dataset, enabling segmentation without groundtruth labels. However, naive re-purposing of CycleGAN without carefully-designed regularizations may lead to inferior performance in color microscopy images where the background patterns are much more complicated than in grayscale images. In our empirical experiments, we observe issues such as contrast inversion between foreground and background, as well as limited image diversity (see Fig. 2).

In this paper, we propose a novel unified microscopy image synthesis and segmentation pipeline that uses only point annotation and image pairs during training. In particular, the synthesis component takes a point label as the input, then transforms the points into a stochastic shape-regularized instance mask, and finally creates a point-regularized microscopy image. Once trained, our synthesis pipeline can generate a diverse set of image-segmentation pairs from a set of real/synthetic point labels. The synthetic data is used for training a segmentation backbone under supervised learning objectives. Our contributions are threefold.

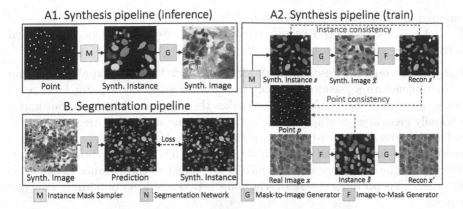

Fig. 1. Framework overview. A1/A2 illustrate the inference/training of our synthesis pipeline that takes a point label as input and samples an instance/segmentation pair. B. is the segmentation backbone trained with the synthetic data in a supervised fashion.

First, we introduce a unified microscopy synthesis and segmentation framework that requires training images with only point annotations. Secondly, we incorporate stochasticity and regularizations into the synthesis pipeline to enhance the diversity of the synthetic dataset while maintaining object-consistency between the generated instance masks and synthetic images. Finally, we train a segmentation network using the synthetic dataset and demonstrate superior performance compared to existing benchmarks at both pixel and object levels. Our results are comparable to those obtained using training on real images with dense annotations, which indicates the potential of our approach to significantly reduce annotation costs.

2   Methods

Formulation. Figure 1 gives an overview of our framework consisting of **A**. synthesis and **B**. segmentation components. The synthesis pipeline samples an instance mask given the input point label with shape priors, and translates the instance mask to a microscopy image. After obtaining a set of point annotations, a synthetic dataset is generated with both synthetic images and instance mask pairs. The point annotations can be either manually created or randomly generated. This dataset is then used to train the segmentation model B.

Formally, we assume access during training to a set of microscopy images $X = \{x_1, x_2, \ldots, x_n\} \in \mathcal{X}$ along with their point annotations $P = \{p_1, p_2, \ldots, p_n\} \in \mathcal{P}$. The notation $\mathcal{X}, \mathcal{S}, \mathcal{P}$ stands for image space, segmentation space, and point mask space separately. The instance mask sampler $M : \mathcal{P} \rightarrow \mathcal{S}$ takes the point labels and samples a set of stochastic instance masks $S = \{s_1, s_2, \ldots, s_n\}$, where $s_i = M(p_i)$. Then, a conditional generator $G : \mathcal{S} \rightarrow \mathcal{X}$ translates the masks to synthetic microscopy images $\tilde{X} = \{\tilde{x}_1, \tilde{x}_2, \ldots, \tilde{x}_n\} \in \mathcal{X}, \tilde{x}_i = G(s_i)$, trained in an unpaired manner as in CycleGAN, which involves a reverse mapping $F : \mathcal{X} \rightarrow \mathcal{S}$ (Fig. 1A2). $(\tilde{X}, S)$ then constitute a synthetic pairwise dataset that can be used to train the segmentation backbone N.

Shape-Regularized Instance Mask Sampler. We use shape distribution priors to generate a pseudo instance mask from a given input point label map. The generation process (M in Fig. 1A) takes the object centroids as input and it randomly generates an ellipse from each point using a sampled area $\mathcal{A}$, angle θ, and eccentricity ϵ. The area $\mathcal{A}$ is sampled from a uniform distribution $\mathcal{U}(a, b(\rho))$, where a is the lower bound of the object area, and b is the upper-bound depends inversely on the object density ρ., which is equivalent to the distance to the nearest point. This prevents severe overlapping between objects in densely crowded regions.

Point-Regularized Mask-to-Image Synthesis. To train the mask-to-image generator G without access to mask-image pairs, we construct G under the commonly used unpaired image translation framework CycleGAN [32]. As shown in Fig. 1A2, G maps the instance mask S to an image X so that $G(S)$ is indistinguishable to an image discriminator D_X (we omit D_X and D_S in Fig. 1 for simplicity). In practice, we represent S as a concatenation of the semantic mask and the horizontal/vertical maps [11]. Additionally, an inverse mapping F enforces the cycle consistency $F(G(S)) \approx S$. To ensure that the output distribution of F aligns with our expectations (i.e., a segmentation map), we formulated F using an instance segmentation framework [11], where $F = \{F_{\text{hv}}, F_{\text{seg}}\}$ predicts both the horizontal/vertical distance maps and the semantic mask. Consequently, we replaced its cycle consistency loss with an instance segmentation loss (Eq. 2). We further incorporate two important considerations into the CycleGAN framework to improve the synthesis quality and fidelity.

Diversity. As the domains of the image and the instance mask possess different complexity (i.e., the mapping between a mask and an image is one-to-many), it contradicts the one-to-one mapping in CycleGAN [6]. Empirically, we find this formulation leads to low diversity of the generated images, particularly within the background (see Fig. 2a). We speculate using such synthetic datasets may yield detrimental segmentation outcomes. To this end, we inject a 3D noise tensor at every layer of the generator (including the input layer) to enable the multimodal synthesis that varies in both local and global image appearances. We also replaced the ResNet generator with the OASIS generator [28] where the network architecture is specifically tailored for semantic image synthesis.

Point Regularization. While incorporating randomness allows for the generation of more diverse samples, it may also indicate a less tractable manipulation of the image content, such as inverting the image color and/or contrast [8,31]. In our application, this phenomenon manifests as a color and texture inversion occurring between the foreground and background elements, as illustrated in Fig. 2b, as some organs in the background have a similar elliptical appearance, which can confuse the model if no regularizer is used. A more regularized process [27] is thus necessary to ensure that the generated image and the input instance mask exhibit a high level of object-level consistency, while adhering to the characteristics of the underlying imaging modality. To do so, we employ the point label P shared by both X and $G(S)$ as a foreground indicator to regularize the output of F. In particular, applying the point regularizer to $F(X)$ enforces F to accurately identify foreground and background pixels. In turn, regularization on $F(G(S))$ guarantees that the synthetic image accurately captures the color distribution of objects.

Objectives. The framework is trained end-to-end with the CycleGAN adversarial terms $\mathcal{L}_{GAN}$, the cycle-consistency terms, as well as the point-consistency terms. We employ LSGAN [23] for the adversarial term as:

$$\mathcal{L}_{\text{GAN}}(D_X) = \frac{1}{2}\mathbb{E}_{x \sim X}\left[||1 - D_X(x)||_2^2\right] + \frac{1}{2}\mathbb{E}_{s \sim S}\left[||D_X(G(s))||_2^2\right],$$
$$\mathcal{L}_{\text{GAN}}(G) = \frac{1}{2}\mathbb{E}_{s \sim S}\left[||D_X(G(s)) - 1||_2^2\right]. \tag{1}$$

Analogous terms are used for $\mathcal{L}_{\text{GAN}}(D_S, F)$. To enforce cycle consistency, we use L1 loss between $G(F(X))$ and X, but replace the consistency between $F(G(I))$ and I to an instance-specific loss [11] to accommodate for different domains of X (image) and S (segmentation) defined as follows:

$$\mathcal{L}_{\text{instance}}(F, G) = \mathbb{E}_{s \sim S}\left[\mathcal{L}_{\text{hv}}(F_{hv}, G) + \mathcal{L}_{\text{seg}}(F_{seg}, G)\right],$$
$$\mathcal{L}_{\text{hv}}(F_{hv}, G) = \mathbb{E}_{s \sim S}\left[||F_{hv}(G(s)) - s_{hv}||_2^2 + ||\nabla F_{hv}(G(s)) - \nabla s_{hv}||_2^2\right], \tag{2}$$
$$\mathcal{L}_{\text{seg}}(F_{seg}, G) = \mathbb{E}_{s \sim S}\left[Dice(F_{seg}(G(s)), i_{seg}) + CE(F_{seg}(G(s)), s_{seg})\right].$$

F_{hv} predicts the horizontal and vertical distance maps from the generated image, and F_{seg} predicts the binary semantic mask. The point-consistency loss between $F(G(S))$ and P, and $F(S)$ and P is defined as

$$\mathcal{L}_{\text{point}}(F, G) = \mathbb{E}_{(s,x,p) \sim (S,X,P)}\left[-p \log F(G(s)) - p \log F(x)\right]. \tag{3}$$

s and x by definition share the identical point label p, as shown in Fig. 1A2.

Segmentation with Synthetic Training Data. With the trained synthesis pipeline, we simulate a dataset from a set of point labels which is then used to train an instance segmentation model N with supervised objectives. In practice, N can be instantiated with different network backbones such as [11,17].

3   Experiments

Setup and Metrics. We conduct experiments on the MoNuSeg dataset [16, 17]. A total of 37 2D microscopy images (size 1000×1000) obtained from 9 tissues are provided, and 14 testing images are held-out for evaluating the trained segmentation models. We use FID (Fréchet Inception Distance) and KID (Kernel Inception Distance) [2] to measure the visual fidelity of the generated images. We also calculate the standard deviation of 10 samples to measure the diversity of the generated images for the same input instance mask. Segmentation performance

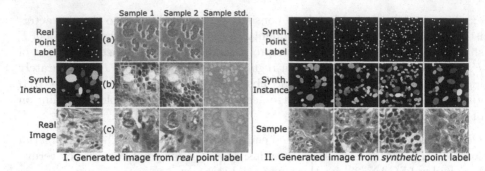

Fig. 2. I. Synthetic samples with a *real* point label from the test set. **(a)** Use of CycleGAN [32] lacks texture diversity. **(b)** Injection of randomness to baseline results in increased diversity but generates incoherent objects and foreground/background color inversion. Our model **(c)** imposes object/point regularization and produces diverse and proper object samples. II. Synthetic samples from fully *synthetic* point labels. Our pipeline generates diverse instance masks and anatomically consistent images.

on the test set is quantified by pixel-level Intersection over Union (IoU) and F1 scores as well as by object-level Dice and Average Jaccard Index (AJI).

Implementation Details. All models are implemented in PyTorch 1.8.1 and trained with Adam optimizer on a single NVIDIA RTX8000 GPU. Training takes around 12 h for the synthesis pipeline and 4 h for the segmentation pipeline. More training/inference details are provided in the appendix.

Microscopy Image Synthesis. We studied the effects of introducing randomness and point regularization on the quality and diversity of samples generated by isolating each components with three different model configurations (Table 1 and Fig. 2): Configuration (a) indicates a baseline CycleGAN; configuration (b) introduces randomness into (a), and (c) is our model with further object regularization. In Fig. 2(a), CycleGAN samples lacked diversity and visual fidelity, as also quantified by the low standard deviation and high FID/KID scores in Table 1. Introducing randomness in (b) improved both FID and KID and increased sample diversity. However, we observed noticeable color and

Table 1. Ablation comparison of image generation quality using inception scores FID, KID, and sample diversity. (a) is a baseline CycleGAN model [32] lacking sample diversity. (b) injects noise, reducing inception distances and increasing diversity, but with erroneous object manipulation (see Fig. 2(b)). Our final model (c) achieves the best inception scores and increased sample diversity.

Config.	Randomness	Point Reg.	FID ↓	KID ↓	Diversity ↑
(a)	–	–	215.58 (1.274)	0.235 (0.003)	4.34e−08
(b)	✓	–	213.45 (2.273)	0.189 (0.002)	0.085
(c)	✓	✓	**102.44 (0.767)**	**0.072 (0.002)**	**0.166**

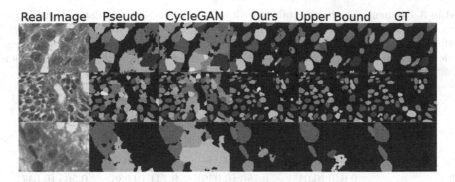

Fig. 3. Comparison of instance segmentation results using an identical segmentation backbone [11] trained on different data pair generation strategies. Models trained with our synthetic data outperforms models trained on pseudo labels or CycleGAN-generated data pairs, approaching the accuracy of models trained on real images with dense annotation. Challenging regions (highlighted by cyan boxes) with fuzzy boundaries are highlighted. More full-slice results are provided in the appendix. (Color figure online)

Table 2. Segmentation results with various backbones. Models using our synthetic data outperform those trained on pseudo labels or using CycleGAN-generated data, approaching the accuracy of models trained on densely annotated real images (Up.bound).

Backbone	Method	Image	Label	Pixel level		Object level	
				IoU ↑	F1 ↑	Dice ↑	AJI ↑
CNN3 [17]	Up.bound	Real	Dense	0.614 (0.05)	0.760 (0.03)	0.734 (0.03)	0.541 (0.05)
	Pseudo [18]	Real	Point	0.508 (0.08)	0.670 (0.06)	0.587 (0.08)	0.311 (0.11)
	CycleGAN [32]	Syn	Point	0.469 (0.11)	0.631 (0.10)	0.547 (0.10)	0.266 (0.12)
	Ours	Syn	Point	**0.600 (0.05)**	**0.749 (0.04)**	**0.691 (0.04)**	**0.463 (0.06)**
HoverNet [11]	Up.bound	Real	Dense	0.644 (0.07)	0.781 (0.01)	0.747 (0.05)	0.572 (0.07)
	Pseudo [18]	Real	Point	0.538 (0.07)	0.697 (0.06)	0.679 (0.05)	0.472 (0.06)
	CycleGAN [32]	Syn	Point	0.483 (0.19)	0.622 (0.23)	0.601 (0.20)	0.413 (0.17)
	Ours	Syn	Point	**0.636 (0.05)**	**0.776 (0.04)**	**0.745 (0.04)**	**0.569 (0.05)**

texture inversion between foreground/background semantics where the colors were incorrectly learned (Fig. 2(b)). Moreover, intractable generation of non-existing objects appeared in the background. Our method (c) with regularization generated visually more realistic samples, and exhibited much higher object-level consistency with the input instance mask. In what follows, we use the generator trained with config (c) for data synthesis and ad-hoc segmentation training (Fig. 3).

Segmentation Results. We evaluate the usability of our synthetic data by training a segmentation model using the generated image-segmentation pairs.

Benchmark. We trained the same segmentation backbone under different data configurations: (1) real images with dense manual annotation which serves as the

Table 3. Segmentation results trained with fully synthetic training data. We train the same backbone (HoverNet) under increasing numbers of generated pairs and observe performance gains at both pixel and object level. Under 92 fully synthetic pairs, the performance surpasses the model trained with 23 real images with dense annotation (see 'Up. bound' under HoverNet in Table 2).

# Synthetic pairs	Pixel level		Object level	
	IoU ↑	F1 ↑	Dice ↑	AJI ↑
23	0.629 (0.046)	0.771 (0.035)	0.718 (0.042)	0.530 (0.055)
46	0.633 (0.045)	0.775 (0.034)	0.728 (0.035)	0.544 (0.047)
69	0.640 (0.045)	0.780 (0.036)	0.741 (0.036)	0.565 (0.047)
92	**0.647 (0.047)**	**0.785 (0.036)**	**0.752 (0.039)**	**0.580 (0.051)**

upper bound for all methods 'Upper bound'; (2) real images with manual point annotation [18] 'Pseudo', where pseudo dense labels are generated from the point annotation; (3) 'CycleGAN' [32] and (4) 'Ours' following the pipeline in Fig. 1 that artificially synthesize the pairwise data given the real point annotations. Table 2 presents pixel/object-level results on the held-out test set. When only point labels are accessible (our assumption), a large performance gap is observed with pseudo labels compared with the upper bound. Training with CycleGAN synthesized dataset does not generalize well to the real test set, indicating a potential lack of data diversity and fidelity as also quantified in Table 1(a). With the same amount of generated data from our pipeline, we achieved highly comparable and/or on-par performance with the upper bound while using only point annotations for training.

Training with Fully Synthetic Dataset. We investigate the performance of a fully synthetic dataset, excluding any real point labels during the data generation process. We randomly sample a set of point labels based on empirical assumptions about the object distribution per image and apply the data generation pipeline accordingly (Fig. 1A). Table 3 presents segmentation results using only synthetic data for training the backbone. As the amount of synthetic data increases, the segmentation performance improves, particularly at the object level, highlighting the effectiveness of our synthetic dataset in enhancing segmentation performance.

4   Discussion

We propose a unified framework for microscopy image segmentation using shape and object regularized data synthesis but only using point-annotated images for training. As demonstrated via comprehensive validation and ablation analysis, our new framework outperforms existing baselines and obtains results similar to models trained on real images with dense annotations while significantly reducing annotation efforts. Our current work leaves some open questions that will be addressed in future research. First, we currently perform offline data synthesis prior to training the segmentation model. Potential benefits of generating data online needs further investigation. Additionally, we plan to incorporate additional prior knowledge, such as accounting for appearance variations among different tissue types, to generate more complex and anatomically-diverse objects.

Data Use Declaration and Acknowledgment. A retrospective analysis was performed on one open-access datasets [16,17], all of whom complied with the Declarations of Helsinki and received approval at their respective institutions. This work is supported by the grants NIH NIBIB R01EB021391, NIH 1R01EY030770-01A1, NIH-NEI 2R01EY013178-15, and the New York Center for Advanced Technology in Telecommunications (CATT).

References

1. Billot, B., et al.: SynthSeg: domain randomisation for segmentation of brain scans of any contrast and resolution. arXiv preprint arXiv:2107.09559 (2021)
2. Bińkowski, M., Sutherland, D.J., Arbel, M., Gretton, A.: Demystifying MMD GANs. In: International Conference on Learning Representations (2018)
3. Butte, S., Wang, H., Vakanski, A., Xian, M.: Enhanced sharp-GAN for histopathology image synthesis. arXiv preprint arXiv:2301.10187 (2023)
4. Butte, S., Wang, H., Xian, M., Vakanski, A.: Sharp-GAN: sharpness loss regularized GAN for histopathology image synthesis. In: 2022 IEEE 19th International Symposium on Biomedical Imaging (ISBI), pp. 1–5. IEEE (2022)
5. Chen, P., et al.: Unsupervised dense nuclei detection and segmentation with prior self-activation map for histology images. arXiv preprint arXiv:2210.07862 (2022)
6. Chu, C., Zhmoginov, A., Sandler, M.: CycleGAN, a master of steganography. arXiv preprint arXiv:1712.02950 (2017)
7. Ciga, O., Xu, T., Martel, A.L.: Self supervised contrastive learning for digital histopathology. Mach. Learn. Appl. **7**, 100198 (2022)
8. Cohen, J.P., Luck, M., Honari, S.: Distribution matching losses can hallucinate features in medical image translation. In: Frangi, A.F., Schnabel, J.A., Davatzikos, C., Alberola-López, C., Fichtinger, G. (eds.) MICCAI 2018, Part I. LNCS, vol. 11070, pp. 529–536. Springer, Cham (2018). https://doi.org/10.1007/978-3-030-00928-1_60
9. Falahkheirkhah, K., Tiwari, S., Yeh, K., Gupta, S., Herrera-Hernandez, L., McCarthy, M.R., Jimenez, R.E., Cheville, J.C., Bhargava, R.: DeepFake histologic images for enhancing digital pathology. Lab. Invest. **103**(1), 100006 (2023)
10. Fu, C., et al.: Three dimensional fluorescence microscopy image synthesis and segmentation. In: Proceedings of the IEEE Conference on Computer Vision and Pattern Recognition Workshops, pp. 2221–2229 (2018)
11. Graham, S., et al.: Hover-net: simultaneous segmentation and classification of nuclei in multi-tissue histology images. Med. Image Anal. **58**, 101563 (2019)
12. Hou, L., Agarwal, A., Samaras, D., Kurc, T.M., Gupta, R.R., Saltz, J.H.: Unsupervised histopathology image synthesis. arXiv preprint arXiv:1712.05021 (2017)
13. Hou, L., Agarwal, A., Samaras, D., Kurc, T.M., Gupta, R.R., Saltz, J.H.: Robust histopathology image analysis: to label or to synthesize? In: Proceedings of the IEEE/CVF Conference on Computer Vision and Pattern Recognition, pp. 8533–8542 (2019)

14. Huang, X., Liu, M.Y., Belongie, S., Kautz, J.: Multimodal unsupervised image-to-image translation. In: ECCV (2018)
15. Isola, P., Zhu, J.Y., Zhou, T., Efros, A.A.: Image-to-image translation with conditional adversarial networks. In: CVPR (2017)
16. Kumar, N., et al.: A multi-organ nucleus segmentation challenge. IEEE Trans. Med. Imaging **39**(5), 1380–1391 (2019)
17. Kumar, N., Verma, R., Sharma, S., Bhargava, S., Vahadane, A., Sethi, A.: A dataset and a technique for generalized nuclear segmentation for computational pathology. IEEE Trans. Med. Imaging **36**(7), 1550–1560 (2017)
18. Li, S., et al.: Point-supervised segmentation of microscopy images and volumes via objectness regularization. In: 2021 IEEE 18th International Symposium on Biomedical Imaging (ISBI), pp. 1558–1562. IEEE (2021)
19. Liu, Q., et al.: Asist: annotation-free synthetic instance segmentation and tracking by adversarial simulations. Comput. Biol. Med. **134**, 104501 (2021)
20. Liu, W., He, Q., He, X.: Weakly supervised nuclei segmentation via instance learning. In: 2022 IEEE 19th International Symposium on Biomedical Imaging (ISBI), pp. 1–5. IEEE (2022)
21. Lou, W., Li, H., Li, G., Han, X., Wan, X.: Which pixel to annotate: a label-efficient nuclei segmentation framework. IEEE Trans. Med. Imaging (2022)
22. Mahmood, F., et al.: Deep adversarial training for multi-organ nuclei segmentation in histopathology images. IEEE Trans. Med. Imaging **39**(11), 3257–3267 (2019)
23. Mao, X., Li, Q., Xie, H., Lau, R.Y., Wang, Z., Paul Smolley, S.: Least squares generative adversarial networks. In: Proceedings of the IEEE International Conference on Computer Vision, pp. 2794–2802 (2017)
24. Park, T., Liu, M.Y., Wang, T.C., Zhu, J.Y.: Semantic image synthesis with spatially-adaptive normalization. In: Proceedings of the IEEE Conference on Computer Vision and Pattern Recognition (2019)
25. Park, T., Liu, M.Y., Wang, T.C., Zhu, J.Y.: Semantic image synthesis with spatially-adaptive normalization. In: Proceedings of the IEEE/CVF Conference on Computer Vision and Pattern Recognition, pp. 2337–2346 (2019)
26. Qu, H., et al.: Weakly supervised deep nuclei segmentation using partial points annotation in histopathology images. IEEE Trans. Med. Imaging **39**(11), 3655–3666 (2020)
27. Ren, M., Dey, N., Fishbaugh, J., Gerig, G.: Segmentation-renormalized deep feature modulation for unpaired image harmonization. IEEE Trans. Med. Imaging **40**(6), 1519–1530 (2021)
28. Sushko, V., Schönfeld, E., Zhang, D., Gall, J., Schiele, B., Khoreva, A.: You only need adversarial supervision for semantic image synthesis. arXiv preprint arXiv:2012.04781 (2020)
29. Tian, K., et al.: Weakly-supervised nucleus segmentation based on point annotations: a coarse-to-fine self-stimulated learning strategy. In: Martel, A.L., et al. (eds.) MICCAI 2020, Part V. LNCS, vol. 12265, pp. 299–308. Springer, Cham (2020). https://doi.org/10.1007/978-3-030-59722-1_29
30. Wang, H., Xian, M., Vakanski, A., Shareef, B.: SIAN: style-guided instance-adaptive normalization for multi-organ histopathology image synthesis. arXiv preprint arXiv:2209.02412 (2022)
31. Zhang, R., Pfister, T., Li, J.: Harmonic unpaired image-to-image translation. arXiv preprint arXiv:1902.09727 (2019)
32. Zhu, J.Y., Park, T., Isola, P., Efros, A.A.: Unpaired image-to-image translation using cycle-consistent adversarial networks. In: 2017 IEEE International Conference on Computer Vision (ICCV) (2017)

A Unified Approach to Learning with Label Noise and Unsupervised Confidence Approximation

Navid Rabbani[1,2](✉) and Adrien Bartoli[1,2]

[1] EnCoV, Institut Pascal, Université Clermont Auvergne, CNRS, Aubière, France
navid_rabbani@yahoo.com
[2] DRCI, CHU Clermont-Ferrand, Clermont-Ferrand, France

Abstract. Noisy label training is the problem of training a neural network from a dataset with errors in the labels. Selective prediction is the problem of selecting only the predictions of a neural network which have sufficient confidence. These problems are both important in medical deep learning, where they commonly occur simultaneously. Existing methods however tackle one problem but not both. We show that they are interdependent and propose the first integrated framework to tackle them both, which we call Unsupervised Confidence Approximation (UCA). UCA trains a neural network simultaneously for its main task (*e.g.* image segmentation) and for confidence prediction, from noisy label datasets. UCA does not require confidence labels and is thus unsupervised in this respect. UCA is generic as it can be used with any neural architecture. We evaluated its performance on the CIFAR-10N and Gleason-2019 datasets. UCA's prediction accuracy increases with the required level of confidence. UCA-equipped networks are on par with the state-of-the-art in noisy label training when used in regular, full coverage mode. However, they have a risk-management facility, showing flawless risk-coverage curves with substantial performance gain over existing selective prediction methods.

Keywords: Noisy labels · Prediction confidence · Instance reweighting

1 Introduction

Deep learning has been very successful in many domains. Effectively training a deep neural network (DNN) generally requires a large amount of carefully labelled data. Medical image datasets, like any real-world dataset, may include noise in the labels. Noisy labels arise when the annotators give a wrong label to the image, either as a random mistake or owing to the ambiguity of the image, leading to inconclusiveness of the annotation task. The rate of label noise can be substantial when the annotators are non-expert humans, automated systems or when the diagnostic uncertainty is intrinsically high, see Fig. 1. While recklessly training a DNN with noisy labels severely degrades performance, specific

Y. Xue et al. (Eds.): DALI 2023, LNCS 14379, pp. 33–42, 2024.
https://doi.org/10.1007/978-3-031-58171-7_4

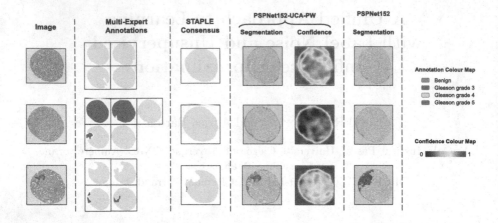

Fig. 1. Test samples from the Gleason-2019 dataset [22] for cancer grading. PSP-Net152 [24] trained from the STAPLE consensus is to date the best performing method (Gleason-2019 challenge). PSPNet152-UCA-PW is PSPNet152 with the proposed UCA trained from STAPLE (very similar results are obtained when trained from the multi-expert annotations). First row: test case with multi-expert agreement, PSPNet152 and PSPNet152-UCA-PW give similar results, PSPNet152-UCA-PW has high confidence. Second row: test case with strong multi-expert disagreement, PSPNet152 and PSPNet152-UCA-PW give similar results, however PSPNet152-UCA-PW indicates low confidence. Third row: test case with mild multi-expert disagreement, PSPNet152 fails to predict the STAPLE consensus, while PSPNet152-UCA-PW does succeed and also indicates low confidence in the disagreement area.

robust training methods exist [4,14,27]. Aside, potential errors are inherent and inevitable in the outputs of any given DNN. To manage the risk caused by these errors, a selective predictor abstains from making predictions when it detects high uncertainty in the DNN predictions. A reliable uncertainty or confidence measure is at the core of selective prediction methods [6]. We claim that the engineering of clinical and healthcare systems would strongly benefit the concurrent features of 1) training from noisy labels and 2) making selective prediction. Both features are well-known but have not been realised concurrently. We show that they are interdependent and solvable in an integrated framework.

We propose Unsupervised Confidence Approximation (UCA), a method to train a DNN for its main task and for confidence prediction, from noisy datasets without confidence labels. UCA gives, for the first time, concurrent solutions for the two mentioned features. It is a major contribution as existing methods solve one of these two problems but fail when they are concurrent. UCA adds a confidence prediction head to the main DNN, whose role is to approximate the confidence for the main task. It is generic, in the sense that it can be used with any neural architecture. The proposed UCA loss makes it possible to train the main network and the UCA head concurrently. It does not require the confidence labels and is thus unsupervised in this respect. We show experimental results on the CIFAR-10N and Gleason-2019 datasets, where UCA shows a strong performance gain over existing selective prediction methods and is on par with the state-of-the-art in noisy label training when used in full coverage mode.

2 Related Work

We review related work in training with noisy labels and predictive uncertainty estimation. *There is no concurrent solution to these two problems.*

Training with noisy labels has been a research focus in machine learning for a decade, see the surveys [4,14,27]. The first approach weights the contribution of samples to the loss. A straightforward method is the confidence-scored instance-dependent noise (CSIDN) weight, which however requires the confidence labels [2]. The weights can also be found during training by constrained optimisation [17]. The second approach iteratively selects samples that are likely to be noise-free [3,12,19,32,35]. These methods use two networks selecting the clean data samples for each other to mitigate the confirmation bias [28]. The third approach uses a noise-resistant loss. The mean absolute error (MAE) was shown to be more robust to noise than cross-entropy (CE) [9]. A generalised cross-entropy (GCE) loss was proposed that combines the advantages of MAE and CE [36]. A loss exploiting class switching probabilities was used [10,13,23]. However, the probabilities are assumed class-dependent and feature-independent, which is not realistic in many cases. The fourth approach uses early training stopping, assuming that the clean data have more impact in the early training steps whilst the noisy samples start corrupting in the later training steps [1].

Predictive uncertainty estimation has recently gained an increased interest, see the survey [6]. The first approach uses the ultimate softmax value of a DNN to predict confidence. A DNN is deemed calibrated when this prediction is valid. A straightforward method is to directly train a calibrated DNN, which however requires the confidence labels [25]. Calibration can also be done by postprocessing from a clean validation dataset [11]. The mixup method regularises the DNN to favour a simple linear behaviour across the training examples, resulting in an improved calibration [29]. The second approach uses a stochastic model. The parameters of Bayesian DNNs are explicitly modelled as random variables, leading to stochastic predictions, from which the confidence can be estimated. Bayesian inference in DNNs is however intractable. This was addressed by Deep Ensembles [18,20,26] and Monte Carlo Dropout (MC-Dropout) [5]. Both techniques are highly resource-intensive and require several forward passes. The probabilistic U-Net [16] is a generative segmentation model based on a combination of a U-Net with a conditional variational autoencoder that is capable of efficiently producing an unlimited number of plausible hypotheses. In [15], a Bayesian deep learning framework combining input-dependent aleatoric uncertainty together with epistemic uncertainty is presented. Aleatoric uncertainty captures data noise rather than label noise inherent in the observations. In [8], an automatic system is proposed that learns not only the probabilistic estimate on the presence of an abnormality, but also an explicit uncertainty measure which captures the confidence of the system in the predicted output. This method is applicable solely to binary classification. While these methods address the uncertainty in the predictions, they are not designed to handle noise in the labels.

3   Method

We predict confidence as a measure of prediction uncertainty [21]. We first describe the 'global UCA', which implements a per sample confidence.

3.1   Noisy Labels and Confidence Score Approximation

We formulate the problem of learning with noisy labels following [34]. Let D be the distribution of the noise-free samples, modelled as a pair of random variables $(X, Y) \in \mathcal{X} \times \mathcal{Y}$, where $\mathcal{X} \subseteq \mathbb{R}^d$ is the input space and $\mathcal{Y} = \{1, 2, \ldots, C\}$ is the target set. In contrast, the samples of a noisy dataset $(X, \bar{Y}) \in \mathcal{X} \times \mathcal{Y}$ are drawn from the noisy distribution $\bar{D}$. A relationship between the two distributions is given by the clean probability of the sample $(x, \bar{y})$:

$$r(x, \bar{y}) = P(Y = \bar{y} \mid \bar{Y} = \bar{y}, X = x). \tag{1}$$

We assume the label noise is structured, image-dependent and label-independent [30,37], which holds very well for human annotations [33]. It means the label noise statistics are highly correlated to the visual features, hence images with similar features have similar noise statistics. Concretely, the human-annotated label noise is due in large part to the image being ambiguous, low quality, inconclusive or confusing, and in small part to random mistakes. The clean probability (1) thus becomes independent of $\bar{y}$; we propose to model it by a DNN $\bar{r}(x; \phi) \approx P(Y = \bar{Y} \mid X = x_i)$ with parameters ϕ. Assuming an effective training of $\bar{r}(x; \phi)$, it provides the average clean probability distribution. As the reliability of the DNN's output for the main task is compromised in regions where training samples have a low clean probability, we can consider $\bar{r}(x; \phi)$ as an approximation for the confidence score.

3.2   Unsupervised Confidence Approximation Loss

We model the DNN for the main task as $y = f(x; \theta)$ with parameters θ. We denote the loss for the main task and the i-th training sample as $L(x_i, \bar{y}_i; \theta) \geq 0$, for $i = 1, \ldots, N$. For per-sample weights $\{w_i\}$, the DNN parameters θ^* are classically found by solving:

$$\theta^* = \operatorname*{argmin}_{\theta} \sum_{i=1}^{N} w_i \, L(x_i, \bar{y}_i; \theta). \tag{2}$$

We propose to use $w_i = \alpha \, \bar{r}(x_i; \phi)$ as sample weights so as to downweight the samples prone to noise. Considering that:

$$\sum_{i=1}^{N} \bar{r}(x_i; \phi) \approx N \mathbb{E}_X \bar{r}(x_i; \phi) = N \sum_i P(Y = \bar{Y} \mid X = x_i) P(X = x_i) = N P(Y = \bar{Y}),$$
$$\tag{3}$$

and normalising the weights to $\sum_{i=1}^{N} w_i = 1$, we have:

$$\alpha = \frac{1}{\sum_{i=1}^{N} \bar{r}(x_i; \phi)} \approx \frac{1}{N P(Y = \bar{Y})} = \frac{1}{NA}, \tag{4}$$

where A is the total labelling accuracy of the training data, considered as a hyperparameter if not known a priori. A naive approach is then to train θ, ϕ by solving:

$$\theta^*, \phi^* = \underset{\theta, \phi}{\arg\min} \sum_{i=1}^{N} \frac{\bar{r}(x_i; \phi)}{NA} L(x_i, \bar{y}_i; \theta). \tag{5}$$

This has trivial spurious solutions, such as weighting all samples with zero except one. We thus add a regularisation term $D(w, u)$ penalising divergence of the discrete weight distribution w, with $w_i = \frac{1}{NA}\bar{r}(x_i; \phi)$, to a prior weight distribution u. We use the non-informative uniform distribution $u_i = \frac{1}{N}$ by default; any other distribution constructed for instance from inter-expert variability may be used instead. We arrive at the proposed UCA loss for training in the presence of noisy data with hyperparameter $\beta > 0$ as:

$$\theta^*, \phi^* = \underset{\substack{\theta, \phi \\ \bar{r}(x;\phi)>0 \\ \sum_{i=1}^{N} \bar{r}(x_i;\theta)=NA}}{\arg\min} \sum_{i=1}^{N} \bar{r}(x_i; \phi) L(x_i, \bar{y}_i; \theta) + \beta D(w, u). \tag{6}$$

The UCA loss is the core of our approach: it allows one to train $f(x; \theta)$ and $\bar{r}(x; \phi)$ end-to-end without needing confidence labels while handling noisy data.

3.3 Unsupervised Confidence Approximation Architecture

We name the DNN $\bar{r}(x; \phi)$ as UCA head, as it learns the instance-based confidence without requiring its label. The UCA head is connected to the features of the main network $f(x; \theta)$, as shown in Fig. 2. We present two versions of the UCA head. The global UCA head implements the method as described thus far, with a per-sample weight $\bar{r}(x; \phi)$. It has a global averaging layer and K fully connected hidden layers with ReLU activation. We use a sigmoid as last activation, enforcing $\bar{r}(x; \phi) > 0$. We use a special batch normalisation layer in the output, enforcing $\sum_i \bar{r}(x_i; \theta) = NA$ in each training batch. The pixelwise UCA head is described in Sect. 3.5.

3.4 Confidence-Selective Prediction

Following the concept of selective classifiers [7], we define the confidence-selective predictor $\tilde{f}$ as a pair of functions (f, r) where $f : \mathcal{X} \to \mathcal{Y}$ is the prediction function and $r : \mathcal{X} \to [0, 1]$ is the confidence function. Defining $t \in [0, 1]$ as the minimum acceptable confidence, the confidence-selective predictor is:

$$\tilde{f}(x) = \begin{cases} f(x), & r(x) \geq t \\ \text{reject} & \text{otherwise.} \end{cases} \tag{7}$$

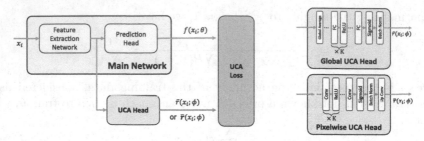

Fig. 2. Unsupervised Confidence Approximation (UCA) architecture.

Concretely, $r(x)$ is obtained by UCA, softmax confidence or any other confidence measure. By varying t, one controls the coverage and consequently the risk. Coverage is the probability mass of the non-rejected region in $\mathcal{X}$ and risk is the expected value of $l(f(x), y)$ on the same region, where $l : \mathcal{Y} \times \mathcal{Y} \to \mathbb{R}$ is a given evaluation loss function. For classification, we use the classification error and for segmentation, we use Jaccard dissimilarity. A risk-coverage (RC) curve is a plot of prediction risk and coverage for a varying t. The RC curve can be used to choose a balancing point with an acceptable trade-off between risk and coverage. We use area under RC curve (AURC) as a performance metric of selective predictors.

3.5   Pixelwise UCA

The above described UCA, which we name global UCA, estimates a single confidence per sample. This is very restricted for complex images and pixelwise tasks such as segmentation, for which one may be interested in accessing the local confidence of the DNN prediction, as shown in Fig. 1. We propose an extension named pixelwise UCA, which predicts a per-pixel confidence map $\bar{\mathbf{r}}_q(x_i; \phi)$ per sample, where $q \in \mathcal{I}$ is the pixel coordinates within the set of image pixel coordinates $\mathcal{I}$. We write the training loss as $\mathbf{L}_q(x_i, \bar{y}_i; \theta)$ for training sample x_i at pixel q. Defining the number of pixels as $M = \text{card}(\mathcal{I})$, we set the weights as $\mathbf{w}_{i,q} = \frac{1}{MNA}\bar{\mathbf{r}}_q(x_i; \phi)$ and the uniform prior distribution as $\mathbf{u}_{i,q} = \frac{1}{MN}$. We arrive at the proposed pixelwise UCA loss as:

$$\theta^*, \phi^* = \underset{\substack{\theta, \phi \\ \bar{\mathbf{r}}_q(x;\phi)>0 \\ \sum_{i=1}^N \sum_{q\in\mathcal{I}} \bar{\mathbf{r}}_q(x_i;\theta)=MNA}}{\operatorname{argmin}} \sum_{i=1}^N \sum_{q\in\mathcal{I}} \bar{\mathbf{r}}_q(x_i; \phi)\, \mathbf{L}_q(x_i, \bar{y}_i; \theta) + \beta\, D(\mathbf{w}, \mathbf{u}). \quad (8)$$

The confidence is modelled by the pixelwise UCA head shown in Fig. 2, which is similar to the global UCA head without the global averaging layer and with convolutional hidden layers instead of fully connected ones. Pixelwise UCA allows pixelwise selective prediction. Concretely, the selective predictor can reject the predicted class for low confidence pixels. The Jaccard index is then computed on the selected pixel set $\mathcal{I}_c = \{q \in \mathcal{I} \mid \bar{\mathbf{r}}_q(x; \phi) \geq t\}$.

4   Experimental Results

Evaluation Metrics. We use standard metrics. We evaluate the ability to cope with noisy labels using the Full Coverage Accuracy (FC-Acc) and Full Coverage Jaccard index (FC-Jac), for classification and segmentation respectively. Full Coverage metrics are computed averaging over the complete test dataset. We evaluate selective prediction using the RC curve and AURC. An effective method must both cope with noisy labels and perform well in selective prediction.

Table 1. FC-Acc and AURC for image classification on CIFAR-10N.

Method	FC-Acc↑	AURC↓
MC-Dropout [5]	82.92%	4.43%
Divide-Mix [19]	89.64%	4.87%
Co-Teaching+ [35]	89.83%	1.75%
ResNet34-CE (Baseline)	86.79%	3.76%
ResNet34-UCA (ours)	89.64%	2.01%
PES (semi) [1]	95.12%	1.60%
PES-UCA (ours)	94.62%	0.96%

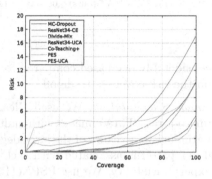

Fig. 3. RC curves on CIFAR-10N.

Image Classification. We use CIFAR10-N [33]. This dataset uses the same images as CIFAR-10 but the training dataset labels are substituted by human-annotated noisy labels. The test dataset labels are kept unchanged. We use ResNet34 trained with CE as baseline, named ResNet34-CE. We connect the global UCA head with $K = 1$ and 128 neurons to the output of layer 4. We train using Eq. (6) and CE as main task loss, with fixed hyperparameters $A = 0.5$ and $\beta = 5$ forming method ResNet34-UCA. We also combined PES [1] and UCA, forming method PES-UCA. We trained in three steps: the main network using PES, then the UCA head and finally the complete DNN, both using Eq. (6). We compare UCA-equipped DNNs with existing methods, all trained on the Random1 subset of CIFAR-10N, whose noise rate is 17.23%. The results are in Table 1 and Fig. 3. Comparing FC-Acc values between ResNet34-CE and ResNet34-UCA shows that UCA successfully downweights the impact of noisy samples. The performance of ResNet34-UCA is substantially better than ResNet34-CE and on par with PES [1], Co-Teaching+ [35] and Divide-Mix [19], which are solid methods in noisy label training. We also observe that MC-Dropout [5], representing uncertainty quantification methods, does not cope with noisy labels. The RC curves and AURCs show that ResNet34-CE performs poorly, but that ResNet34-UCA brings a significant boost. While PES has a satisfactory AURC, its RC curve is mostly flat, making it nearly impossible to trade off coverage for gaining accuracy. In contrast, PES-UCA shows the best RC performance. The AURC is

Table 2. FC-Jac and AURC for image segmentation on Gleason-2019.

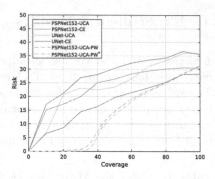

Method	FC-Jac↑	AURC↓
UNet-CE	64.48%	27.79%
UNet-UCA (ours)	64.02%	24.11%
PSPNet152-CE	69.47%	23.74%
PSPNet152-UCA (ours)	71.65%	17.77%
PSPNet152-UCA-PW (ours)	68.56%	13.32%
PSPNet152-UCA-PW* (ours)	68.74%	12.74%

Fig. 4. RC curves on Gleason-2019.

considerably decreased compared to PES and the RC curve gives better control on the risk-coverage trade-off.

Image Segmentation. We used Gleason-2019 [22], Fig. 1. The dataset is tissue micro-array (TMA) images with multiple segmentation masks by up to six expert pathologists. Because of the large degree of heterogeneity in the cellular and glandular patterns associated with each Gleason grade, there is a significant inter-expert variability. We use PSPNet152 and UNet trained with CE as baselines, named PSPNet152-CE and UNet-CE. We connect the global UCA head with $K = 2$ hidden layers with 512 and 128 neurons to the last layer of PSPNet152 and to the last layer of the contracting path of UNet. We trained with STAPLE consensus [31] using Eq. (6) and CE as main task loss forming methods PSPNet152-UCA and UNet-UCA. We also connect the pixelwise UCA head to PSPNet152 with $K = 2$ convolutional layers with 512 and 128 filters and trained using Eq. (8) with STAPLE consensus and with the multi-expert annotations, forming methods PSPNet152-UCA-PW and PSPNet152-UCA-PW* respectively. We use the same hyperparameters $A = 0.75$ and $\beta = 12$ in all cases. The noisy label training methods evaluated above [1,19,35] are not applicable to segmentation. The results are in Table 2 and Fig. 4. UNet-UCA has a similar FC-Jac as the original UNet but decreases AURC by more than 3pp. PSPNet152, as winner of the Gleason-2019 challenge [24], represents the state of the art for this dataset. PSPNet152-UCA boosts the FC-Jac and AURC by more than 5pp and 6pp respectively. UCA thus brings a significant boost to both baselines. PSPNet152-UCA-PW and PSPNet152-UCA-PW* have remarkably better AURCs with an FC-Jac on par with the global one. PSPNet152-UCA-PW* has the benefit of being self-sufficient and to not dependent on STAPLE.

5   Conclusion

We have proposed UCA, the first method to handle training from noisy labels and confidence selective prediction simultaneously. UCA is generic: it does not require additional labels (specifically, confidence labels) and adapts to any existing neural architecture for various tasks, making it an adapted solution in the medical context. It shows a strong performance gain over existing selective prediction methods and is on par with the state-of-the-art in noisy label training when used in full coverage mode. Future work will test UCA in highly subjective medical image computing problems.

References

1. Bai, Y., et al.: Understanding and improving early stopping for learning with noisy labels. In: NeurIPS (2021)
2. Berthon, A., Han, B., Niu, G., Liu, T., Sugiyama, M.: Confidence scores make instance-dependent label-noise learning possible. In: ICML (2021)
3. Cheng, H., Zhu, Z., Li, X., Gong, Y., Sun, X., Liu, Y.: Learning with instance-dependent label noise: a sample sieve approach. arXiv preprint: arXiv:2010.02347 (2020)
4. Cordeiro, F.R., Carneiro, G.: A survey on deep learning with noisy labels: how to train your model when you cannot trust on the annotations? In: SIBGRAPI (2020)
5. Gal, Y., Ghahramani, Z.: Dropout as a Bayesian approximation: representing model uncertainty in deep learning. In: ICML (2016)
6. Gawlikowski, J., et al.: A survey of uncertainty in deep neural networks. arXiv preprint: arXiv:2107.03342 (2021)
7. Geifman, Y., El-Yaniv, R.: Selective classification for deep neural networks. In: NeurIPS (2017)
8. Ghesu, F.C., et al.: Quantifying and leveraging classification uncertainty for chest radiograph assessment. In: Shen, D., et al. (eds.) Medical Image Computing and Computer Assisted Intervention – MICCAI 2019. Lecture Notes in Computer Science(), vol. 11769. Springer, Cham (2019). https://doi.org/10.1007/978-3-030-32226-7_75
9. Ghosh, A., Kumar, H., Sastry, P.S.: Robust loss functions under label noise for deep neural networks. In: AAAI (2017)
10. Goldberger, J., Ben-Reuven, E.: Training deep neural-networks using a noise adaptation layer. In: ICLR (2017)
11. Guo, C., Pleiss, G., Sun, Y., Weinberger, K.Q.: On calibration of modern neural networks. In: ICML (2017)
12. Han, B., et al.: Co-teaching: robust training of deep neural networks with extremely noisy labels. In: NeurIPS (2018)
13. Hendrycks, D., Mazeika, M., Wilson, D., Gimpel, K.: Using trusted data to train deep networks on labels corrupted by severe noise. In: NeurIPS (2018)
14. Karimi, D., Dou, H., Warfield, S.K., Gholipour, A.: Deep learning with noisy labels: exploring techniques and remedies in medical image analysis. Med. Image Anal. **65**, 101759 (2020)
15. Kendall, A., Gal, Y.: What uncertainties do we need in Bayesian deep learning for computer vision? In: Advances in Neural Information Processing Systems, vol. 30 (2017)
16. Kohl, S., et al.: A probabilistic U-Net for segmentation of ambiguous images. In: Advances in Neural Information Processing Systems, vol. 31 (2018)
17. Kumar, A., Amid, E.: Constrained instance and class reweighting for robust learning under label noise. arXiv preprint: arXiv:2111.05428 (2021)
18. Lakshminarayanan, B., Pritzel, A., Blundell, C.: Simple and scalable predictive uncertainty estimation using deep ensembles. In: NeurIPS (2017)

19. Li, J., Socher, R., Hoi, S.C.: DivideMix: learning with noisy labels as semi-supervised learning. arXiv preprint: arXiv:2002.07394 (2020)
20. Liu, J., et al.: Detecting out-of-distribution via an unsupervised uncertainty estimation for prostate cancer diagnosis. In: MIDL (2021)
21. Malinin, A., Gales, M.: Predictive uncertainty estimation via prior networks. In: NeurIPS (2018)
22. Nir, G., et al.: Automatic grading of prostate cancer in digitized histopathology images: learning from multiple experts. Med. Image Anal. **50**, 167–180 (2018)
23. Patrini, G., Rozza, A., Krishna Menon, A., Nock, R., Qu, L.: Making deep neural networks robust to label noise: a loss correction approach. In: CVPR (2017)
24. Qiu, Y., et al.: Automatic prostate Gleason grading using pyramid semantic parsing network in digital histopathology. Front. Oncol. **12**, 1–13 (2022)
25. Raghu, M., Blumer, K., Sayres, R., Obermeyer, Z., Kleinberg, B., Mullainathan, S., Kleinberg, J.: Direct uncertainty prediction for medical second opinions. In: ICML (2019)
26. Rodriguez-Puigvert, J., Recasens, D., Civera, J., Martinez-Cantin, R.: On the uncertain single-view depths in colonoscopies. In: Wang, L., Dou, Q., Fletcher, P.T., Speidel, S., Li, S. (eds.) Medical Image Computing and Computer Assisted Intervention – MICCAI 2022. Lecture Notes in Computer Science, vol. 13433. Springer, Cham (2022). https://doi.org/10.1007/978-3-031-16437-8_13
27. Song, H., Kim, M., Park, D., Shin, Y., Lee, J.G.: Learning from noisy labels with deep neural networks: a survey. IEEE Trans. Neural Netw. Learn. Syst. (2022)
28. Tarvainen, A., Valpola, H.: Mean teachers are better role models: weight-averaged consistency targets improve semi-supervised deep learning results. In: NeurIPS (2017)
29. Thulasidasan, S., Chennupati, G., Bilmes, J.A., Bhattacharya, T., Michalak, S.: On mixup training: improved calibration and predictive uncertainty for deep neural networks. In: NeurIPS (2019)
30. Wang, J., Liu, Y., Levy, C.: Fair classification with group-dependent label noise. In: ACM FAccT (2021)
31. Warfield, S.K., Zou, K.H., Wells, W.M.: Simultaneous truth and performance level estimation (staple): an algorithm for the validation of image segmentation. IEEE Trans. Med. Imaging **23**(7), 903–921 (2004)
32. Wei, H., Feng, L., Chen, X., An, B.: Combating noisy labels by agreement: a joint training method with co-regularization. In: CVPR (2020)
33. Wei, J., Zhu, Z., Cheng, H., Liu, T., Niu, G., Liu, Y.: Learning with noisy labels revisited: a study using real-world human annotations. arXiv preprint: arXiv:2110.12088 (2021)
34. Xia, X., et al.: Are anchor points really indispensable in label-noise learning? In: NeurIPS (2019)
35. Yu, X., Han, B., Yao, J., Niu, G., Tsang, I., Sugiyama, M.: How does disagreement help generalization against label corruption? In: ICML (2019)
36. Zhang, Z., Sabuncu, M.: Generalized cross entropy loss for training deep neural networks with noisy labels. In: NeurIPS (2018)
37. Zhu, Z., Song, Y., Liu, Y.: Clusterability as an alternative to anchor points when learning with noisy labels. In: ICML (2021)

Transesophageal Echocardiography Generation Using Anatomical Models

Emmanuel Oladokun[1(✉)]🆔, Musa Abdulkareem[2]🆔, Jurica Šprem[2]🆔,
and Vicente Grau[1]🆔

[1] Institute of Biomedical Engineering, University of Oxford, Oxford, UK
emmanuel.oladokun@eng.ox.ac.uk
[2] GE HealthCare, Cardiovascular Ultrasound R&D, Chicago, USA

Abstract. Through automation, deep learning (DL) can enhance the
analysis of transesophageal echocardiography (TEE) images. However,
DL methods require large amounts of high-quality data to produce accurate results, which is difficult to satisfy. Data augmentation is commonly
used to tackle this issue. In this work, we develop a pipeline to generate synthetic TEE images and corresponding semantic labels. The proposed data generation pipeline expands on an existing pipeline that generates synthetic transthoracic echocardiography images by transforming
slices from anatomical models into synthetic images. We also demonstrate that such images can improve DL network performance through
a left-ventricle semantic segmentation task. For the pipeline's unpaired
image-to-image (I2I) translation section, we explore two generative methods: CycleGAN and contrastive unpaired translation. Next, we evaluate
the synthetic images quantitatively using the Fréchet Inception Distance
(FID) Score and qualitatively through a human perception quiz involv-
ing expert cardiologists and the average researcher.

In this study, we achieve a dice score improvement of up to 10%
when we augment datasets with our synthetic images. Furthermore, we
compare established methods of assessing unpaired I2I translation and
observe a disagreement when evaluating the synthetic images. Finally,
we see which metric better predicts the generated data's efficacy when
used for data augmentation.

Keywords: Image Generation · Data Augmentation · Ultrasound

1 Introduction

Medical imaging is an essential tool in cardiovascular medicine. Its use can be
found in screening, early diagnosis, treatment, and follow-up. Echocardiography
(Echo) is a key contributor to the assessment and management of cardiac diseases
[19]. Transesophageal Echocardiography (TEE), specifically, is an invasive form

---

Supplementary Information The online version contains supplementary material
available at https://doi.org/10.1007/978-3-031-58171-7_5.

of echo that provides additional and relatively clear visualisation of the heart [12]. Due to its invasive nature, it is uncommonly used and researched relative to other forms, e.g. transthoracic echocardiography (TTE). TEE provides information that is key for diagnosing cardiac pathologies and assessing cardiac performance, including calculating quantitative metrics.

The acquisition process for relevant physiological variables would benefit from automation, which could be accomplished using state-of-the-art computer vision methods. Deep learning (DL) methods have been proven effective in modern image analysis, especially Convolutional Neural Networks (CNNs) [7,11,15,18]. However, the large amount of high-quality labelled data generally required for training, is a challenge. Medical professionals are required to generate the labels (i.e., gold standard approximations to the ground truth), which is often expensive and time-consuming. Furthermore, it has been shown that there is significant inter-observer variability in the labelling of echo images by experienced cardiologists, resulting in up to 22% variability in the calculation of physiological variables [1,3]. Differences occur in the labels because echo images are noisy and often contain artefacts. As a result, boundaries delineating structures are blurred and become open to interpretation. Finally, updating manual labels in light of new information is also time-consuming. In addition to these difficulties, acquiring large amounts of TEE data is especially difficult due to its relatively infrequent use.

Datasets of inadequate size and quality are a common problem in DL, motivating many attempts at finding a solution. A common approach is data augmentation, which aims to increase the size and diversity of a dataset. Most notably, Ronneberger et al. [21] showed that successfully training a deep CNN for semantic segmentation with a small, labelled set of images is possible by randomly applying augmentations, such as rotation and scaling, to existing data to generate 'new' data. However, traditional data augmentation methods are restricted by the strong correlation between the original and augmented samples. Rather than only using real datasets, some researchers have resorted to generating synthetic datasets using synthetic augmentation methods. These methods generally fall into two categories namely, same-domain and cross-domain synthesis. The former involves creating data in the same domain, and the latter involves using data from a source domain to create data in a target domain. The data synthesis approach has largely been spurred on by advancement in generative adversarial networks (GANs), especially the advent of the CycleGAN [24]. For example, conditional GANs (cGANs) have been used to synthesise X-ray images [23], and pairs of MRI and CT images were synthesised using a CycleGAN [6]. Echo images are considerably more difficult to synthesise due to the complex speckle patterns and numerous artefacts. Attempts to synthesise echo images have traditionally taken a modelling approach where the physics behind the observed noise patterns are simulated [4]. Unfortunately, this approach often lacks realism and has poor scalability due to the large computational power needed to run the simulations. Abdi et al. [2] successfully took a synthetic augmentation approach to synthesise echo images by training a patch-based cGAN, but did so using a paired, scarcely annotated dataset.

Using detailed 3D anatomical models and a CycleGAN, Gilbert et al. [9] developed a pipeline where synthetic images are generated from existing high-quality annotations. Using this approach, they generated a synthetic labelled dataset of echo images and trained a CNN for left ventricle (LV) and left atrium segmentation. However, their example only presents two views, apical 4-chamber and apical 2-chamber, which are characteristic views of transthoracic echo. The TEE modality, however, is more data-deprived due to its invasive nature and the large variety of acquired views, making dataset acquisition more challenging. Since the inception of [9], newer methods for unpaired image-to-image (I2I) translation have been developed, such as contrastive unpaired translation (CUT) [17]. Unlike the CycleGAN, CUT is one-sided and does not require as many auxiliary networks and loss functions. Consequently, it has lower memory requirements and requires fewer computational resources to train. Now, with other promising unpaired I2I methods available, we explore whether CUT improves upon the CycleGAN in this context. Furthermore, it is desirable to have a metric that predicts whether the synthetic images from a generator will improve segmentation performance without having to train a segmentation network on each augmented dataset to compare. This contrasts with current metrics for predicting augmentation impact that require training networks to perform the downstream task (segmentation in this case) using clean and augmented datasets [10], which is unrealistic for GAN training. Therefore, we also investigate whether the metrics used to evaluate I2I translation methods can predict augmentation impact. The contributions of this paper are as follows:

1. For the first time, we develop a pipeline[1] capable of automatically generating realistic, labelled synthetic images showing 19^2 standard views of TEE (as defined by the American Society of Echocardiography [12]).
2. We show that these synthetic images can be used to improve performance when tested on a LV segmentation task
3. For the first time, we investigate the link between Fréchet Inception Distance (FID) Score [13] and human-judged realism in synthetic TEE images and explore if either metric can also predict augmentation benefit

2 Methods

2.1 Pseudo-Image Generation

Anatomical Models. Figure 1 shows the journey from anatomical models to usable synthetic images and eventually, augmentation. These models were generated using CT images of asymptomatic hearts acquired at end-diastole. Firstly, the main heart structures were automatically segmented and post-processed, then a mesh was constructed following methods described in [20]. The models contain a full set of tissue labels and labels for all four chambers. The major

---

[1] Code is available at https://github.com/adgilbert/pseudo-image-extraction.git.
[2] Details of which 19 views can be found in the supplementary material.

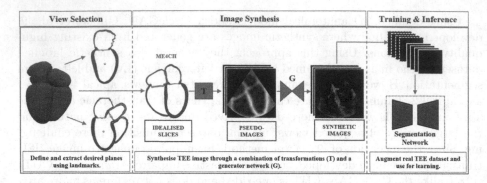

Fig. 1. Synthetic TEE Generation and Image Segmentation Pipeline Using landmarks, desired TEE planes are extracted from each heart model. These ideal slices are the ground truth labels for the synthetic images. Next, pseudo-images are made by adding the acquisition cone and some transformations e.g. Gaussian blurring, shadowing etc., The image synthesis phase concludes with pseudo-images being passed through a trained generator. The synthetic images and their masks can then be used to augment a real dataset for the chosen task

vessels: aorta, pulmonary veins, pulmonary arteries, and both venae cavae are also labelled. More information on the model creation process can be found in the following works [20,22]. From a set of 19 subject-specific anatomical models, Principal Component Analysis was used to create a statistical model. We sampled from this to generate 99 models, which we then used to generate pseudo-images. Full details of this expansion can be found in [9].

TEE View Extraction. According to the American Society of Echocardiography [12], there are 28 standard views acquired in a comprehensive TEE examination. These views can be defined by prescribing which structures should be visible in the echo images. Figure 1 shows how we create pseudo-images for specific views (e.g. Mid-Esophageal 4-Chamber (ME4CH)) extending on the method described in [9]. Three structures that should be present in the image are selected and used to define a unique slice plane. In the case of ME4CH, the three landmarks are the centres of mass of the mitral valve, tricuspid valve, and LV. Furthermore, to mimic the natural variations in ultrasounds during acquisition, we rotate the extracted slice about two mutually perpendicular axes to produce images where only some landmarks are in-plane. The rotation axes were defined by using two landmarks to generate a line along the long- or short-axis of the heart. This process was repeated with different heart models, and the results were visually assessed to ensure the extracted slice was similar to the expected view, despite variations in the heart morphology. Following the slice extraction, an ultrasound cone mask, random noise, shadows, and blurring are added to the image to complete the pseudo-image generation. The parameters of these transformations are randomly sampled from a predefined range to introduce more variability (details on exact parameters can be seen in the GitHub repository) Using this approach, we extended the pipeline by providing functionality to generate 19 of the possible 28 standard views. Our current methodology cannot generate the remaining 9 views, either because the structures present in a view were not available in the shape models or because there were insufficient landmarks to define the plane robustly.

2.2 Image Synthesis

Unpaired I2I Models. Given unpaired datasets X (source domain), and Y (target domain), both the CUT [17] and CycleGAN [24] methods attempt to find an optimal generator $\hat{G}$ that best maps from $X \to Y$. The CycleGAN's two generators $\{G, F\}$ try and fool their respective discriminators $\{D_X, D_Y\}$. High-quality mappings can be attained by combining these networks and adding a cyclic-consistency loss. The CycleGAN's loss function is

$$\mathcal{L}(G, F, D_X, D_Y) = \mathcal{L}_{adv}(G, D_Y, X, Y) + \mathcal{L}_{adv}(F, D_X, Y, X) + \\ \lambda_{cyc}\mathcal{L}_{cyc}(G, F) + \lambda_{idt}\mathcal{L}_{idt}(G, F), \tag{1}$$

where $\mathcal{L}_{\{adv, cyc, idt\}}$ corresponds to the adversarial, cyclic and identity losses, and $\lambda_{\{cyc,idt\}}$ allow the weighting of individual loss terms.

CUT takes a different approach and leverages contrastive learning to encourage content preservation while allowing changes in appearance. CUT samples patches from the original and generated images then via a projection head H, maps patches in the same position together in latent spaces and distances patches from different positions. Its loss function is

$$\mathcal{L}(G, H, D) = \mathcal{L}_{adv}(G, D, X, Y) + \lambda_x\mathcal{L}_{PatchNCE}(G, H, X) + \\ \lambda_y\mathcal{L}_{PatchNCE}(G, H, Y), \tag{2}$$

where $\mathcal{L}_{PatchNCE}$ is the contrastive loss used for the patches, and $\lambda_{\{x,y\}}$ are weighting hyperparameters

Data. The set of real ME4CH echos used in this study consists of 2,914 images sourced from 26 subjects. The images are sampled freely from all parts of the cardiac cycle and were sourced from several institutions in different countries by GE HealthCare. Splits were made on a subject basis. Images from 12 subjects were removed to generate R_{I2I}, which contains 1,959 images. From the remaining 14 subjects, 182 images were sampled, labelled, and then split into train (R_{train}) and test (R_{test}) sets of sizes 155 and 27, respectively. The labelling was performed by two expert cardiologists who use echo daily.

Using the extended pipeline, we generated 854 pseudo-images and the corresponding labels of the ME4CH plane. This dataset was split into sets P_{I2I} and P_{seg}, each containing 503 and 351 images, respectively.

Generative Training. To train the generators discussed in "Unpaired I2I Models", we made use of P_{I2I} and R_{I2I} as the source domain and target domain data. At train time, we manually review and sample results every five epochs.

The best-performing generators in terms of realism were selected by the first author, giving generators $\hat{G}_{cyc}$ and $\hat{G}_{cut}$ (Details of networks, hyperparameters and training schedules can be seen in the supplementary Table 2). Next, synthetic datasets were generated by passing P_{seg} through each generator, thereby generating synthetic sets $\hat{S}_{cyc}$ and $\hat{S}_{cut}$ which both contain 351 images.

Evaluation. The synthetic images were then evaluated in three separate ways. To test realism, we conducted a Turing-like test where two expert cardiologists and six researchers in our group were tasked with labelling echos as real or synthetic. Using VGG's Image Annotator [8], we developed a User Interface (UI) to show the participant an image and ask whether they believed it was real or synthetic. Before the test began, participants were shown several real ME4CH echos. The user could then toggle back and forth through the images, providing responses. The quiz dataset comprised 120 images, 60 real, 30 from CUT, and 30 from CycleGAN. Secondly, we calculate each set's FID score, which quantifies the similarity between two datasets and is commonly used in I2I translation literature [16].

Finally, to evaluate the synthetic data augmentation impact, we use the trusted nnunet framework [14] to train U-Nets for segmenting the LV. Firstly, we generate baselines by training nnunet models on datasets containing a randomly sampled percentage of the original train set. Then, we independently add $\hat{S}_{cyc}$ and $\hat{S}_{cut}$ to the real image sets, giving: purely synthetic datasets, mixed datasets with varying fractions of the real images, and a set containing all real images and all synthetic images from a particular generator. We term the performance metric difference between the real baseline and the augmented sets the 'delta (Δ) metric'. In all cases, we used 3-fold cross-validation and ensured only real images were present in the validation set, thereby only evaluating performance on real images. Standard shape and texture augmentations were included for all runs as they are cheap to run, and we believe the addition of synthetic images can improve performance alongside such transformations.

3   Results and Discussion

Generative Results. Table 1 shows the confusion matrices for each expert and the researcher cohort. The experts were especially adept at identifying real images compared to the researchers. Moreover, the experts had significantly fewer false negatives (Real as Synthetic), showing strong knowledge of what TEE images should look like. Observing the F1-Score, a score which helps measure precision and recall simultaneously, we see that the experts were noticeably better classifiers than the average researcher. This is despite Expert-2's accuracy being close to the average researcher's accuracy range. Interestingly, Expert-1 performed extremely well in identifying the synthetic images as well. Consequently, we further investigated how they made their decisions. They commented that the real image's grey areas and black cavities were more homogeneous and that there were differences in the myocardium.

Table 1. Participant results on the quiz with expert performance and researcher performance separated. Each person was shown 60 real (R) and 60 synthetic (S) images. *Accuracy was rounded to 1 d.p whilst frequencies were rounded to the nearest integer. ** 95% confidence interval

Human Perception Quiz						
Participant	Accuracy [%]	R as R	R as S	S as R	S as S	F1-Score
Expert 1	95.0	55	5	1	59	94.8
Expert 2	79.2	60	0	25	35	82.8
Researchers*	69.7 $[60.2, 79.2]$**	39	21	15	45	68.4

Table 2. FID Score between an unseen set of TEE images and the synthetic sets. A lower score represents better fidelity between the generated and real images

FID Score ↓	
$\hat{G}_{cut}$	$\hat{G}_{cyc}$
188	230

Table 3. Accuracy on the synthetic images only. A lower score shows more difficulty in identifying the generator's image as synthetic

Accuracy (%) ↓			
$\hat{G}_{cut}$		$\hat{G}_{cyc}$	
Experts	Researchers	Experts	Researchers
96.7	91.1	60.0	58.3

Tables 2 and 3 show the FID score for each generator and how successful they were at fooling the quiz participants, respectively. Interestingly, the two metrics do not agree, which suggests that the FID score may not correlate well with human-judged realism, perhaps for medical images in general, but at least for ME4CH TEE images. In Table 3, we see that $\hat{G}_{cyc}$ creates more realistic images compared to $\hat{G}_{cut}$. Furthermore, the expert and researcher cohorts performed similarly in identifying synthetic images from each generator, showing that expert opinion is not required to assess the quality of a generator's synthetic images properly.

LV Segmentation. In Table 4, we see the dice score achieved on the test set (R_{test}) by the models trained on datasets with differing mixtures of real and synthetic data. In all columns except R_{train}^{20}, the networks trained on mixed sets performed best, showing improvements of up to 10%. The maximum dice score achieved (72.9) was by a network trained with mixed data and shows a 5.9% improvement on the baseline. This is especially significant when considering the dataset's realistic size and its heterogeneity in time and source institutions. Moreover, this improvement occurred due to leveraging unlabelled data via the pipeline, and despite the synthetic images only depicting the heart at end-diastole, just like the anatomical models they were sourced from.

Interestingly, the models trained on $[\emptyset \cup R_{train}^{20}]$ and $[\hat{S}_{cut} \cup R_{train}^{20}]$ performed better than expected compared to some sets with more real data. One explanation for this could be the randomness of the data added from 20% to 40%.

Adding training data only improves performance when the added data is relevant to the task at hand. Given the heterogeneity of the data, it is likely that the domain gap between datasets in the R_{train}^{40} column and the test set is larger than the domain gap between the R_{train}^{20} column and test set. This would likely lead to a drop in performance, as seen here.

Table 4. Dice score achieved on the test set. The column headers show real datasets with varying percentages of R_{train}, whilst the first column shows the source of the synthetic data and delta scores. Each non-grey element corresponds to the performance of an nnunet trained on the union of the column and row datasets ($< column > \bigcup < row >$). **Blue** = Best Column Delta Score; **Bold** = Best Overall Dice Score

		Dice Score (x100) ↑				
	$\emptyset$	R_{train}^{20}	R_{train}^{40}	R_{train}^{60}	R_{train}^{80}	R_{train}
$\emptyset$	-	54.7	47.9	51.1	53.5	67.0
$\hat{S}_{cut}$	34.9	50.2	48.2	49.5	63.6	69.5
Δ_{cut}	-	**-4.5**	+0.3	-1.6	**+10.1**	+2.5
$\hat{S}_{cyc}$	20.9	44.2	50.4	53.7	61.8	**72.9**
Δ_{cyc}	-	-10.5	**+2.5**	**+2.6**	+8.3	**+5.9**

When we observe the generative model metrics in tandem with the segmentation results, we see that human realism is a better predictor for augmentation impact than FID Score. $\hat{S}_{cyc}$ produced the better delta score in more mixes and was responsible for the largest overall dice score. This agrees more with the quiz results; notably, the average researcher should be able to make this assessment. This disagreement in evaluation metrics is not unfeasible as even though FID Score usually correlates well with human perception, there is doubt as to whether this is true for medical images [5]. The Inception Net used to calculate the FID Score is pre-trained on natural scene images. Unlike natural scene images, echo images can often hold valuable information in the noise and speckle patterns. Therefore, the FID Score may not be as meaningful for TEE images.

4   Conclusion

In this study, we extended the functionality of an existing pipeline to extract standard TEE views and generate their pseudo-images. We compared image translation methods for transforming pseudo-images into synthetic TEE images, evaluated them with the FID Score, and through a human perception quiz. Next, we showed that these synthetic images improved performance on an LV segmentation task by as much as 10%. Finally, we observed that human perception and the FID Score disagreed in evaluating the realism of synthetic TEE images and that human perception was a better predictor of augmentation impact than the FID Score. Future work could entail exploring the use of these synthetic images for other tasks such as augmenting ultrasound datasets that are not TEE. Another useful path is the development of a quantitative I2I translation metric that can be trusted with medical images.

Acknowledgements. The authors thank D. Kulikova and A. Novikova for their help annotating images and participating in the quiz. We also thank the researchers who participated in the quiz.

References

1. Thorstensen, A., Dalen, H., Amundsen, B.H., Aase, S.A., Stoylen, A.: Reproducibility in echocardiographic assessment of the left ventricular global and regional function, the HUNT study. Eur. J. Echocardiogr. : J. Working Group Echocardiogr. Eur. Soc. Cardiol. **11**(2), 149–156 (2010). https://doi.org/10.1093/EJECHOCARD/JEP188
2. Abdi, A.H., Tsang, T., Abolmaesumi, P.: GAN-enhanced conditional echocardiogram generation (2019). https://arxiv.org/abs/1911.02121v2
3. Armstrong, A.C., et al.: Quality control and reproducibility in m-mode, two-dimensional, and speckle tracking echocardiography acquisition and analysis: the CARDIA study, year 25 examination experience. Echocardiogr. (Mount Kisco, N.Y.) **32**(8), 1233–1240 (2015). https://doi.org/10.1111/ECHO.12832
4. Alessandrini, M., et al.: A pipeline for the generation of realistic 3D synthetic echocardiographic sequences: methodology and open-access database. IEEE Trans. Med. Imaging **34**(7) (2015). https://doi.org/10.1109/TMI.2015.2396632
5. Bargsten, L., Schlaefer, A.: SpeckleGAN: a generative adversarial network with an adaptive speckle layer to augment limited training data for ultrasound image processing. Int. J. Comput. Assist. Radiol. Surg. **15**(9), 1427–1436 (2020). https://doi.org/10.1007/S11548-020-02203-1/TABLES/2
6. Chartsias, A., Joyce, T., Dharmakumar, R., Tsaftaris, S.A.: Adversarial image synthesis for unpaired multi-modal cardiac data. In: Tsaftaris, S., Gooya, A., Frangi, A., Prince, J. (eds.) Simulation and Synthesis in Medical Imaging. Lecture Notes in Computer Science(), vol. 10557. Springer, Cham. https://doi.org/10.1007/978-3-319-68127-6_1
7. Chi, J., Walia, E., Babyn, P., Wang, J., Groot, G., Eramian, M.: Thyroid nodule classification in ultrasound images by fine-tuning deep convolutional neural network. J. Digit. Imaging **30**(4), 477–486 (2017). https://doi.org/10.1007/S10278-017-9997-Y
8. Dutta, A., Zisserman, A.: The VIA annotation software for images, audio and video. In: MM 2019 - Proceedings of the 27th ACM International Conference on Multimedia, pp. 2276–2279 (2019). https://doi.org/10.1145/3343031.3350535
9. Gilbert, A., Marciniak, M., Rodero, C., Lamata, P., Samset, E., McLeod, K.: Generating synthetic labeled data from existing anatomical models: an example with echocardiography segmentation. IEEE Trans. Med. Imaging (2021). https://doi.org/10.1109/TMI.2021.3051806
10. Gontijo-Lopes, R., Smullin, S.J., Dyer, E.: Affinity and diversity: quantifying mechanisms of data augmentation (2020)
11. Hafiane, A., Vieyres, P., Delbos, A.: Deep learning with spatiotemporal consistency for nerve segmentation in ultrasound images (2017). https://arxiv.org/abs/1706.05870v1

12. Hahn, R.T., et al.: ASE guidelines and standards guidelines for performing a comprehensive transesophageal echocardiographic examination: recommendations from the American society of echocardiography and the society of cardiovascular anesthesiologists (2013). https://doi.org/10.1016/j.echo.2013.07.009

13. Heusel, M., Ramsauer, H., Unterthiner, T., Nessler, B., Hochreiter, S.: GANs trained by a two time-scale update rule converge to a local Nash equilibrium (2017)

14. Isensee, F., et al.: nnU-Net: self-adapting framework for U-Net-based medical image segmentation. Informatik aktuell, 22 (2018). https://doi.org/10.1007/978-3-658-25326-4_7

15. Li, Z., Kamnitsas, K., Glocker, B.: Overfitting of neural nets under class imbalance: analysis and improvements for segmentation. In: Shen, D., et al. (eds.) Medical Image Computing and Computer Assisted Intervention – MICCAI 2019. Lecture Notes in Computer Science(), vol. 11766, pp. 402–410. Springer, Cham (2019). https://doi.org/10.1007/978-3-030-32248-9_45, https://arxiv.org/abs/1907.10982v2

16. Maximilian Seitzer: pytorch-fid: FID Score for PyTorch. GitHub (2020). https://github.com/mseitzer/pytorch-fid

17. Park, T., Efros, A.A., Zhang, R., Zhu, J.Y.: Contrastive learning for unpaired image-to-image translation. In: Vedaldi, A., Bischof, H., Brox, T., Frahm, JM. (eds.) Computer Vision – ECCV 2020. Lecture Notes in Computer Science(), vol. 12354, pp. 319–345. Springer, Cham (2020). https://doi.org/10.48550/arxiv.2007.15651

18. PM, C., HS, M.: Transfer learning with convolutional neural networks for classification of abdominal ultrasound images. J. Digit. Imaging 30(2), 234–243 (2017). https://doi.org/10.1007/S10278-016-9929-2

19. Potter, A., Pearce, K., Hilmy, N.: The benefits of echocardiography in primary care. Brit. J. Gen. Pract. 69(684), 358–359 (2019). https://doi.org/10.3399/BJGP19X704513

20. Rodero, C., et al.: Linking statistical shape models and simulated function in the healthy adult human heart (2021). https://doi.org/10.1371/journal.pcbi.1008851

21. Ronneberger, O., Fischer, P., Brox, T.: U-Net: convolutional networks for biomedical image segmentation. In: Navab, N., Hornegger, J., Wells, W., Frangi, A. (eds.) Medical Image Computing and Computer-Assisted Intervention – MICCAI 2015. Lecture Notes in Computer Science(), vol. 9351, pp. 234–241. Springer, Cham (2015). https://doi.org/10.1007/978-3-319-24574-4_28, https://arxiv.org/abs/1505.04597v1

22. Strocchi, M., et al.: A publicly available virtual cohort of four-chamber heart meshes for cardiac electro-mechanics simulations. PLOS ONE 15(6), e0235145 (2020). https://doi.org/10.1371/JOURNAL.PONE.0235145

23. Tang, Y., Tang, Y., Xiao, J., Summers, R.M.: XLSor: a robust and accurate lung segmentor on chest x-rays using criss-cross attention and customized radiorealistic abnormalities generation. In: Proceedings of Machine Learning Research, pp. 1–11 (2019). https://arxiv.org/abs/1904.09229v1

24. Zhu, J.Y., Park, T., Isola, P., Efros, A.A.: Unpaired image-to-image translation using cycle-consistent adversarial networks. In: Proceedings of the IEEE International Conference on Computer Vision 2017-October, pp. 2242–2251 (2017). https://arxiv.org/abs/1703.10593v7

Data Augmentation Based on DiscrimDiff for Histopathology Image Classification

Xianchao Guan[1], Yifeng Wang[1], Yiyang Lin[2], and Yongbing Zhang[1(✉)]

[1] Harbin Institute of Technology (Shenzhen), Shenzhen, China
{guanxianchao,wangyifeng}@stu.hit.edu.cn, ybzhang08@hit.edu.cn
[2] Tsinghua Shenzhen International Graduate School, Tsinghua University,
Beijing, China
lyy20@mails.tsinghua.edu.cn

Abstract. Histopathological analysis is the present gold standard for cancer diagnosis. Accurate classification of histopathology images has great clinical significance and application value for assisting pathologists in diagnosis. However, the performance of histopathology image classification is greatly affected by data imbalance. To address this problem, we propose a novel data augmentation framework based on the diffusion model, DiscrimDiff, which expands the dataset by synthesizing images of rare classes. To compensate for the lack of discrimination ability of the diffusion model for synthesized images, we design a post-discrimination mechanism to provide image quality assurance for data augmentation. Our method significantly improves classification performance on multiple datasets. Furthermore, histomorphological features of different classes concerned by the diffusion model may provide guiding significance for pathologists in clinical diagnosis. Therefore, we visualize histomorphological features related to classification, which can be used to assist pathologist-in-training education and improve the understanding of histomorphology.

Keywords: Computational pathology · Diffusion models · Data augmentation · Histomorphological features

1 Introduction

The classification of histopathology images has great clinical significance for the diagnosis of cancer [1–3]. However, the phenomenon of data imbalance will inevitably occur due to the high annotation costs and scarcity of rare class lesion samples [4]. Imbalanced datasets may lead the model to overfit the minority class and focus excessively on the majority class, thereby degrading the classification

---

X. Guan, Y. Wang and Y. Lin—Co-first authors.

Supplementary Information The online version contains supplementary material available at https://doi.org/10.1007/978-3-031-58171-7_6.

performance. While traditional data augmentation methods can improve the generalization performance to some extent, the inability to expand the rare data impairs their ability to deal with insufficient data for rare classes. Therefore, it is desirable to design novel methods addressing the imbalance of histopathology images for improving classification accuracy [5].

As a typical data augmentation tool, Generative Adversarial Networks can improve the performance of classification by generating images different from the original data [13,14]. However, the presence of discriminators may affect the diversity of generated images [7]. In addition, the problem of unstable training also hinders its practical application. Recently, diffusion models [6,7] have emerged as a promising method for generating high-quality images, which use continuous-time probabilistic models to describe the dynamic evolution of pixels and can synthesize more complex image structures while avoiding the problem of pattern collapse during training. Therefore, diffusion models hold great promise for generating high-quality histopathology images [8–10].

Another crucial factor for improving classification performance is how to ensure the quality of synthetic images used to expand the imbalanced dataset [11,12]. Since the diffusion model lacks the ability to discriminate synthetic images from the real ones [7], we cannot directly use synthetic images to complement the imbalanced dataset. This is because the poor-quality synthetic images will affect the overall distribution of the data set, leading to the degradation of classification performance. To address this problem, we propose a post-discrimination mechanism to guarantee image quality by screening synthetic images.

In summary, the main contributions of this paper are as follows: (1) We propose a DiscrimDiff framework for addressing the data imbalance problem in histopathology image classification. To compensate for the lack of discrimination ability of the diffusion model to synthetic images, we propose a post-discrimination mechanism to provide image quality assurance for data augmentation. (2) Experimental results show that the method significantly improves the classification performance on multiple datasets, which can be used to assist pathologists in improving the accuracy of clinical diagnosis. (3) We visualize histomorphological features related to classification, which can be used to assist pathologist-in-training education to improve pathologists' understanding of histomorphology.

2   Method

To address the data imbalance problem in histopathology image classification, we propose a DiscrimDiff framework for data augmentation, as shown in Fig. 1. We train a diffusion model on histopathology images based on class labels to synthesize the corresponding class image. Due to insufficient discrimination capabilities of the diffusion model to the synthesized images, some images are unsuitable for data augmentation. To address this problem, we design a post-discrimination mechanism to provide image quality assurance for data augmentation. Details will be introduced in subsequent subsections.

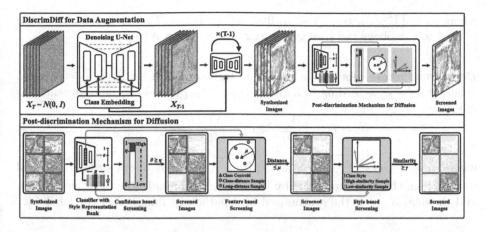

Fig. 1. The panel above shows the overall framework of the proposed DiscrimDiff for Data Augmentation. The panel below shows the details of the post-discrimination mechanism for diffusion.

2.1 Synthesizing Histopathology Images Based on Diffusion Model

Problem Formulation. Suppose a histopathology image dataset D contains R classes, denoted by labels $L_j (j = 1, 2, ..., R)$. There are S images in class L_j expressed by $I_k (k = 1, 2, ..., S)$:

$$D_{L_j} = \{I_k\}. \tag{1}$$

For the task of synthesizing the corresponding classes of histopathology images based on diffusion models, the objective function F can be expressed as:

$$F\{L_j, z \sim N(0, I)\} = \tilde{I}. \tag{2}$$

In the above objective function F, $\tilde{I}$ denotes the synthesized image.

Diffusion Models. The diffusion model is a generative model which consists of two essential processes: the diffusion process and the denoising process. During the diffusion process, the image is gradually added with noise until it becomes random noise. During the denoising process, the image is recovered from Gaussian noise by progressively removing prediction noise at each step using a series of Markov chains. The diffusion model synthesizes high-quality and diverse images through these two processes. In the following, we describe the two processes in detail.

Diffusion Process Suppose X_{0,L_q} is a real histopathology image sample labeled with L_q, and X_{t,L_q} is a noisy image generated by X_{0,L_q} at time $t(t = 1, 2..., T)$, then X_{t,L_q} can be derived based on X_{0,L_q} according to:

$$X_{t,L_q} = \sqrt{\bar{\alpha}_t} X_{0,L_q} + \sqrt{1 - \bar{\alpha}_t} z, \tag{3}$$

where $\bar{\alpha}_t = \prod_{i=1}^{T} \alpha_i$, $\alpha_t = 1 - \beta_t$, $0 < \beta_t (t = 1, 2, ..., T) < 1$ is the noise scale related to t, z obeys the standard normal distribution $N(0, I)$.

Denoising Process. As shown in Fig. 1, we use U-Net with parameter ϵ_θ to generate X_{t-1, L_q} according to a given X_{t, L_q}. The process can be represented as follows:

$$X_{t-1, L_q} = \frac{1}{\sqrt{\alpha_t}} \left(X_{t, L_q} - \frac{1 - \alpha_t}{\sqrt{1 - \bar{\alpha}}} \epsilon_\theta \right) + \sigma_t z, \tag{4}$$

where $\sigma_t = 1 - \sqrt{\frac{(1 - \bar{\alpha}_{i-1})\beta_t}{1 - \bar{\alpha}_t}}$. Starting from X_{T, L_q} that obeys standard normal distribution, the noise predicted by U-Net is subtracted in the iterative process, and the final X_{0, L_q} is the synthesized histopathology image with the label L_q.

Loss Function. The loss function for training the diffusion model is defined as the mean square error (MSE) loss of the actual noise added on the real image and the U-Net estimated one. It can be represented as:

$$L(\theta) = \mathbb{E}_{t, X_{0, L_q}, \epsilon} \left[\left\| \epsilon - \epsilon_\theta \left(\sqrt{\bar{\alpha}_t} X_{0, L_q} + \sqrt{1 - \bar{\alpha}_t} \epsilon, t \right) \right\|^2 \right], \tag{5}$$

where ϵ obeys the standard normal distribution.

2.2   Post-discrimination Mechanism for Diffusion

The diffusion model lacks the ability to discriminate generated images. Therefore, to avoid some poor-quality synthetic images degrading the subsequent classification performance, we propose a post-discrimination mechanism, which ensures the image quality for data augmentation by screening synthetic images. The framework is shown in Fig. 1. Specifically, all synthetic images are then passed into the Classifier with Style Representation Bank, aiming to eliminate those lacking substantial and meaningful informational content. Then a classification model is trained with both original and synthetic images. The trained classification model can be used for inference on test data.

Classifier with Style Representation Bank. We pre-train a specific classifier on the original histopathology dataset to assist in screening synthesized images. The classifier contains a style representation bank of $R \times Q$, where R represents the number of classes, and Q represents the dimension of the style vector. During the training process, we use the Gram matrix of each image as its style, calculate its cosine similarity with the corresponding vector in the representation bank, and update its parameters by minimizing the cosine similarity between them. When the classifier converges, it can not only classify histopathology images and extract features but also store the class-specific styles in each column of the representation bank.

Confidence-Based Screening. The lack of discrimination ability of the diffusion model may cause the synthesized images not to match the given labels. So we only select images with high classification confidence. Specifically, we set a confidence score threshold $\mu(0 < \mu < 1)$. We only select images with confidence score θ higher than threshold μ as candidates for the subsequent screening process.

Feature-Based Screening. Except for the problem of mismatched labels, the diffusion model may also cause the synthesized images to contain fewer class-specific features. So we extract the high-dimensional features from each synthetic image selected in the previous step and calculate the Euclidean distance with the class centroid of the original histopathology dataset. We set a threshold value η for the Euclidean distance and only screen the images whose distance is less than η as candidate images in the subsequent screening process.

Style-Based Screening. To make the synthetic images used for data augmentation closer to real images, we only screen synthetic images whose style is highly similar to that of the corresponding class in the actual dataset. Specifically, we extract style vectors for each synthetic image and perform cosine similarity calculations with the corresponding class style vectors stored in the style representation bank. We set a cosine similarity threshold γ and only screen images with cosine similarity higher than γ as the data augmentation samples for the imbalanced dataset.

Suppose the set of images synthesized by the diffusion model is X, and $|X| = N$, the post-discrimination mechanism can be expressed as:

$$\tilde{X} = \{X_i | \theta_i \geq \eta, d_i \leq \mu, s_i \geq \gamma, i = 1, 2, ..., N\}, \tag{6}$$

where $\tilde{X}$ is the set of images selected for expanding the imbalanced dataset, θ is the classification confidence score, d is the Euclidean distance between each synthetic image's feature and the original dataset's class centroid, s is the cosine similarity between each synthetic image's style vector and the original dataset's class style vector.

3   Experiments

3.1   Datasets and Implementation

We evaluate our method on five publicly available unbalanced histopathology datasets. Table 1 presents the characteristics of these datasets.

Training Details. Our method is implemented with Python based on PyTorch on a computer with Intel(R) Xeon(R) Silver 4210R CPU, 128 GB RAM, and 1 NVidia GTX 3090 GPU. We set $T = 1000$ for all experiments, and the diffusion

Table 1. The datasets used in this paper.

Datasets	Cancer types	Total patches	Number of classes and number of patches in each class
MHIST [16]	Colorectum	3,152	2 (2,161/991)
NCT [17]	Colorectum	100,000	9 (15,550/14,128/12,191/11,851/11, 745/11,413/10,867/9,931/9,504)
BreakHis [18]	Breast	9,109	8 (862/264/196/163/140/135/111/108)
Osteosarcoma [19]	Osteosarcoma	1,144	3 (536/345/263)
WSSS4LUAD [20]	Lung	4,698	3 (1,837/1,680/1,181)

process variances increase linearly from $\beta_1 = 0.0001$ to $\beta_T = 0.02$. The diffusion model is trained for $100,000$ iterations. During training, we use the AdamW optimizer. The learning rate is set as 0.0001 initially and decreases using linear decay. To evaluate the improvement of our method on classification performance, we divided the original dataset into the training set and the test set in an 8:2 ratio, and we identified the category with the largest number of patches in the training set. Then we supplemented the number of patches in other categories to achieve an equal number of patches per category. For example, the training set of MHIST changes from (1544, 632) to (1544, 1544). For model evaluation, we employed 5-fold cross-validation and trained for 100 epochs. Subsequently, we tested the model with the lowest loss on the validation set. Finally, we calculated the average of the final results.

3.2   Result and Discussion

Feature Distribution Visualization. To illustrate the effect of the post-discrimination mechanism on the feature distribution of synthetic images, we performed feature extraction on original and synthetic images of MHIST and NCT using the classifier proposed in Fig. 1. We use the Unified Manifold Approximation and Projection (UMAP) algorithm [15] to visualize the distribution of features across classes explicitly. As shown in Fig. 2, the synthetic image's features without screening are confused, which is inconsistent with the feature distribution of the original dataset. In contrast, the features of the screened synthetic image are distinguishable and consistent with the feature distribution of the original dataset. It demonstrates that the post-discrimination mechanism can fully compensate for the lack of discrimination ability of the diffusion model.

Classification Results. We only expand the data with insufficient samples in the original dataset to demonstrate the effectiveness of our proposed data augmentation method. In Table 2, we list the performance improvement of our classifier using the ResNet18 [21] backbone network under the same hyperparameter settings. The data in brackets represent the specific value of performance

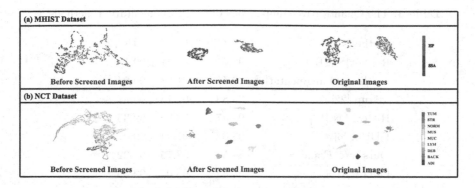

Fig. 2. UMAP diagram of the feature distribution for the synthetic image before and after screening and the original image.

improvement. It demonstrates that our method significantly improves the classification performance on all the evaluation metrics(ACC, F1, and AUC).

Table 2. The classification results without and with DiscrimDiff.

Dataset	Without DiscrimDiff			With DiscrimDiff		
	ACC(%)	F1(%)	AUC(%)	ACC(%)	F1(%)	AUC(%)
MHIST	81.66	80.24	89.75	83.38(+1.72)	82.43(+2.19)	90.96(+1.21)
NCT	92.77	91.41	99.18	96.58(+3.81)	95.14(+3.73)	99.56(+0.38)
BreakHis	88.04	85.98	98.36	89.87(+1.83)	89.30(+3.32)	98.59(+0.23)
Osteosarcoma	95.70	95.40	98.98	96.14(+0.44)	95.69(+0.29)	99.09(+0.11)
WSSS4LUAD	96.57	96.80	99.50	96.89(+0.32)	97.11(+0.31)	99.55(+0.05)

Comparison Results. We compared the quantitative results of our method (including ablation results) with other different augmentation methods, such as traditional augmentation, Mixup [22], HistoGAN [12], and DDPM [6] on the NCT dataset, as shown in Table 3. Here, F represents the feature based screening, and S represents the style based screening. Notably, our method consistently demonstrates significant advantages across all evaluation metrics. Specifically, our method achieves a remarkable enhancement of nearly 4% in classification accuracy compared to the baseline model. Furthermore, our method can better select high-quality images for augmentation than other methods.

3.3 Visualization of Class-Specific Image Features

Since the histomorphological features of different classes concerned by the diffusion model may provide guiding significance for pathologists in clinical diagnosis, we visualize the features related to classification, which can be used to

Table 3. The Quantitative comparisons different augmentation methods.

Methods	ACC(%)	F1(%)	AUC(%)
ResNet18 [21]	92.77	91.41	99.18
Traditional augmentation	93.41	91.88	99.24
Mixup [22]	93.89	92.13	99.31
HistoGAN [12]	94.47	93.02	99.35
DDPM [6]	93.02	91.54	99.07
Ours w/o F and S	94.51	93.75	99.22
Ours w/o S	96.44	95.04	99.39
Ours	**96.58**	**95.14**	**99.56**

assist pathologist-in-training education and improve histomorphological understanding.

By passing the same Gaussian noise to the diffusion model and changing only
the class embeddings, we can observe the apparent differences in the organizational structure between different classes. As shown in Fig. 3(a). For the MHIST
dataset, Hyperplastic Polyp (HP) has a superficial serrated architecture and
elongated crypts. In contrast, Sessile Serrated Adenoma (SSA) is characterized
by broad-based crypts, often with complex structures and heavy serration. To
create transition images from one class to another, as shown in Fig. 3(b), we
perform linear interpolation between the two class embeddings to achieve the
generation of image details transitioning progressively, and we can observe the
tissue structure changes progressively in images.

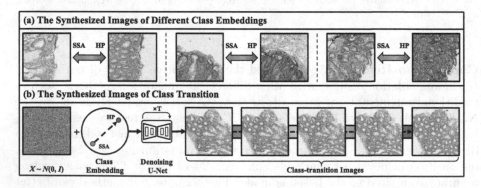

Fig. 3. The visualization of histomorphological features related to the class transition.

4 Conclusion

In this paper, we propose a DiscrimDiff for data augmentation to address data imbalance in histopathology image classification. To compensate for the diffusion model's lack of discrimination capabilities for synthesized images, we design a post-discrimination mechanism to provide image quality assurance for data augmentation. Experimental results demonstrate that our method significantly improves classification performance on multiple datasets. Furthermore, we visualize the influence of class embeddings and their inputting steps on histomorphological features. The visualization reveals key histomorphological features that determine classes, which is helpful to augment pathologist-in-training education and improve the understanding of histomorphology.

Acknowledgements. This work was supported in part by the National Natural Science Foundation of China (62031023), in part by the Shenzhen Science and Technology Project (JCYJ20200109142808034&GXWD20220818170353009), and in part by Guangdong Special Support (2019TX05X187).

References

1. Fuchs, T.J., Buhmann, J.M.: Computational pathology: challenges and promises for tissue analysis. Comput. Med. Imaging Graph. **35**(7–8), 515–530 (2011)
2. Lu, M.Y., Williamson, D.F., Chen, T.Y., Chen, R.J., Barbieri, M., Mahmood, F.: Data-efficient and weakly supervised computational pathology on whole-slide images. Nat. Biomed. Eng. **5**(6), 555–570 (2021)
3. Cui, M., Zhang, D.Y.: Artificial intelligence and computational pathology. Lab. Invest. **101**(4), 412–422 (2021)
4. Abada, E., Anaya, I.C., Abada, O., Lebbos, A., Beydoun, R.: Colorectal adenocarcinoma with enteroblastic differentiation: diagnostic challenges of a rare case encountered in clinical practice. J. Pathol. Transl. Med. **56**(2), 97–102 (2022)
5. Abbasniya, M.R., Sheikholeslamzadeh, S.A., Nasiri, H., Emami, S.: Classification of breast tumors based on histopathology images using deep features and ensemble of gradient boosting methods. Comput. Electr. Eng. **103**, 108382 (2022)
6. Ho, J., Jain, A., Abbeel, P.: Denoising diffusion probabilistic models. In: Advances in Neural Information Processing Systems, vol. 33, pp. 6840–6851 (2020)
7. Dhariwal, P., Nichol, A.: Diffusion models beat GANs on image synthesis. In: Advances in Neural Information Processing Systems, vol. 34, pp. 8780–8794 (2021)
8. Moghadam, P.A., et al.: A morphology focused diffusion probabilistic model for synthesis of histopathology images. In: Proceedings of the IEEE/CVF Winter Conference on Applications of Computer Vision, pp. 2000–2009 (2023)
9. Carrillo-Perez, F., Pizurica, M., Zheng, Y., Shen, J., Gevaert, O.: RNA-to-image multi-cancer synthesis using cascaded diffusion models. bioRxiv (2023)
10. Jeong, J., Kim, K.D., Nam, Y., Cho, C.E., Go, H., Kim, N.: Stain normalization using score-based diffusion model through stain separation and overlapped moving window patch strategies. Comput. Biol. Med. **152**, 106335 (2023)
11. Xue, Y., et al.: Synthetic augmentation and feature-based filtering for improved cervical histopathology image classification. In: Shen, D., et al. (eds.) Medical Image Computing and Computer Assisted Intervention - MICCAI 2019. Lecture

Notes in Computer Science(), vol. 11764, pp. 387–396. Springer, Cham (2019). https://doi.org/10.1007/978-3-030-32239-7_43

12. Xue, Y., et al.: Selective synthetic augmentation with HistoGAN for improved histopathology image classification. Med. Image Anal. **67**, 101816 (2021)

13. Dravid, A., Schiffers, F., Gong, B., Katsaggelos, A.K.: medXGAN: visual explanations for medical classifiers through a generative latent space. In Proceedings of the IEEE/CVF Conference on Computer Vision and Pattern Recognition, pp. 2936–2945(2022)

14. Dolezal, J.M., et al.: Deep learning generates synthetic cancer histology for explainability and education. arXiv preprint: arXiv:2211.06522 (2022)

15. McInnes, L., Healy, J., Melville, J.: UMAP: uniform manifold approximation and projection for dimension reduction. arXiv preprint: arXiv:1802.03426 (2018)

16. Wei, J., et al.: A petri dish for histopathology image analysis. In: Tucker, A., Henriques Abreu, P., Cardoso, J., Pereira Rodrigues, P., Riano, D. (eds.) Artificial Intelligence in Medicine. Lecture Notes in Computer Science(), vol. 12721, pp. 11–24. Springer, Cham (2021). https://doi.org/10.1007/978-3-030-77211-6_2

17. Kather, J. N., Halama, N., Marx, A.: 100,000 histological images of human colorectal cancer and healthy tissue (v0.1) [Data set]. Zenodo (2018). https://doi.org/10.5281/zenodo.1214456

18. Spanhol, F.A., Oliveira, L.S., Petitjean, C., Heutte, L.: A dataset for breast cancer histopathological image classification. IEEE Trans. Biomed. Eng. **63**(7), 1455–1462 (2015)

19. Leavey, P., Sengupta, A., Rakheja, D., Daescu, O., Arunachalam, H.B., Mishra, R.: Osteosarcoma data from UT Southwestern/UT Dallas for Viable and Necrotic Tumor Assessment [Data set]. The Cancer Imaging Archive (2019). https://doi.org/10.7937/tcia.2019.bvhjhdas

20. Han, C., et al.: WSSS4LUAD: grand challenge on weakly-supervised tissue semantic segmentation for lung adenocarcinoma. arXiv preprint: arXiv:2204.06455 (2022)

21. He, K., Zhang, X., Ren, S., Sun, J.: Deep residual learning for image recognition. In: Proceedings of the IEEE Conference on Computer Vision and Pattern Recognition, pp. 770–778 (2016)

22. Zhang, H., Cisse, M., Dauphin, Y.N., Lopez-Paz, D.: mixup: beyond empirical risk minimization. arXiv preprint: arXiv:1710.09412 (2017)

Clinically Focussed Evaluation of Anomaly Detection and Localisation Methods Using Inpatient CT Head Data

Antanas Kascenas[1,2(✉)], Chaoyang Wang[1,5], Patrick Schrempf[1,3],
Ryan Grech[6], Hui Lu Goh[6], Mark Hall[6], and Alison Q. O'Neil[1,4]

[1] Canon Medical Research Europe, Edinburgh, UK
{antanas.kascenas,chaoyang.wang,patrick.schrempf,
alison.oneil}@mre.medical.canon
[2] University of Glasgow, Glasgow, UK
[3] University of St Andrews, St Andrews, UK
[4] University of Edinburgh, Edinburgh, UK
[5] NHS Lothian, Edinburgh, UK
[6] NHS Greater Glasgow & Clyde, Glasgow, UK

Abstract. Anomaly detection approaches in medical imaging show promise in reducing the need for labelled data. However, the question of how to evaluate anomaly detection algorithms remains challenging, both in terms of the data and the metrics. In this work, we take a cohort of inpatient CT head scans from an elderly stroke patient population containing a variety of anomalies, and treat the associated radiology reports as the reference for clinically relevant findings which should be detected by an anomaly detection algorithm. We apply two state-of-the-art anomaly detection methods to the data, namely denoising autoencoder (DAE) and context-to-local feature matching (CLFM) models. We then extract bounding boxes from the predicted anomaly score heatmaps, which we treat as candidate anomaly detections. A clinical evaluation is then conducted in which 3 radiologists rate the candidate anomalies with respect to their detection and localisation accuracy, by assigning the corresponding report sentence where a clinically relevant anomaly is correctly detected, and rating localisation according to a 3-point scale (good, partial, poor). We find that neither method exhibits sufficiently high recall for clinical use, even at low detection thresholds, although anomaly detection shows promise as a scalable approach for detecting clinically relevant findings. We highlight that selection of the optimal thresholds and extraction of discrete anomaly predictions (e.g. bounding boxes) are underexplored topics in anomaly detection.

Keywords: Anomaly Detection · Head CT · Localisation Evaluation

Supplementary Information The online version contains supplementary material available at https://doi.org/10.1007/978-3-031-58171-7_7.

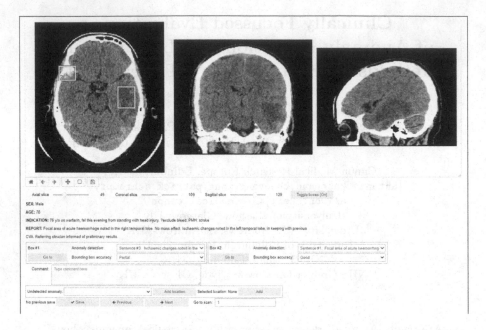

Fig. 1. Our Evaluation User Interface showing a synthetic report and a sample scan from the publicly available CQ500 data [5]. Predicted anomalies are indicated with bounding boxes in the axial images (left), with coronal (middle) and sagittal (right) images available for context. The user can scroll up and down through the volume to view each candidate bounding box set. Candidates are rated on their detection and localisation accuracy using the multiple choice options in the dropdown boxes below.

1   Introduction

In this paper, we consider the task of anomaly detection, specifically the detection and localisation of focal pathologies. Automated detection of pathology could play a role in scan triage and prioritisation, for flagging incidental findings, and even as a second reader for interpreting radiological images.

Anomaly detection methods in medical imaging are an attractive prospect as they are typically unsupervised or semi-supervised, with limited or no need for annotated training examples [22]. However, most proposed methods assume a clean training dataset of healthy samples. Moreover, the evaluation suffers from limited access to test anomalies. Due to data limitations, authors commonly report performance on datasets with single (annotated) pathologies [4,17].

We propose that common evaluation methods of anomaly detection and localisation models using standard image classification and segmentation metrics do not reflect the practical priorities of anomaly detection methods. For example, accurate image classification (as measured by metrics such as scan-level recall, precision and accuracy) is important but for many clinical use cases, a clinician will desire to see the exact region that was detected as anomalous. On the other hand, approximate localisation of anomalies is important, but precise segmentation (as measured by metrics such as Dice score or Hausdorff distance) is usually not necessary, whilst being time-consuming to measure. We thus propose alternative methods of evaluation. Our contributions are as follows:

- We propose a manual evaluation method in which discrete candidate anomaly detections are extracted from the voxel-level model predictions and presented for manual rating of detection and localisation accuracy with reference to the original radiology reports.
- We apply two contrasting state-of-the-art anomaly detection methods [8, 10] to inpatient CT head data.
- We run a blinded evaluation by 3 radiologists, finding the proposed evaluation method to be fast and intuitive for human evaluators to follow, yielding metrics which allow clinically applicable assessment and visualisation of the model behaviour. In common with existing literature [13], we find that neither anomaly detection method yet exhibits sufficiently high recall for clinical use.

2   Related Work

Several prior works have explored the evaluation of anomaly detection methods in medical imaging, as described below.

Baur et al. [4] performed a systematic evaluation of 17 autoencoder anomaly detection method variations on 4 datasets. They highlighted remaining open challenges, of healthy training data acquisition, operating point selection, and the lack of suitable benchmark datasets.

Lagogiannis et al. [12] performed a deep dive into the state of the art of unsupervised pathology detection and compared a selection of image-reconstruction, feature-modelling, attention-based, self-supervised, and self-supervised pretraining anomaly detection methods on 4 datasets. The evaluation concludes that feature-modelling methods are underexplored and raises the question of context-dependent notion of normality/anomaly which is lacking in current approaches.

The medical out-of-distribution (MOOD) analysis challenge [24] is an annual challenge for anomaly detection methods on MRI head and CT abdomen data, using a hidden test set containing natural and synthetic anomalies. The methods are evaluated at sample level for detection and voxel level for localisation.

Our use of NLP to obtain a healthy training set is similar to work on scan triage via anomaly detection by Lee et al. [13]. A generative CN-StyleGAN anomaly detection model was evaluated at sample-level for emergency case detection and by clinical simulation for case prioritisation. It was demonstrated to improve wait and radiology turnaround time, however, high false positive and false negative rates point to the need for further improvements in detection. Localisation accuracy was not quantitatively assessed.

3   Dataset

iCAIRD CT Head Dataset: We use pseudonymised CT head scans obtained through the Industrial Centre for Artificial Intelligence Research in Digital Diagnostics (iCAIRD)[1], for which we obtained ethical approval[2]. The data comes from hospitals in the Greater Glasgow & Clyde (GG&C) region in Scotland and comprises all patients who were diagnosed with a stroke in the period 2013–2018 (mean age of 72 years). The data is held at the West of Scotland Safe Haven; we access it remotely via the Safe Haven Artificial Intelligence Platform [23].

The dataset was assembled by identifying hospital admissions which were assigned International Classification of Diseases (ICD-10 [15]) codes relating to stroke diagnoses, and includes CT head images from the stroke admission as well as any prior CT head images held at GG&C, plus the associated radiology reports. We use 16,559 CT head images available from 7,122 patients. The data contains a variety of naturally occurring anomalies caused by pathologies, unusual anatomy, scanning artefacts, as well as heterogeneous hardware and scan protocols.

Healthy Training Scan Selection: Radiology reports are routinely written by medical doctors to describe the findings in each scan. These text reports can be mined using natural language processing techniques to extract mentions of the presence or absence of findings. For training anomaly detection models, we exclude volumes containing positive findings to obtain a dataset of healthy scans. Specifically, we apply the method of Schrempf et al. [19] to the iCAIRD CT head reports, extracting labels for 14 radiographic findings and 19 clinical impressions, as listed in Appendix B. Each label is predicted as one of 4 classes: *positive, negative, uncertain* or *not mentioned*. Since the dataset is from an elderly stroke population, reports without *any* positive findings are rare. Hence, we consider scans to be healthy for which the only positive findings/impressions are those commonly found in the elderly, namely *calcification, atrophy, cerebral small vessel disease* and *hypodensity* (the latter is highly correlated with atrophy and small vessel disease). To remove follow-up reports (e.g. "No change since last scan."), we filter the remaining cases via keywords and pattern matching using spaCy [6], removing reports which contain references to previous imaging. A manual image quality review is then performed by non-experts, to filter out scans with obvious artefacts. The resulting training dataset contains 804 scans from 757 patients.

Preprocessing: We rigidly register the scans to a reference volume and crop to a fixed field-of-view of the head region. Scans are resampled to 2mm^3 resolution and the voxel intensities are windowed to Hounsfield Unit (HU) values from 0 to 80, then rescaled to the range $[0, 1]$. Random flipping and affine transformation data augmentations are applied during model training.

4   Anomaly Detection Models

Firstly, we use the 3D version of a **denoising autoencoder method (DAE)** [8, 9] which is trained to remove coarse noise and produces dense anomaly scores via

---

[1] https://icaird.com.
[2] West of Scotland Safe Haven ethical approval number GSH19NE004.

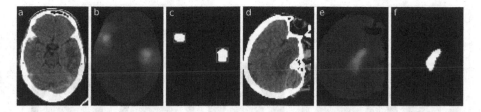

Fig. 2. Images show bounding box extraction for a scan with haemorrhage and ischaemia: (a) axial slice (b) corresponding heatmap from CLFM and (c) derived binarised prediction masks and respective bounding boxes, (d) (rotated) sagittal slice overlaid with outline of 2D bounding box set (e) corresponding heatmap and (f) derived prediction mask and bounding box set outline.

image reconstruction error. The model was trained with 32, 64, 138 convolution output channels in the three stages of the U-Net architecture. We use the Adam [18] optimiser with a "one cycle" learning rate schedule [21] with max_lr = 0.001, batch size of 3 and training duration of 25,600 iterations.

Secondly, we adapt a discriminative **context-to-local feature matching model (CLFM)** [10] for 3D, training it in a supervised fashion with data-augmentation based negatives. We use TorchIO [16] implementations of randomised noise, blur, spike artefact, bias artefact, flip, affine and gamma intensity change transforms in addition to randomised contrast, additive and multiplicative intensity transformations to generate the negatives. We use 32, 64, 128 convolutional output channels in the three stages of CLFM architecture. The context embeddings, instensity embeddings and coordinate embeddings have a dimensionality of 32, 8, 8 respectively. We use the same optimiser and learning rate schedule as for the DAE and train for 32,000 iterations.

Both models were transferred to the 3D iCAIRD data and hyperparameter-tuned on a small validation set of haemorrhage/ischaemia ground truth.

5   Clinical Evaluation Methodology

We run an evaluation on 100 randomly selected scans (selected from a different patient cohort to the training set), by transforming model predictions into discrete anomaly detections which evaluators must rate.

Bounding Box Set Generation: We developed an algorithm to transform 3D heatmap predictions into sets of 2D axial slice anomaly instance masks which in turn are converted into sets of 2D axial slice bounding boxes. This process is visualised in Fig. 2 and described in Appendix D. Each anomaly candidate has an associated anomaly score that is used to rank the candidates from most to least confident i.e. predicted anomalousness. We choose a low threshold t to determine which candidates are presented to evaluators for rating, and subsequently simulate higher detection thresholds for the purpose of computing metrics.

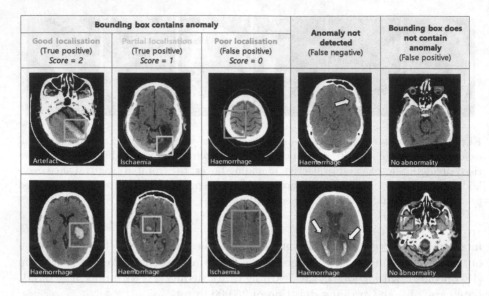

Fig. 3. Illustrative examples for detection rating categories. Samples from the publicly available CQ500 data [5].

Evaluation Interface and Workflow: We implemented an interface using Jupyter notebooks [11], interactive widgets [3] and matplotlib [7] interactive plots [2] for easy viewing and browsing of the anomaly predictions within the context of the original image (see Fig. 1). For each bounding box set, the evaluator assigns the corresponding sentence in the report which describes the detected anomaly (finding), with options for unreported anomalies and false detections. Each positive detection is further evaluated on localisation quality on a 3-point scale (poor, partial, good). Reported but undetected anomalies (false negatives) are also recorded. Figure 3 shows examples for each of the rating categories; these are a subset of the reference examples provided to evaluators in the evaluation protocol. Details of the evaluation workflow are provided in Appendix A.

Study Design: Scans were evaluated by a radiology consultant and two radiology trainees. Of the 100 evaluation scans, 25 were evaluated by all 3 evaluators and 75 scans were split evenly. Detections from both models were presented but the scans were shuffled and evaluators were blinded to which model generated the detections for each scan. In the following analysis, we use the overlapping subset of 25 scans to estimate inter-evaluator agreement, and arbitrarily choose to use annotations from evaluator #2 for the model results.

Metrics: Below we define our precision (P), recall (R) and F_1 metrics. Metrics are expressed in terms of the anomalousness detection threshold t, the number C of candidate bounding box sets which are either detected C_{t+} or undetected C_{t-} at the chosen threshold t, the report sentences assigned by the evaluators to the

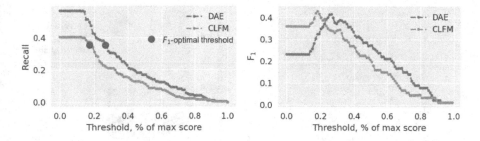

Fig. 4. Recall and F_1 scores across bounding box set anomaly score thresholds t (thresholds expressed as a percentage of the maximum anomaly score for each algorithm).

detected $S_{C_{t+}}$ or undetected $S_{C_{t-}}$ candidates, and the false negative anomaly instances undetected at any threshold A_{FN}.

$$P(C,t) = \frac{\{S_{C_{t+}}\}}{C_{t+}} \quad R(C,t) = \frac{\{S_{C_{t+}}\}}{\{S_{C_{t+}}\} + \{S_{C_{t-}}\} + A_{\mathrm{FN}}} \quad F_1 = 2\frac{P \times R}{P + R}$$

Note that we assume that in each report there is one main sentence to be linked to each positive finding, and therefore by taking the set of unique sentences, we penalise multiple detections of the same anomaly. There are rare cases of bounding box sets containing unreported anomalies, or of sentences describing multiple anomalies, which will lead to a degree of inaccuracy in our metrics.

6   Results

Anomaly Detection Accuracy: Figure 4 shows the recall and F_1 for different detection thresholds. The recall plot shows that at the most generous threshold, the models retrieve only a modest 40% to 60% anomalous findings. Quantitative results are shown in Table 1. Similar performance is reached by both models despite their contrasting modelling principles. We also see that both peaks are relatively "sharp", indicating that selection of the threshold is an important consideration in a practical setting that is often underexplored as many commonly used metrics (e.g. AUPRC, ⌈Dice⌉) do not require a threshold to be set.

Qualitatively, the behaviour of the DAE model is more consistent in picking up anomalies with high contrast (e.g. bright hemorrhages). The CLFM model is capable of detecting more subtle anomalies (e.g. acute ischaemic lesions) but also produces more hard-to-interpret false positives.

Anomaly Localisation Accuracy: We evaluate the localisation quality for different detection thresholds by assigning numerical scores of 0, 1, and 2 to "Poor", "Partial" and "Good" localisations respectively and then calculating the average localisation score across all positive bounding box set predictions. Figure 5 shows the results. The CLFM model produces better localised bounding box sets on

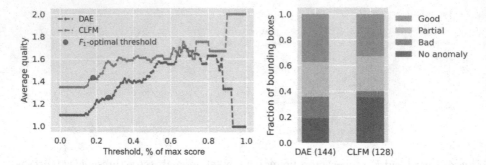

Fig. 5. Positive prediction average anomaly localisation quality across the thresholds t of bounding box set anomaly scores (left) and proposed bounding box set distribution by quality at the F_1-optimal threshold (right).

Table 1. Precision, Recall, F_1 (at F_1-optimal anomaly score threshold) and area under the precision-recall curve (AUPRC) of the two evaluated methods.

Detection method	AUPRC	Precision	Recall	F_1
Denoising autoencoder (DAE) [9]	0.299	0.477	**0.371**	0.417
Context-to-local feature matching (CLFM) [10]	**0.304**	**0.516**	**0.371**	**0.432**

average, however, it also proposes more bounding box sets with no anomalies. We also see that the DAE localisation quality does not fully correlate with the threshold (see thresholds above 0.8); this may indicate that anomaly scores that in part rely on reconstruction error [8] might not be reflective of detection confidence. This is a recognised issue in reconstruction-error-based anomaly detection models (see Meissen et al. [14] for a deeper exploration).

Evaluator Agreement: Finally, we examine evaluation consistency across the three evaluators. We show the F_1 scores of individual evaluators on the 25 commonly evaluated scans in Appendix C, observing similar rating trends across evaluators at different thresholds and for the two algorithms, with only modest absolute variation between evaluators. As the difference across evaluators is similar to the difference in peak F_1 recorded between DAE and CLFM we cannot conclude a significant advantage for one model over the other using our metrics.

7 Conclusion

We have applied two anomaly detection methods to a practical setting of inpatient CT head data, assembling a suitable training dataset of healthy scans by mining the associated radiology reports. Our focus was to obtain clinically meaningful metrics for model performance on this general task, whilst avoiding time-consuming voxel-level annotation or comprehensive re-reading of scans. We first converted the voxelwise anomaly score heatmaps into structured predictions that could be easily rated by clinicians. We then designed an intuitive evaluation UI in collaboration with our clinical evaluators. We finally devised simple rating schemes for detection and localisation accuracy. Since we defined the original radiology reports as the reference, evaluators did not need to comprehensively search for findings that were originally missed. We also made some simplifying assumptions in our analysis (e.g. one main sentence per anomaly in each report) to avoid the need for annotation of the radiology reports.

In common with prior literature [13], we do not find sufficient recall for clinical use, even at low thresholds, although anomaly detection shows promise as a scalable approach for detecting clinically relevant findings. The anomaly detection method and our evaluation could work across patient populations and medical imaging datasets beyond head CT of stroke patients. However, further investigation into handling diffuse pathologies and evaluating anomaly significance might be required for a broader range of clinical situations.

We further highlight the selection of the optimal thresholds and extraction of discrete anomaly predictions (e.g. bounding boxes) as underexplored topics in anomaly detection.

References

1. Flood fill - skimage v0.19.2 docs. https://scikit-image.org/docs/stable/auto_examples/segmentation/plot_floodfill.html. Accessed 24 Apr 2023
2. Interactive figures - matplotlib 3.6.3 documentation. https://matplotlib.org/stable/users/explain/interactive.html. Accessed 24 Apr 2023
3. Jupyter widgets - jupyter widgets 8.0.2 documentation. https://ipywidgets.readthedocs.io/en/stable/. Accessed 24 Apr 2023
4. Baur, C., Denner, S., Wiestler, B., Navab, N., Albarqouni, S.: Autoencoders for unsupervised anomaly segmentation in brain MR images: a comparative study. Med. Image Anal. 101952 (2021)
5. Chilamkurthy, S., et al.: Deep learning algorithms for detection of critical findings in head CT scans: a retrospective study. Lancet **392**(10162), 2388–2396 (2018)
6. Honnibal, M., Montani, I., Van Landeghem, S., Boyd, A.: spaCy: industrial-strength natural language processing in Python (2020). https://doi.org/10.5281/zenodo.1212303
7. Hunter, J.D.: Matplotlib: a 2D graphics environment. Comput. Sci. Eng. **9**(3), 90–95 (2007). https://doi.org/10.1109/MCSE.2007.55
8. Kascenas, A., Pugeault, N., O'Neil, A.Q.: Denoising autoencoders for unsupervised anomaly detection in brain MRI. In: International Conference on Medical Imaging with Deep Learning, pp. 653–664. PMLR (2022)
9. Kascenas, A., et al.: The role of noise in denoising models for anomaly detection in medical images. arXiv preprint arXiv:2301.08330 (2023)
10. Kascenas, A., Young, R., Jensen, B.S., Pugeault, N., O'Neil, A.Q.: Anomaly detection via context and local feature matching. In: 2022 IEEE 19th International Symposium on Biomedical Imaging (ISBI), pp. 1–5. IEEE (2022)
11. Kluyver, T., et al.: Jupyter notebooks - a publishing format for reproducible computational workflows. In: Loizides, F., Scmidt, B. (eds.) Positioning and Power in Academic Publishing: Players, Agents and Agendas, pp. 87–90. IOS Press, The Netherlands (2016). https://eprints.soton.ac.uk/403913/

12. Lagogiannis, I., Meissen, F., Kaissis, G., Rueckert, D.: Unsupervised pathology detection: a deep dive into the state of the art. arXiv preprint arXiv:2303.00609 (2023)
13. Lee, S., et al.: Emergency triage of brain computed tomography via anomaly detection with a deep generative model. Nat. Commun. **13**(1), 4251 (2022)
14. Meissen, F., Wiestler, B., Kaissis, G., Rueckert, D.: On the pitfalls of using the residual as anomaly score. In: Medical Imaging with Deep Learning (2022). https://openreview.net/forum?id=ZsoHLeupa1D
15. Organization, W.H.: ICD-10: international statistical classification of diseases and related health problems: tenth revision (2004)
16. Pérez-García, F., Sparks, R., Ourselin, S.: TorchIO: a python library for efficient loading, preprocessing, augmentation and patch-based sampling of medical images in deep learning. Comput. Methods Program. Biomed. 106236 (2021). https://doi.org/10.1016/j.cmpb.2021.106236, https://www.sciencedirect.com/science/article/pii/S0169260721003102
17. Pinaya, W.H., et al.: Fast unsupervised brain anomaly detection and segmentation with diffusion models. In: Wang, L., Dou, Q., Fletcher, P.T., Speidel, S., Li, S. (eds.) MICCAI 2022. LNCS, vol. 13438, pp. 705–714. Springer, Cham (2022). https://doi.org/10.1007/978-3-031-16452-1_67
18. Reddi, S., Kale, S., Kumar, S.: On the convergence of Adam and beyond. In: International Conference on Learning Representations (2018)
19. Schrempf, P., et al.: Templated text synthesis for expert-guided multi-label extraction from radiology reports. Mach. Learn. Knowl. Extract. **3**(2), 299–317 (2021). https://doi.org/10.3390/make3020015, https://www.mdpi.com/2504-4990/3/2/15
20. Smith, A.R.: Tint fill. In: Proceedings of the 6th Annual Conference on Computer Graphics and Interactive Techniques, SIGGRAPH 1979, pp. 276–283. Association for Computing Machinery, New York (1979). https://doi.org/10.1145/800249.807456
21. Smith, L.N., Topin, N.: Super-convergence: very fast training of neural networks using large learning rates. In: Artificial Intelligence and Machine Learning for Multi-domain Operations Applications, vol. 11006, pp. 369–386. SPIE (2019)
22. Tschuchnig, M.E., Gadermayr, M.: Anomaly detection in medical imaging - a mini review. In: Haber, P., Lampoltshammer, T.J., Leopold, H., Mayr, M. (eds.) Data Science – Analytics and Applications, pp. 33–38. Springer, Wiesbaden (2022). https://doi.org/10.1007/978-3-658-36295-9_5
23. Wilde, K., Anderson, L., Boyle, M., Pinder, A., Weir, A.: Introducing a new trusted research environment – the safe haven artificial platform (SHAIP). Int. J. Popul. Data Sci. **7**(3) (2022)
24. Zimmerer, D., et al.: MOOD 2020: a public benchmark for out-of-distribution detection and localization on medical images. IEEE Trans. Med. Imaging **41**(10), 2728–2738 (2022)

LesionMix: A Lesion-Level Data Augmentation Method for Medical Image Segmentation

Berke Doga Basaran[1,2(✉)], Weitong Zhang[1], Mengyun Qiao[2,3],
Bernhard Kainz[1,4], Paul M. Matthews[3,5], and Wenjia Bai[1,2,3]

[1] Department of Computing, Imperial College London, London, UK
[2] Data Science Institute, Imperial College London, London, UK
bdb19@imperial.ac.uk
[3] Department of Brain Sciences, Imperial College London, London, UK
[4] Friedrich-Alexander University Erlangen-Nürnberg, DE, Erlangen, Germany
[5] UK Dementia Research Institute, Imperial College London, London, UK

Abstract. Data augmentation has become a de facto component of deep
learning-based medical image segmentation methods. Most data augmentation techniques used in medical imaging focus on spatial and intensity transformations to improve the diversity of training images. They
are often designed at the image level, augmenting the full image, and
do not pay attention to specific abnormalities within the image. Here,
we present LesionMix, a novel and simple lesion-aware data augmentation method. It performs augmentation at the lesion level, increasing the
diversity of lesion shape, location, intensity and load distribution, and
allowing both lesion populating and inpainting. Experiments on different
modalities and different lesion datasets, including four brain MR lesion
datasets and one liver CT lesion dataset, demonstrate that LesionMix
achieves promising performance in lesion image segmentation, outperforming several recent Mix-based data augmentation methods. The code
will be released at https://github.com/dogabasaran/lesionmix.

Keywords: Data augmentation · Lesion populating · Lesion
inpainting · Image synthesis · Lesion image segmentation

1 Introduction

Availability of labelled medical imaging data has been a long-term challenge
for developing robust machine learning methods for medical image segmentation. In particular, when dealing with lesions or abnormality detection, datasets
often follow a long-tail distribution [11,21], which means there can be a variety
of categories for abnormal cases but with each category only containing very

---

Supplementary Information The online version contains supplementary material
available at https://doi.org/10.1007/978-3-031-58171-7_8.

few samples. In medical imaging, most data augmentation methods are developed at the image level, aiming to increase the diversity of the full image [8]. They often lack the capability to model specific abnormalities in the images. Recently, several disease-specific augmentation methods have been proposed for brain tumors, multiple sclerosis, and skin lesions [1,2,19]. Unfortunately, the majority of these methods are either disease or organ-specific, or are difficult to train and implement due to their complexity.

In this work, we propose LesionMix, a novel and simple lesion-level data augmentation method for medical image segmentation. LesionMix is able to populate lesions with various properties, including shape, location, intensity and lesion load, as well as inpaint existing lesions by using a dual-branch iterative 3D framework. With LesionMix, we are able to train lesion segmentation models in a low-data setting, even if there are very few samples of lesion images. We perform a comprehensive evaluation of LesionMix using different imaging modalities and datasets, including four brain MR lesion datasets and one liver CT lesion dataset. Experiments show that LesionMix achieves promising lesion segmentation performance on various datasets and outperforms several state-of-the-art (SOTA) data augmentation methods.

1.1   Related Works

Non-generative Data Augmentation. Traditional data augmentation (TDA) techniques are widely used for training medical image segmentation models [12]. TDA include flipping, rotating, scaling, intensity changes, and elastic deformations. These augmentations do not dramatically change the lesion properties, such as the shape and location of lesions with respect to the surrounding tissue. Zhang et al. proposed CarveMix, derived from CutMix [26], which uses a lesion-aware Mix-based technique to carve lesion regions from one image and insert them into another image [28]. Zhu et al. developed another Mix-based data augmentation method, SelfMix, which performs augmentation by mixing tumours with non-tumour regions [29]. Lebbos et al. introduced semantic mixing for rare lesions in ultrasound images [16]. Zhang et al. presented ObjectAug, an object-level augmentation method for semantic image segmentation [27]. These methods provide valuable insights for lesion-level data augmentation. However, they directly mix original lesion masks for augmentation without augmenting individual lesion volumes, with no attention to location of the augmentation, or the lesion load of augmented images.

Generative Data Augmentation. Generative methods provide an alternative way for data augmentation by performing abnormality synthesis. Salem et al. synthesises multiple sclerosis lesions using an encoder-decoder U-Net structure [22]. Bissoto, Jin, and Li et al. utilise generative adversarial networks (GANs) to synthesise skin lesions or brain tumours [5,14,17]. Reinhold et al. creates lesions with a predetermined lesion load using a structural casual model [20]. Xia et al. employs an adversarial framework for subject-specific pathological to healthy image synthesis, referred to as pseudo-healthy synthesis [25]. Similarly, Basaran et al. performs lesion image synthesis and pseudo-healthy synthesis by using cyclic attention-based generators [3]. Lin et al. proposes InsMix, a data augmentation method for nuclei segmentation, by employing a Copy-Paste-Smooth principle with a smooth-GAN for achieving contextual smoothness [18]. While generative augmentation methods have potential for diverse abnormality generation, they are often disease-specific and not easy to extend to different applications and datasets.

1.2 Contributions

There are three main contributions of this work: (1) We propose a novel non-deep data augmentation method, which augments images at the lesion level and accounts for lesion shape, location, intensity as well as load distribution. (2) The method is easy to implement and can be added to a segmentation pipeline to complement traditional data augmentations. (3) It is generic and can be applied to datasets of various modalities (MRI, CT, etc.).

2 Method

2.1 LesionMix

The objective is to develop an efficient and easy-to-implement augmentation method that is aware of lesions in medical images, accounting for the spatial and load distribution of the lesions. Figure 1 illustrates the proposed LesionMix method, which consists of two branches, namely for lesion populating and lesion inpainting. LesionMix takes a lesion image, X, and its corresponding lesion mask, Y, as input, and generates an augmented lesion image, X', and lesion mask, Y', as output, which achieves a target lesion load, v_{tar}. If the target lesion load, v_{tar}, is greater than the current load, v_{cur}, the lesion load is increased via the populating branch. Otherwise, the lesion load is decreased via the inpainting branch. To generate diverse lesion samples, lesion-level augmentations are performed during populating. To maintain the fidelity of the samples, lesions are augmented according to learnt spatial and load distributions.

2.2 Lesion Populating

Lesion-Level Augmentation. Given the input image, X, and its lesion mask, Y, a lesion is randomly selected and augmented. We apply 3D spatial augmentations, brightness augmentations (multiplicative), and Gaussian noise augmentations. Lesion-level spatial augmentations include flipping, rotating, resizing, and elastic deformation. Augmentations are applied by extracting the selected 3D lesion volume, applying the augmentation, and inserting the augmented lesion back into the image. By iteratively inserting lesions into the images, augmented lesions can overlap one another, allowing for unique lesion formations. Augmentation parameters are set empirically and described in the supplementary

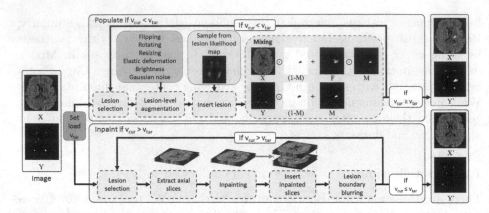

Fig. 1. Illustration of the augmentation process of LesionMix. It consists of lesion populating (top) and lesion inpainting (bottom) branches to iteratively augment images to a desired lesion load.

material. The original image, lesion mask, and the augmented lesion region are mixed using the following equations to generate the augmented image and mask,

$$X' = X \odot (1 - M) + F \odot M \tag{1}$$

$$Y' = Y \odot (1 - M) + M, \tag{2}$$

where F denotes the augmented lesion intensity image, M denotes the mask of the augmented lesion region, and $\odot$ denotes element-wise multiplication. To generate X' we use a soft mask M, in which the boundary pixels of the lesion mask are weighted by 0.66 and the inner pixels are weighted by 1. This allows the lesion boundary to blend more naturally with the input image. Lesion populating can be performed iteratively. At each iteration, lesion-level augmentation is applied to a randomly selected lesion and inserted into the image, until the lesion load, v_{cur}, reaches the target lesion load, v_{tar}.

Lesion Likelihood Map. The augmented lesion is inserted into the original image at a location sampled from a spatial heatmap, termed the lesion likelihood map, which describes the probability that a lesion appears at a specific spatial location in the anatomy. The map is learnt by summing the labels of the images to produce a lesion heatmap and normalising it into a probability map. The map is computed once for each organ dataset before model training. For brain datasets, augmented lesions can occur on both the white matter and gray matter. Although white matter lesions may be more common, gray matter lesions have been recorded in clinical literature [6].

2.3   Lesion Inpainting

Given the input image and lesion mask, a 3D lesion volume is randomly selected. 2D axial slices of the volume are inpainted using the fast marching method [24], which fills in the intensities within the lesion mask with neighbouring intensities from the normal region, formulated by,

$$I(p) = \frac{\sum_{q \in N(p)} w(p, q)[I(q) + \nabla I(q)(p - q)]}{\sum_{q \in N(p)} w(p, q)}, \tag{3}$$

where I denotes the intensity, p denotes a pixel within the lesion mask, $q \in N(p)$ denotes pixels in the neighbourhood of q that belong to the normal region, $\nabla I(q)$ denotes the image gradient at q and $w(p, q)$ denotes a weighting function determined by the distance and direction from q to p [24]. After inpainting, we insert the inpainted slices back into the original image. 2D inpainting is implemented on axial slices of the lesions, due to the simplicity in implementation and fast computation. To ensure 3D continuity of the inpainted lesion, Gaussian blurring is performed on the boundary of inpainted lesions along all three dimensions,

$$X' = G(f(X, M)) \odot \partial M + f(X, M) \odot (1 - \partial M) \tag{4}$$

$$Y' = Y - M, \tag{5}$$

where $f(X, M)$ denotes the inpainting function using fast marching, G denotes the Gaussian blurring function, and ∂M denotes the boundary of the lesion mask. Lesion inpainting can be performed iteratively for randomly selected lesions, until the lesion load, v_{cur}, reaches the target lesion load, v_{tar}.

2.4 Lesion Load Distribution

Unlike other Mix-based methods, LesionMix allows for the generation of datasets with varying lesion load distribution. The load distribution, $P(v)$, is a probability distribution function for lesion volume, v. It characterises the degree of severity of the disease. We experiment with six different lesion load distributions: low, medium, high, uniform, Gaussian, and Real. Real denotes the real distribution learnt from the data. The other five are parametric distribution functions, with parameters described in the supplementary material. For each image to be augmented, we sample the target lesion load, v_{tar}, from the distribution and apply lesion populating or inpainting iteratively to achieve this target. We present the algorithm of LesionMix in Algorithm 1.

2.5 Properties of LesionMix

We compare LesionMix with other Mix-based data augmentation methods, including CutMix [26], CarveMix [28] and SelfMix [29]. LesionMix offers greater control in augmentation, compared to CarveMix and SelfMix. LesionMix is spatially-aware, utilising the lesion likelihood map for drawing locations and thus mixes different backgrounds with the lesion. LesionMix performs shape and intensity augmentations at the lesion level, thus increasing sample diversity. Apart from populating lesions, it is also able to inpaint lesions and control the lesion load distribution. We summarise further in the supplementary material and present a qualitative comparison against CutMix and CarveMix in Fig. 2.

Algorithm 1: LesionMix: Lesion-level augmentation

    Input Training images and annotations $\{(X_1, Y_1), ..., (X_N, Y_N)\}$; the desired number of augmented images T, the desired load distribution $P(v)$.

    Output Augmented training data $\{(X'_1, Y'_1), ..., (X'_T, Y'_T)\}$

for $t=1,2,...,T$ **do**

    Sample target load from the distribution, $v_{tar} \sim P(v)$

    if $v_{cur} < v_{tar}$ **then**

        while $v_{cur} < v_{tar}$ **do**

            1) Randomly select lesion from (X_i, Y_i)

            2) Sample lesion location from the lesion likelihood map

            3) Apply lesion-level augmentations and generate F and M

            4) Apply mixing in Eq. 1 and 2

        end

    else

        while $v_{cur} > v_{tar}$ **do**

            1) Randomly select lesion from (X_i, Y_i) and extract axial slice

            2) Apply inpainting in Eq. 4 and 5 and reinsert slices

        end

    end

    return (X'_i, Y'_i)

end

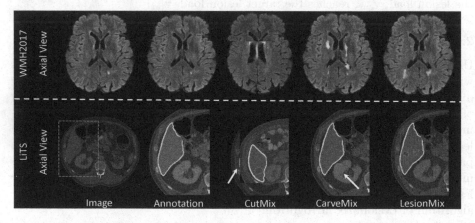

Fig. 2. Original image, annotation and augmented data by Mix-based methods (lesions: red, liver: green). CutMix produces discontinuities in the image. CarveMix can place lesions outside the organ, indicated by arrows. (Color figure online)

3 Experiments

3.1 Data

As a generic method for lesion data augmentation, LesionMix is evaluated on brain lesion MR images and liver lesion CT images.

Brain Lesion Data. Four brain lesion datasets are used, the MICCAI 2008 multiple sclerosis (MS) lesion dataset (MS2008, n=20) [23], ISBI 2015 longitudinal MS lesion dataset (MS2015, n=21) [7], MICCAI 2016 MS lesion dataset (MS2016, n=15) [9], and MICCAI 2017 white matter hyperintensity dataset (WMH2017, n_{train}=60, n_{test}=110) [15]. We use the WMH2017 training set for training a lesion segmentation network with the proposed augmentation method and evaluate its performance on the WMH2017 test set and MS2008, MS2015, MS2016 datasets. For all datasets, FLAIR images are used and resampled to $1 \times 1 \times 1$ mm^3 voxel spacing, followed by brain extraction using FSL [13] and rigid registration into the MNI space [10].

Liver Lesion Data. We use the MICCAI 2017 liver tumor segmentation dataset (LiTS) [4]. The training set contains CT scans for 131 subjects, which are split into batch 1 (n=28) and batch 2 (n=103) by the challenge organisers. We use the LiTS batch 1 dataset for training a liver lesion segmentation network and evaluate its performance on the LiTS batch 2 dataset. The in-plane image resolution ranges from 0.56mm to 1.0mm, and 0.45mm to 6.0mm in slice thickness. The LiTS dataset has high variance of data size and organ shape, therefore we use the normalised label map of the liver as the lesion likelihood map. This ensures the placed lesion is within the liver.

3.2   Implementation Details

The proposed method is developed on PyTorch. All augmentation methods are evaluated with the same segmentation model, nnU-Net with 3D full resolution configuration, and trained for 1,000 epochs on NVIDIA Tesla T4 GPUs.

3.3   Results

Lesion Load Distribution. We perform an ablation study to select the optimal lesion load distribution for LesionMix. We simulate a low-data setting by selecting just training image from WMH2017, perform data augmentation using LesionMix to generate 100 augmented images, and train a segmentation network. Table 1 reports the lesion segmentation performance when six different lesion load distributions are used, and compared against the *None* method, which is trained with a single image without augmentation.

Comparison to Other Data Augmentation Methods. Following the ablation study, we choose the uniform lesion load distribution for the remaining experiments. We compare LesionMix to SOTA data augmentation methods, including traditional data augmentations (TDA), which come default with nnU-Net [12], CutMix [26] and CarveMix [28]. TDA includes rotation, scaling, mirroring, elastic deformation, intensity perturbation and simulation of low resolution. We add CutMix, CarveMix, or the proposed LesionMix onto TDA. We re-implement CutMix [26] for 3D medical images, and use the public code for

Table 1. Mean and standard deviations of lesion segmentation Dice scores (%), when different lesion load distributions are used for LesionMix. Best results are in bold.

Test set	None	Low	Medium	High	Uniform	Gaussian	Real
MS2008	$16.46_{15.43}$	$22.90_{18.59}$	$22.23_{17.63}$	$23.57_{18.72}$	$\mathbf{24.07_{19.04}}$	$22.22_{17.59}$	$22.66_{17.84}$
MS2015	$37.58_{16.05}$	$\mathbf{40.51_{9.05}}$	$37.09_{12.20}$	$40.37_{15.64}$	$39.38_{15.68}$	$36.64_{14.34}$	$37.68_{14.21}$
MS2016	$24.35_{20.07}$	$36.75_{21.33}$	$38.10_{20.37}$	$49.08_{18.05}$	$\mathbf{50.72_{18.96}}$	$41.16_{20.04}$	$50.32_{16.43}$
WMH2017	$39.30_{25.16}$	$49.79_{24.88}$	$51.59_{23.80}$	$58.99_{21.26}$	$\mathbf{59.42_{21.25}}$	$53.23_{22.85}$	$55.24_{21.56}$
LiTS	$3.34_{4.94}$	$9.40_{6.25}$	$12.18_{10.34}$	$13.33_{5.94}$	$\mathbf{13.65_{8.02}}$	$12.88_{7.20}$	$11.99_{7.82}$

CarveMix [28]. We are unable to compare against SelfMix [29] due to unavailability of public code. For fair comparison, all methods use nnU-net as the segmentation network and augment the WMH2017 training set for brain lesions and the LiTS batch 1 dataset for liver lesions by five times. We conduct experiments when different sizes of the training data is used. Table 2 reports the lesion

Table 2. Mean and standard deviations of lesion segmentation Dice scores (%), at different sizes of training data. Best results are in bold. Asterisks indicate statistical significance (*: p≤ 0.05, **: p ≤ 0.01, ***: p ≤ 0.005) when using a paired Student's t-test comparing LesionMix's performance to baseline methods.

Size	Test set	TDA [12]	CutMix [26]	CarveMix [28]	LesionMix
100%	MS2008	$36.72^{*}_{18.07}$	$37.67_{19.09}$	$36.69^{*}_{17.82}$	$\mathbf{38.30_{17.67}}$
	MS2015	$71.59_{11.14}$	$\mathbf{72.81_{7.53}}$	$71.33_{9.96}$	$72.33_{11.41}$
	MS2016	$57.85_{17.50}$	$63.22_{15.04}$	$\mathbf{65.85_{14.26}}$	$65.62_{14.56}$
	WMH2017	$79.13_{10.59}$	$80.14_{9.69}$	$79.74_{9.94}$	$\mathbf{80.95_{9.45}}$
	LiTS	$61.93_{24.30}$	$58.39^{*}_{29.40}$	$60.20_{29.04}$	$\mathbf{63.51_{24.97}}$
50%	MS2008	$35.11_{21.16}$	$35.83_{19.55}$	$32.71^{*}_{19.95}$	$\mathbf{36.04_{18.93}}$
	MS2015	$70.59_{11.14}$	$71.77_{7.16}$	$67.44^{**}_{9.78}$	$\mathbf{71.82_{7.40}}$
	MS2016	$55.75^{***}_{17.82}$	$57.90^{**}_{14.24}$	$62.27_{16.64}$	$\mathbf{62.64_{16.26}}$
	WMH2017	$73.65_{17.30}$	$74.26_{12.69}$	$72.45^{*}_{18.25}$	$\mathbf{75.65_{17.60}}$
	LiTS	$52.40_{29.21}$	$49.60^{*}_{31.32}$	$51.98_{27.99}$	$\mathbf{52.59_{29.18}}$
25%	MS2008	$34.35_{21.49}$	$33.86_{20.21}$	$30.64^{*}_{21.17}$	$\mathbf{34.51_{20.04}}$
	MS2015	$66.09^{**}_{8.82}$	$67.69^{*}_{6.10}$	$67.12^{*}_{8.13}$	$\mathbf{70.73_{8.20}}$
	MS2016	$55.72^{**}_{18.78}$	$58.24_{15.67}$	$60.64_{17.67}$	$\mathbf{60.94_{16.66}}$
	WMH2017	$71.50^{*}_{17.88}$	$72.02_{14.29}$	$72.12_{16.95}$	$\mathbf{73.92_{15.81}}$
	LiTS	$29.88^{***}_{26.52}$	$36.35^{*}_{30.12}$	$36.77_{29.45}$	$\mathbf{39.25_{30.01}}$
10%	MS2008	$28.77^{**}_{17.77}$	$31.32_{18.28}$	$29.57^{*}_{21.66}$	$\mathbf{32.28_{22.11}}$
	MS2015	$63.97^{**}_{9.97}$	$64.97^{*}_{10.15}$	$58.10^{***}_{13.35}$	$\mathbf{67.13_{10.73}}$
	MS2016	$43.07^{***}_{17.03}$	$49.58^{***}_{13.65}$	$50.34^{***}_{13.71}$	$\mathbf{61.02_{15.56}}$
	WMH2017	$71.16_{16.70}$	$70.18^{*}_{14.79}$	$67.80^{**}_{19.97}$	$\mathbf{72.03_{15.48}}$
	LiTS	$24.23^{***}_{25.76}$	$27.99_{29.26}$	$20.53^{***}_{26.84}$	$\mathbf{30.12_{27.47}}$

segmentation Dice scores for different data augmentation methods. LesionMix improves lesion segmentation against SOTA methods in the majority of experiments. We notice greater statistical significance in experiments with smaller dataset sizes. We present example segmentations against benchmark methods in Fig. 3.

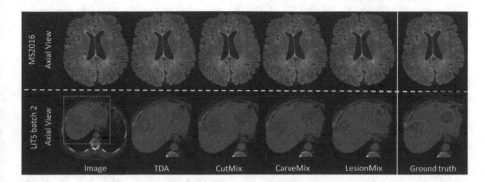

Fig. 3. Qualitative comparison of segmentation performance when 10% of dataset size is used. Models with LesionMix detect more lesions and segment them more accurately.

4 Conclusion

We present LesionMix, a simple lesion-level data augmentation method. It is aware of the lesion likelihood distribution and produces augmented data with varying lesion load. LesionMix improves segmentation performance against other Mix-based augmentation methods across datasets of different modalities and organs. It is modality- and organ-agnostic and can serve as a useful tool for medical image segmentation.

Acknowledgements. This work is supported by the UKRI CDT in AI for Healthcare http://ai4health.io (Grant No. EP/S023283/1).

References

1. Abdelhalim, I.S.A., Mohamed, M.F., Mahdy, Y.B.: Data augmentation for skin lesion using self-attention based progressive generative adversarial network. Expert Syst. Appl. **165**, 113922 (2021)
2. Barile, B., Marzullo, A., Stamile, C., Durand-Dubief, F., Sappey-Marinier, D.: Data augmentation using generative adversarial neural networks on brain structural connectivity in multiple sclerosis. Comput. Methods Programs Biomed. **206**, 106113 (2021)

3. Basaran, B.D., Qiao, M., Matthews, P.M., Bai, W.: Subject-specific lesion generation and pseudo-healthy synthesis for multiple sclerosis brain images. In: Zhao, C., Svoboda, D., Wolterink, J.M., Escobar, M. (eds.) Simulation and Synthesis in Medical Imaging. Lecture Notes in Computer Science, vol. 13570, pp. 1–11. Springer, Cham (2022). https://doi.org/10.1007/978-3-031-16980-9_1

4. Bilic, P., et al.: The liver tumor segmentation benchmark (LiTS). Med. Image Anal. **84**, 102680 (2023)

5. Bissoto, A., Perez, F., Valle, E., Avila, S.: Skin lesion synthesis with generative adversarial networks. In: OR 2.0 Context-Aware Operating Theaters, Computer Assisted Robotic Endoscopy, Clinical Image-Based Procedures, and Skin Image Analysis (2018)

6. Calabrese, M., Favaretto, A., Martini, V., Gallo, P.: Grey matter lesions in MS. Prion (2013)

7. Carass, A., et al.: Longitudinal multiple sclerosis lesion segmentation: resource and challenge. Neuroimage **148**, 77–102 (2017)

8. Chlap, P., Min, H., Vandenberg, N., Dowling, J.A., Holloway, L., Haworth, A.: A review of medical image data augmentation techniques for deep learning applications. J. Med. Imaging Radiat. Oncol. **65**, 545–563 (2021)

9. Commowick, O., et al.: Objective evaluation of multiple sclerosis lesion segmentation using a data management and processing infrastructure. Sci. Rep. **8**, 13650 (2018)

10. Fonov, V., Evans, A., McKinstry, R., Almli, C., Collins, D.: Unbiased nonlinear average age-appropriate brain templates from birth to adulthood. Neuroimage **47**, S102 (2009)

11. Galdran, A., Carneiro, G., González Ballester, M.A.: Balanced-mixup for highly imbalanced medical image classification. In: de Bruijne, M., et al. (eds.) Medical Image Computing and Computer Assisted Intervention – MICCAI 2021. Lecture Notes in Computer Science(), vol. 12905. Springer, Cham (2021). https://doi.org/10.1007/978-3-030-87240-3_31

12. Isensee, F., Jaeger, P.F., Kohl, S.A.A., Petersen, J., Maier-Hein, K.H.: nnU-Net: a self-configuring method for deep learning-based biomedical image segmentation. Nat. Methods **18**, 203–211 (2021)

13. Jenkinson, M., Beckmann, C.F., Behrens, T.E., Woolrich, M.W., Smith, S.M.: FSL. Neuroimage **62**, 782–790 (2012)

14. Jin, Q., Cui, H., Sun, C., Meng, Z., Su, R.: Free-form tumor synthesis in computed tomography images via richer generative adversarial network. Knowl.-Based Syst. **218**, 106753 (2021)

15. Kuijf, H.J., et al.: Standardized assessment of automatic segmentation of white matter hyperintensities and results of the WMH segmentation challenge. IEEE Trans. Med. Imaging **38**, 2556–2568 (2019)

16. Lebbos, C., et al.: Adnexal mass segmentation with ultrasound data synthesis. In: Aylward, S., Noble, J.A., Hu, Y., Lee, S.L., Baum, Z., Min, Z. (eds.) Simplifying Medical Ultrasound. Lecture Notes in Computer Science, vol. 13565, pp. 106–116. Springer, Cham (2022). https://doi.org/10.1007/978-3-031-16902-1_11

17. Li, Q., Yu, Z., Wang, Y., Zheng, H.: TumorGAN: a multi-modal data augmentation framework for brain tumor segmentation. Sensors **20**, 4203 (2020)

18. Lin, Y., Wang, Z., Cheng, K.T., Chen, H.: InsMix: towards realistic generative data augmentation for nuclei instance segmentation. In: Wang, L., Dou, Q., Fletcher, P.T., Speidel, S., Li, S. (eds.) Medical Image Computing and Computer Assisted Intervention – MICCAI 2022. Lecture Notes in Computer Science, vol. 13432, pp. 140–149. Springer, Cham (2022). https://doi.org/10.1007/978-3-031-16434-7_14

19. Mok, T.C.W., Chung, A.C.S.: Learning data augmentation for brain tumor segmentation with coarse-to-fine generative adversarial networks. In: Crimi, A., Bakas, S., Kuijf, H., Keyvan, F., Reyes, M., van Walsum, T. (eds.) Brainlesion: Glioma, Multiple Sclerosis, Stroke and Traumatic Brain Injuries. Lecture Notes in Computer Science(), vol. 11383, pp. 70–80. Springer, Cham (2019). https://doi.org/10.1007/978-3-030-11723-8_7

20. Reinhold, J.C., Carass, A., Prince, J.L.: A structural causal model for MR images of multiple sclerosis. In: de Bruijne, M., et al. (eds.) Medical Image Computing and Computer Assisted Intervention - MICCAI 2021. Lecture Notes in Computer Science(), vol. 12905, pp. 782–792. Springer, Cham (2021). https://doi.org/10.1007/978-3-030-87240-3_75

21. Roy, A.G., et al.: Does your dermatology classifier know what it doesn't know? Detecting the long-tail of unseen conditions. Med. Image Anal. **75**, 102274 (2022)

22. Salem, M., et al.: Multiple sclerosis lesion synthesis in MRI using an encoder-decoder U-NET. IEEE Access **7**, 25171–25184 (2019)

23. Styner, M., et al.: 3D segmentation in the clinic: a grand challenge II: MS lesion segmentation. MIDAS J. (2008)

24. Telea, A.: An image inpainting technique based on the fast marching method. J. Graph. Tools (2004)

25. Xia, T., Chartsias, A., Tsaftaris, S.A.: Pseudo-healthy synthesis with pathology disentanglement and adversarial learning. Med. Image Anal. **64**, 101719 (2020)

26. Yun, S., Han, D., Oh, S.J., Chun, S., Choe, J., Yoo, Y.: CutMix: regularization strategy to train strong classifiers with localizable features. In: IEEE/CVF International Conference on Computer Vision (2019)

27. Zhang, J., Zhang, Y., Xu, X.: ObjectAug: object-level data augmentation for semantic image segmentation. In: 2021 International Joint Conference on Neural Networks (IJCNN) (2021)

28. Zhang, X., et al.: CarveMix: a simple data augmentation method for brain lesion segmentation. In: de Bruijne, M., et al. (eds.) Medical Image Computing and Computer Assisted Intervention - MICCAI 2021. Lecture Notes in Computer Science(), vol. 12901, pp. 196–205. Springer, Cham (2021). https://doi.org/10.1007/978-3-030-87193-2_19

29. Zhu, Q., Wang, Y., Yin, L., Yang, J., Liao, F., Li, S.: SelfMix: a self-adaptive data augmentation method for lesion segmentation. In: Wang, L., Dou, Q., Fletcher, P.T., Speidel, S., Li, S. (eds.) Medical Image Computing and Computer Assisted Intervention - MICCAI 2022. Lecture Notes in Computer Science, vol. 13434, pp. 683–692. Springer, Cham (2022). https://doi.org/10.1007/978-3-031-16440-8_65

Knowledge Graph Embeddings for Multi-lingual Structured Representations of Radiology Reports

Tom van Sonsbeek[✉], Xiantong Zhen, and Marcel Worring

University of Amsterdam, Amsterdam, The Netherlands
{t.j.vansonsbeek,x.zhen,m.worring}@uva.nl

Abstract. The way we analyse clinical texts has undergone major changes over the last years. The introduction of language models such as BERT led to adaptations for the (bio)medical domain like PubMedBERT and ClinicalBERT. These models rely on large databases of archived medical documents. While performing well in terms of accuracy, both the lack of interpretability and limitations to transfer across languages limit their use in clinical setting. We introduce a novel light-weight graph-based embedding method specifically catering radiology reports. It takes into account the structure and composition of the report, while also connecting medical terms in the report through the multi-lingual SNOMED Clinical Terms knowledge base. The resulting graph embedding uncovers the underlying relationships among clinical terms, achieving a representation that is better understandable for clinicians and clinically more accurate, without reliance on large pre-training datasets. We show the use of this embedding on two tasks namely disease classification of X-ray reports and image classification. For disease classification our model is competitive with its BERT-based counterparts, while being magnitudes smaller in size and training data requirements. For image classification, we show the effectiveness of the graph embedding leveraging cross-modal knowledge transfer and show how this method is usable across different languages.

Keywords: Knowledge graphs · Disease classification · Multi-modal learning

1 Introduction

Processing of medical text underwent major changes with the emergence of Transformer-based models. Fine-tuned versions of the Bidirectional Encoder Representation of Transformers (BERT) [11] model, such as ClinicalBERT [1] and BioBERT [21] are highly effective [13]. In particular ClinicalBERT works well in tasks regarding radiology reports of X-ray scans, such as text based disease classification and report generation [7]. However, there are crucial complications of directly applying general NLP methods to the medical domain making

© The Author(s), under exclusive license to Springer Nature Switzerland AG 2024
Y. Xue et al. (Eds.): DALI 2023, LNCS 14379, pp. 84–94, 2024.
https://doi.org/10.1007/978-3-031-58171-7_9

a case for creating more domain-specific solutions to processing of medical text: (1) BERT produces embeddings that are computationally expensive and data-inefficient. Since there is no prior content knowledge, high parameter count and deep models are needed to optimally model text. To bridge the gap between generic text and medical text there is a dependency on fine-tuning with large medical text datasets. (2) BERT and its fine-tuned versions are self-supervised methods. Effective connections and patterns are learnt, but these certainly are not equivalent to medical knowledge. The lack of explainability and intuition behind them complicates their usage in synergy with clinicians, who need to understand how these models work before they can trust them [22]. (3) BERT models largely focus on English language. These large language models can not be adapted for multi-lingual use with the same effectiveness. Spanish equivalents of BERT (BETO [8]) and ClinicalBERT (Bio-cli-52k [6]) are trained with around ten times less data and hence have lower performance.

As an alternative to self-supervision we can use formalized medical knowledge. The Universal Medical Language System (UMLS) contains standardized definitions and relationships within medical terminologies and vocabularies across 25 languages [4]. Examples are ontologies for primary care (ICPC), genes (GO), clinical terms (SNOMED CT), drugs (Rxnorm) and even billing (ICD10). The UMLS can be used among various national hospitals, but also across countries. This can be especially beneficial to countries that do not have access to large medical datasets, due to their smaller population size or lack of financial resources.

The specific ontologies within the UMLS can provide additional advantages. SNOMED CT provides relationships between concepts within their respective ontology. The added information from this knowledge base can be beneficial, since expert-level annotation is not in abundance in the medical domain. One particularly useful application of SNOMED CT is in radiology reports, which are widely available in public datasets, but are largely un-annotated. The structure of UMLS and SNOMED CT make them suitable for representation with knowledge graphs, which can efficiently represent structured sets of entities [9,18].

In this paper we propose the first graph embedding based method for structured representation of radiology reports which incorporates information from existing medical knowledge by leveraging the structure and composition of the text. (i) Experiments show that the proposed graph embedding achieves competitive performance. These report embeddings are a computationally more efficient, more explainable and intuitive alternative to existing embedding methods. (ii) We show that the usage of UMLS and SNOMED CT allows for easy translation across languages. (iii) Lastly, the proposed report graph can be used in a multi-modal setting for cross-modal knowledge transfer to images, enabling improved image-based disease classification.

Related Work. There are two methods currently used most for embedding of medical text. The first one is BioWordVec [34], a word2vec [25] inspired embedding pre-trained on biomedical datasets. The second is a class of methods,

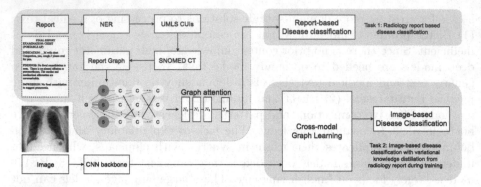

Fig. 1. Schematic representation of construction and evaluation methods for knowledge graph embeddings for representations of radiology reports. We evaluate the proposed graph embeddings for text (task 1) and image (task 2) based disease classification.

namely fine-tuned versions of BERT and BETO, such as BioBERT [21], PubMed-BERT [12], ClinicalBERT [1] and Bio-cli-52k [6]. These models are fine-tuned using respectively (bio)medical and clinical datasets. These type of embeddings are currently used in most recent state-of-the-art methods which use chest X-ray reports and outperform previous methods by a large margin. A new embedding should be compared against these BERT-based methods.

Knowledge graphs have been used to improve diagnosis based on patient records [14], for improvement of entity extraction from radiology reports [17] and to supplement X-ray image diagnosis [27]. Numerous methods were developed for using knowledge graphs in radiology report generation. The graph to generate a report is typically a small graph (∼15 nodes) containing disease labels. This proves to be an effective way to capture the global context of a report [15,16,20, 23,24,31–33,35]. Our method proposes an embedding *from* a radiology report, instead of *for the generation of* a radiology report. There have not been prior works on structured representations encompassing full radiology reports with knowledge graphs and medical ontologies.

2 Methodology

Our proposed method consists of three components: entity extraction from the radiology report, graph construction, and graph encoding, as illustrated in Fig. 1. The nodes in the graph correspond to words in the report that match terms from clinical databases. Graph edges encode relationships between those terms and their location in the report[1].

Named Entity Recognition. Clinical concepts in the plain text of the radiology report R are extracted using Named Entity Recognition (NER). A widely

---

[1] github.com/tjvsonsbeek/knowledge_graphs_for_radiology_reports.git.

used tool for NER on English UMLS concepts is MetaMap [2]. For Spanish we use UMLSMapper [26]. We can extract UMLS Concept Unique Identifiers (CUIs): $\{\mathbf{u}^0, \mathbf{u}^1, ..\} = \mathrm{NER}(R)$ from R. The corresponding SNOMED CT concept for each CUI forms the final set of clinical concepts from report $R : \{\mathbf{c}^0, \mathbf{c}^1, ..\}$.

Graph Construction. We consider undirected graph $G_R = (N_R, E_R)$ defined by a set of nodes $N_R = \{n_0, n_1, ..\}$ and edges $E_R = \{e^{l \leftrightarrow m}, ..\}$, with $e^{l \leftrightarrow m} = (n_l, n_m)$. To capture the structure of the radiology report we consider each sentence of the report separately with sentence node $\mathbf{s}^j$ of sentence j. SNOMED CT concepts extracted from report R yield a set of concepts per sentence: $\{\mathbf{c}^{j,0}, \mathbf{c}^{j,1}, ..\}$.

Global connection node $\mathbf{g}$ captures context between nodes. This gives us the following set of nodes: $N_R = \{\mathbf{s}^j, \mathbf{g}, \mathbf{c}\}$. We consider three different types of edges:

$$E_R = \{e^{c \leftrightarrow c}, e^{s \leftrightarrow c}, e^{g \leftrightarrow s}, e^{g \leftrightarrow c}\} = \{(\mathbf{c}^l, \mathbf{c}^m)\}, \{(\mathbf{c}^l, \mathbf{s}^j)\}, \{(\mathbf{s}^j, \mathbf{g})\}, \{(\mathbf{c}^l, \mathbf{g})\}\}$$

1. Edges $e^{c \leftrightarrow c}$ between concept nodes c that hold a contextual connection to each other due to a corresponding relation in the SNOMED CT ontology.
2. Edges $e^{s \leftrightarrow c}$ from the sentence nodes $\mathbf{s}^j$ to all $\mathbf{c}$ within their respective sentence capturing the local composition of the report.
3. Global connection node $\mathbf{g}$ is connected to every concept node node through edges $e^{g \leftrightarrow c}$ and $e^{g \leftrightarrow s}$ to enable interaction across the entire report.

Graph Encoding. Graph attention networks leverage the self-attention mechanism to enable nodes in G_R to efficiently attend to their neighborhoods [30]. This is the current preferred method in encoding of (knowledge) graphs [36]. We consider node N_R^p and neighboring nodes N_R^q, with their respective weight matrices $\mathbf{W} \in \mathbb{R}^{F' \times F}$, in which F is the node feature length. The normalized attention score between those nodes can be defined as:

$$a_{pq} = softmax(LeakyRELU(\mathbf{W}_{att}^t[\mathbf{W}_{N_R^p} \| \mathbf{W}_{N_R^q}])).$$

The encoded representation of node N_R^p is: $N_R^{p'} = \sigma(\sum \alpha_{pq} \cdot \mathbf{W}_{N_R^q})$, with nonlinearity σ. The encoding of the entire graph with n stacked GAT layers can be represented as: $G_R' = f_{GAT}^n(N_R, E_R)$.

Evaluation Tasks. To evaluate whether the constructed graph embeddings contain information representative of the content of the radiology report, we evaluate them on two types of tasks centered around disease classification as shown in Fig. 1. We first evaluate the effectiveness of our knowledge graph embedding for a diagnosis classification task based on the radiology report. We make comparisons against BERT and its bio(medical) variations. Disease classification is done on the global report. This is achieved through a max pooling operation on encoded node representations N_R', followed by a classification MLP: $f_{MLP}(\cdot)$.

The capability of out graph embedding to transfer the information it contains across modalities is tested by deploying the embeddings in the variational knowledge distillation framework (VKD) [29], where graph embeddings will be used to aid image-based disease classifications. In VKD, a conditional latent variable model is introduced in which information is distilled from radiology report R to chest X-ray scan I through variational inference. This architecture is inspired by conditional variational inference (CVI) [28]. The evidence lower bound objective (ELBO) of CVI is composed of a reconstruction term and a Kullback-Leibler (KL) divergence term: $\mathcal{L} = \mathbb{E}[\log p(\mathbf{y}|I, \mathbf{z}_I)] - D_{KL}[q(\mathbf{z})||p(\mathbf{z}_I|I)]$ in which $\mathbf{z}_I$ is a latent representation of I, classification labels are denoted by $\mathbf{y}$ and prior distribution $p(\mathbf{z}_I|I)$. $q(\mathbf{z})$ is the posterior distribution over $\mathbf{z}$, which is usually set to an isotropic Gaussian distribution $\mathcal{N}(0, I)$. In VKD the posterior is set as $q(\mathbf{z}_R|R)$, with z_R being a latent representation of R. This new posterior makes it possible to distill information from R to I by minimizing the following KL term: $D_{KL}[q(\mathbf{z}_R|R)||p(\mathbf{z}_I|I)]$. Through this process we are able to transfer information from the radiology report to the medical image. During the training stage of this method both image and radiology report are required as input, while during testing only image input is required. With this method we use our report graph embeddings to improve image representations.

3   Experimental Setup

Datasets. The datasets used for training and evaluation are: 1) *MIMIC-CXR* [19] consisting of $377,110$ chest X-rays (both frontal and/or sagittal views) and $227,827$ anonymized radiology reports, with disease labels generated with a rule-based labeller. 2) *OpenI* [10] with $7,470$ chest X-rays and $3,955$ anonymized reports which are similarly labelled 3) *PadChest* [5] contains $160,000$ radiology images and Spanish reports. It contains 174 disease labels similarly extracted as above and which can be condensed in the same label space as the other datasets.

Experimental Settings. No limit is enforced on the number of entities that can be extracted from a report with NER through MetaMap or on the number of edges within a graph. We adopt vectorized representations of single UMLS concepts to initialize the nodes. These were obtained by pre-training on datasets with (bio)medical data [3]. These 200-dimensional non-contextual embeddings were inspired by word2vec and can be used in our method without additional processing steps. Embedding initializations for $\mathbf{s}^j$ and $\mathbf{g}$ are computed by averaging the node embeddings $\mathbf{c}$ over the sentence and whole graph respectively.

The graph attention encoder consists of one, three, six or twelve sequential graph attention layers with hidden size 512, 1024 or 2048. Graph classification is done through an MLP with dimensions $\{512, 256, 14\}$, using cross-entropy loss. Results are reported with the AUC metric, consistent with existing benchmarks. Evaluation on VKD is done with a latent space size of 2048 and 12 sequential graph attention layers for encoding. Other hyper-parameter settings are directly adopted from [29]. A dropout rate of 0.5 is applied to all layers of the architecture.

Training is done on one Ryzen 2990WX CPU and one NVIDIA RTX 2080ti GPU, with Adam optimization using early stopping with a tolerance of 1%.

Table 1. Comparison of our graph-based disease classification to BERT-based methods. Our Graph MLP Small and Graph MLP Large embeddings have one and three encoder layers and encoder hidden size 512 and 1024 respectively.

		OpenI							MIMIC-CXR							PadChest			
		BioWordVec	BERT	BioBERT	PubMedBERT	ClinicalBERT	Graph MLP S	Graph MLP L	BioWordVec	BERT	BioBERT	PubMedBERT	ClinicalBERT	Graph MLP S	Graph MLP L	BETO	Bio-cli-52k	Graph MLP S	Graph MLP L
Inference rate (1/s)	CPU	-	17	17	18	18	41	24	-	18	19	18	18	39	33	23	23	46	43
	GPU	-	208	213	212	216	398	325	-	203	204	203	203	368	312	241	243	412	428
No Finding		.924	.796	.861	.907	.804	.917	.926	.817	.891	.914	.923	.923	.882	.902	.923	.954	.980	.980
Enl. cardiomed		.559	.715	.784	.854	.864	.852	.861	.863	.855	.866	.870	.966	.518	.870	.645	.809	.863	.906
Cardiomegaly		.944	.922	.941	.941	.909	.935	.937	.921	.917	.925	.937	.979	.904	.920	.861	.895	.866	.873
Lung Opacity		.953	.820	.902	.950	.973	.966	.978	.910	.923	.936	.942	.978	.930	.940	.858	.923	.917	.914
Lung Lesion		.961	.814	.869	.941	.971	.945	.968	.918	.917	.921	.930	.972	.911	.927	.801	.826	.928	.932
Edema		.984	.859	.924	.946	.976	.951	.965	.898	.916	.927	.935	.979	.921	.930	.632	.913	.929	.957
Consolidation		.969	.923	.926	.968	.962	.955	.968	.905	.920	.935	.942	.979	.958	.965	.701	.749	.871	.914
Pneumonia		.953	.878	.900	.940	.962	.947	.968	.932	.925	.930	.949	.949	.940	.948	.794	.823	.853	.877
Atelectasis		.961	.847	.897	.957	.947	.929	.974	.918	.942	.952	.967	.976	.936	.952	.963	.921	.849	.861
Pneumothorax		.960	.975	.982	.968	.973	.944	.956	.894	.936	.942	.959	.979	.926	.951	.711	.898	.861	.963
Pleural Effusion		.968	.917	.974	.962	.976	.943	.969	.896	.921	.933	.945	.981	.923	.941	.891	.937	.867	.968
Pleural Other		.939	.945	.985	.969	.958	.971	.961	.803	.904	.914	.925	.964	.921	.930	.872	.893	.931	.939
Fracture		.926	.860	.892	.893	.935	.935	.942	.532	.886	.898	.906	.958	.975	.978	.861	.875	.896	.907
Support Devices		.904	.813	.847	.872	.912	.899	.903	.877	.919	.921	.934	.983	.925	.941	.924	.924	.860	.889
Average AUC		.959	.930	.930	.965	.970	.947	.964	.896	.919	.921	.947	.974	.931	.948	.582	.919	.951	.967
Recall		.817	.769	.815	.818	.863	.867	.863	.827	.743	.841	.847	.868	.842	.848	.510	.679	.923	.841
Precision		.697	.561	.572	.602	.629	.615	.624	.526	.525	.504	.601	.611	.614	.631	.220	.491	.544	.587
F1		.719	.681	.718	.700	.721	.729	.716	.603	.615	.688	.714	.726	.713	.718	.586	.575	.656	.681

4   Results and Discussion

Report Classification. Table 1 shows disease classification results of our graph embeddings. Results are shown for an encoder that performed best on average with hidden size 1024 and three graph attention layers. Our method yields competitive performance compared to BioBERT and PubMedBERT, and slightly lower compared to ClinicalBERT, while being 200× smaller in terms of parameters (Table 2). On the Spanish PadChest dataset our method outperforms BERT-based methods. This can be attributed to the size of the training corpora of these models, which is ten times smaller than their English counterparts. Next to this, both CPU and GPU inference rates (samples per second) are faster for our method. Our method performs relatively better on the smaller OpenI dataset, emphasising the effectiveness of our embedding for report representation without relying on large datasets.

Cross-Modal Knowledge Transfer. The application of graphs in a multi-modal setting can give a better understanding on how well the graph captures complex information structures that can pass across modalities. Table 2 shows the results of our method on disease classification of chest X-rays with cross modal knowledge transfer, compared to existing methods using ClinicalBERT as report embedding. Training of this framework showed that convergence of this model is complex for graphs with shallow encoders with hidden layers of smaller size. Table 2 thus shows results with an encoder of 12 graph attention layers and hidden size 2048.

Table 2. Comparison of disease classification metrics on variational knowledge distillation (VKD) based chest X-ray classification. Performance is reported on single-modal image classification, VKD with ClinicalBERT/Bio-cli-52k report embeddings and VKD with our proposed graph embeddings.

	OpenI			MIMIC-CXR			PadChest		
	Img only	ClinicalBERT	Ours	Img only	ClinicalBERT	Ours	Img only	Bio-cli-52k	Ours
Recall	.568	.582	**.578**	.546	**.565**	.526	.519	.529	**.533**
Precision	.487	**.534**	.527	.530	**.538**	.536	.487	.510	**.530**
F1	.491	**.510**	.495	.468	**.509**	.487	.468	**.481**	.473
AUC	.837	**.885**	.862	.807	**.839**	.823	.802	.815	**.819**

While not outperforming the existing ClinicalBERT method, graph embeddings show to work on both MIMIC-CXR and OpenI. There is increased performance compared to image-only classification so we can successfully transfer information across modalities without requiring large pre-training datasets.

Ablation Studies. We analyze graph encoders for disease classification in Fig. 2, showing the effect of encoder count and hidden size on performance. Parameter count is crucial, with ClinicalBERT performing best but requiring more resources. The performance difference between the smallest (0.4M parameters) and largest (62M parameters) models is small, indicating that graph construction captures medical knowledge well regardless of encoder size. We also conduct an ablation on the components of the graph in Table 3. The role of node types is shown by removing them from the graph. Key elements in the graph structure appear to be the global node and edges between SNOMED CT concepts. This accentuates how the combined report composition and the incorporation of medical knowledge base SNOMED CT creates a rich representation of the report.

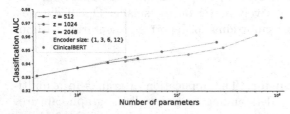

Fig. 2. Graph size and performance for a set of models with hidden size z and varying encoder size.

Table 3. Graph ablations on disease classification.

	OpenI	MIMIC-CXR	PadChest
Full graph	0.947	0.931	0.951
w/o g	0.940	0.925	0.942
w/o g&s	0.932	0.918	0.934
w/o $e^{c\leftrightarrow c}$	0.936	0.918	0.926
w/o g&s&$e^{c\leftrightarrow c}$	0.916	0.920	0.921

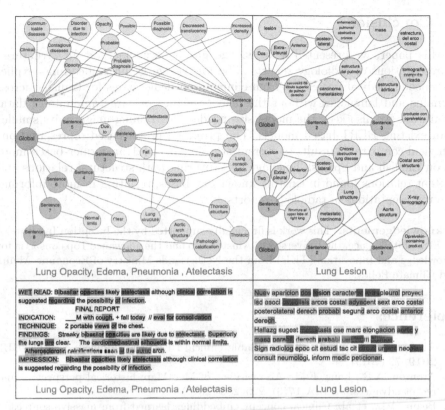

Fig. 3. Examples of our graph embedding (top), compared to ClinicalBERT embedding weights (bottom), with predicted disease labels. Green means correct classification and red false negative. Global node edges are omitted for clarity. (Color figure online)

Graph Visualization and Explainability. Fig. 3 shows two examples of our graph embedding and attention weights of ClinicalBERT with results of these methods on disease classification. The left report shows how disease labels are verbatim present in the detected SNOMED CT concepts, contributing to interpretability. Concepts that reoccur in the report or have a high 'connectedness' are often important. The graph handles repeated terms more efficiently than clinicalBERT: our graph consists of 34 nodes, while tokenization with ClinicalBERT takes as much as 124 tokens. Our report graph captures the word 'opacities' in its entirety. In ClinicalBERT, this is tokenized as 'o', 'pa' and 'cities'. The last token in this sequence obviously has another contextualized meaning in the general language BERT model on which ClinicalBERT is based. This illustrates graphs can captures medical terminology in a more intuitive and interpretable way.

The last example shows a Spanish report graph, and below it the English translation. Translation is straightforward since each content node corresponds to a multi-lingual UMLS concept.

5   Conclusion

In this paper, we presented a knowledge graph based method for structured representations of radiology reports. The knowledge graph embeddings explicitly encode medical knowledge from clinical knowledge bases for transfer across domains and languages without the heavy reliance on large amounts of data. Meanwhile we also keep the model size needed for training magnitudes smaller than existing BERT-based models. The proposed graph based representations can yield comparable results to current state-of-the-art Transformer-based models on English and Spanish language by capturing both structural relations and content relations found in existing knowledge bases, resulting in more informative representations of radiology reports

Acknowledgements. This work is financially supported by the Inception Institute of Artificial Intelligence, the University of Amsterdam and the allowance Top consortia for Knowledge and Innovation (TKIs) from the Netherlands Ministry of Economic Affairs and Climate Policy.

References

1. Alsentzer, E., et al.: Publicly available clinical BERT embeddings. NAACL HLT **2019**, 72 (2019)
2. Aronson, A.R., Lang, F.M.: An overview of MetaMap: historical perspective and recent advances. JAMIA **17**(3), 229–236 (2010)
3. Beam, A.L., et al.: Clinical concept embeddings learned from massive sources of multimodal medical data. In: Pacific Symposium on Biocomputing 2020, pp. 295–306. World Scientific (2019)
4. Bodenreider, O.: The unified medical language system (UMLS): integrating biomedical terminology. Nucleic Acids Res. **32**, D267–D270 (2004)
5. Bustos, A., Pertusa, A., Salinas, J.M., de la Iglesia-Vayá, M.: PadChest: a large chest x-ray image dataset with multi-label annotated reports. Med. Image Anal. **66**, 101797 (2020)
6. Carrino, C.P., et al.: Biomedical and clinical language models for Spanish: on the benefits of domain-specific pretraining in a mid-resource scenario (2021)
7. Casey, A., et al.: A systematic review of natural language processing applied to radiology reports. BMC Med. Inform. Decis. Mak. **21**(1), 1–18 (2021)
8. Cañete, J., Chaperon, G., Fuentes, R., Ho, J.H., Kang, H., Pérez, J.: Spanish pretrained BERT model and evaluation data. In: PML4DC at ICLR 2020 (2020)
9. Chang, D., Balažević, I., Allen, C., Chawla, D., Brandt, C., Taylor, R.A.: Benchmark and best practices for biomedical knowledge graph embeddings. In: Proceedings of the Conference Association for Computational Linguistics Meeting, vol. 2020, p. 167. NIH Public Access (2020)
10. Demner-Fushman, D., et al.: Preparing a collection of radiology examinations for distribution and retrieval. J. Am. Med. Inform. Assoc. **23**(2), 304–310 (2016)
11. Devlin, J., Chang, M.W., Lee, K., Toutanova, K.: BERT: pre-training of deep bidirectional transformers for language understanding, pp. 4171–4186 (2019)
12. Gu, Y., et al.: Domain-specific language model pretraining for biomedical natural language processing (2020)

13. Gu, Y., et al.: Domain-specific language model pretraining for biomedical natural language processing. Trans. Comput. Healthcare **3**(1), 1–23 (2021)
14. Heilig, N., Kirchhoff, J., Stumpe, F., Plepi, J., Flek, L., Paulheim, H.: Refining diagnosis paths for medical diagnosis based on an augmented knowledge graph. arXiv:2204.13329 (2022)
15. Hu, J., et al.: Word graph guided summarization for radiology findings. In: Findings of the Association for Computational Linguistics: ACL-IJCNLP 2021, pp. 4980–4990 (2021)
16. Hu, J., Li, Z., Chen, Z., Li, Z., Wan, X., Chang, T.H.: Graph enhanced contrastive learning for radiology findings summarization. arXiv:2204.00203 (2022)
17. Jain, S., et al.: RadGraph: extracting clinical entities and relations from radiology reports. In: Thirty-fifth Conference on Neural Information Processing Systems Datasets and Benchmarks Track (Round 1) (2021)
18. Ji, S., Pan, S., Cambria, E., Marttinen, P., Philip, S.Y.: A survey on knowledge graphs: representation, acquisition, and applications. IEEE Trans. Neural Netw. Learn. Syst. (2021)
19. Johnson, A.E., et al.: MIMIC-CXR, a de-identified publicly available database of chest radiographs with free-text reports. Sci. Data **6**(1), 1–8 (2019)
20. Kale, K., et al.: Knowledge graph construction and its application in automatic radiology report generation from radiologist's dictation. arXiv preprint:2206.06308 (2022)
21. Lee, J., et al.: BioBERT: a pre-trained biomedical language representation model for biomedical text mining. Bioinformatics **36**(4), 1234–1240 (2020)
22. Litjens, G., et al.: A survey on deep learning in medical image analysis. Med. Image Anal. **42**, 60–88 (2017)
23. Liu, F., Wu, X., Ge, S., Fan, W., Zou, Y.: Exploring and distilling posterior and prior knowledge for radiology report generation. In: CVPR, pp. 13753–13762 (2021)
24. Liu, F., et al.: Auto-encoding knowledge graph for unsupervised medical report generation. NeurIPS **34**, 16266–16279 (2021)
25. Mikolov, T., Chen, K., Corrado, G., Dean, J.: Efficient estimation of word representations in vector space. arXiv preprint arXiv:1301.3781 (2013)
26. Perez, N., et al.: Cross-lingual semantic annotation of biomedical literature: experiments in Spanish and English. Bioinformatics **36**(6), 1872–1880 (2019)
27. Prabhakar, C., et al.: Structured knowledge graphs for classifying unseen patterns in radiographs. In: GeoMeDIA (2022)
28. Sohn, K., Lee, H., Yan, X.: Learning structured output representation using deep conditional generative models. In: NeurIPS, pp. 3483–3491 (2015)
29. van Sonsbeek, T., Zhen, X., Worring, M., Shao, L.: Variational knowledge distillation for disease classification in chest X-rays. In: Feragen, A., Sommer, S., Schnabel, J., Nielsen, M. (eds.) IPMI 2021. LNCS, vol. 12729, pp. 334–345. Springer, Cham (2021). https://doi.org/10.1007/978-3-030-78191-0_26
30. Veličković, P., Cucurull, G., Casanova, A., Romero, A., Liò, P., Bengio, Y.: Graph attention networks. In: International Conference on Learning Representations (2018)
31. Yan, S.: Memory-aligned knowledge graph for clinically accurate radiology image report generation. In: BioNLP, pp. 116–122 (2022)
32. Yang, S., Wu, X., Ge, S., Zhou, S.K., Xiao, L.: Knowledge matters: radiology report generation with general and specific knowledge. arXiv:2112.15009 (2021)
33. Zhang, D., Ren, A., Liang, J., Liu, Q., Wang, H., Ma, Y.: Improving medical x-ray report generation by using knowledge graph. Appl. Sci. **12**(21) (2022)

34. Zhang, Y., Chen, Q., Yang, Z., Lin, H., Lu, Z.: BioWordVec, improving biomedical word embeddings with subword information and MeSH. Sci. data **6**(1), 1–9 (2019)
35. Zhang, Y., Wang, X., Xu, Z., Yu, Q., Yuille, A., Xu, D.: When radiology report generation meets knowledge graph. In: AAAI, vol. 34, pp. 12910–12917 (2020)
36. Zhou, J., et al.: Graph neural networks: a review of methods and applications. AI Open **1**, 57–81 (2020)

Modular, Label-Efficient Dataset Generation for Instrument Detection for Robotic Scrub Nurses

Jorge Badilla-Solórzano[1]([envelope]) [ORCID], Nils-Claudius Gellrich[2] [ORCID], Thomas Seel[1] [ORCID], and Sontje Ihler[1] [ORCID]

[1] Institute of Mechatronic Systems, Leibniz University Hannover, Garbsen, Germany
{jorge.badilla,thomas.seel,sontje.ihler}@imes.uni-hannover.de
[2] Department of Cranio-Maxillofacial Surgery, Hannover Medical School, Hannover, Germany
gellrich.nils-claudius@mh-hannover.de

Abstract. Surgical instrument detection is a fundamental task of a robotic scrub nurse. For this, image-based deep learning techniques are effective but usually demand large amounts of annotated data, whose creation is expensive and time-consuming. In this work, we propose a strategy based on the copy-paste technique for the generation of reliable synthetic image training data with a minimal amount of annotation effort. Our approach enables the efficient in situ creation of datasets for specific surgeries and contexts. We study the amount of employed manually annotated data and training set sizes on our model's performance, as well as different blending techniques for improved training data. We achieve 91.9 box mAP and 91.6 mask mAP, training solely on synthetic data, in a real-world scenario. Our evaluation relies on an annotated image dataset of the wisdom teeth extraction surgery set, created in an actual operating room. This dataset, the corresponding code, and further data are made publicly available (https://github.com/Jorebs/Modular-Label-Efficient-Dataset-Generation-for-Instrument-Detection-for-Robotic-Scrub-Nurses).

Keywords: Synthetic data · Efficient annotation · Robotic Scrub Nurse · MBOI · Copy-paste · Deep learning

1 Introduction

Healthcare systems face a deficit of medical workers [1–4]. To mitigate this, Robotic Scrub Nurses (RSN) can be employed, whose study responds to the growing interest in robot-assisted surgery [5,6]. RSN are autonomous systems designed to aid surgeons during medical procedures by handing surgical instruments. The surgical tools are commonly arranged on a tray in a random configuration (Fig. 1a). An RSN must reliably detect the instruments in order to grip

Supplementary Information The online version contains supplementary material available at https://doi.org/10.1007/978-3-031-58171-7_10.

(a) Real test data   (b) Synthetic training data (c) Prediction on real data

Fig. 1. To perform instrument detection on real data (a), we rely entirely on synthetic multi-instrument training images (b). The generation of the synthetic data is based on copy-paste. We achieve high performance, as illustrated in (c). Each color represents a different instrument class. (Color figure online)

them upon request and hand them to the surgeon. High-performance detection is, thus, essential. Instrument detection for RSN is challenging since typical surgery sets consist of dozens of instruments [7–9], including similar-looking tools, which are difficult to differentiate. Moreover, the heterogeneous lighting of an operating room can drastically change the appearance of the instruments.

High performance can be attained with deep-learning-based instrument detectors but they rely heavily on the use of suitable datasets. While several instrument image datasets are available in the literature [10–14], they are not adequate for RSN. They are either created with unsuitable viewpoints [10–13], e.g., that of laparoscopic surgery, or focus on image classification [14], not including segmentation masks or bounding boxes. In our previous work [15], we introduce an instrument image dataset for RSN but it is heavily imbalanced and it is created in a laboratory with homogeneous backgrounds and lighting, not representing the conditions of an actual operating room.

In general, the creation of manually annotated datasets is expensive and time-consuming, especially in the case of segmentation masks. Annotation efficiency for deep learning is, thus, an active subject of research [16]. In this work, we focus on label-efficient instrument detection for RSN. The typical setup (Fig. 1a), with instruments on a common plane and fairly invariant background, is ideal for the exploitation of copy-paste techniques [17–19] to generate automatically annotated synthetic data. Traditional copy-paste approaches are, however, not optimal for surgical instrument detection, as they do not preserve the relative tool size, which is relevant for their identification. In [15], we introduce the Mask-Based Object Insertion (MBOI) method, a scale-preserving copy-paste approach that provides an effective technique for the generation of synthetic multi-instrument (MI) training data. Our method is tailored for improving instrument detection for RSN and it is originally intended to be used as a complimentary source of training data. Instead, in this work, we focus on its full exploitation for the generation of fully synthetic training sets, which has proven to lead to successful binary instrument segmentation, as presented in [20,21].

We expand upon this by applying copy-paste to the more complex task of instrument instance segmentation for an RSN. With limited annotated data in the form of single-instrument (SI) images (Fig. 2) we generate large amounts of synthetic MI training data. These constitute collages of instrument foregrounds randomly pasted into background (BG) images (Fig. 1b). If competitive detection performance solely on synthetic training data is feasible, modular training set generation with a formidable level of training flexibility would be attained, enabling the adaptation to different contexts simply with the inclusion of additional BG images, with no further annotation effort. Moreover, the addition of new instruments would only require annotating images of each particular tool, allowing for great adaptability.

In this work, we achieve competitive detection performance, as shown in Fig. 1c, by training exclusively on synthetic data from the MBOI method, implying high label-efficiency. Our contributions are: 1) the introduction of a highly efficient training dataset generation strategy for instrument detection for RSN, 2) an in-depth study of our strategy in terms of efficiency by analyzing the employed amount of annotated data and training set sizes, 3) the improvement of the MBOI method with the incorporation of blending techniques, and 4) the publication a MI image dataset of the complete surgery set for wisdom teeth extraction, created in an actual operating room under standard conditions.

2 Dataset

The quality of a dataset is a determining factor in the performance of a deep-learning-based detector. The corresponding images must be collected under conditions that depict the intended working scenario to guarantee suitable performance. This is especially meaningful for the instrument detection task of RSN since errors could hinder the successful completion of a medical procedure. In this section, we describe the gathering process of our data and its characteristics.

2.1 Data Acquisition

Our data is collected in an operating room, under standard conditions (heterogeneous lighting, presence of medical equipment). Our experiments consider a complete surgery set for wisdom teeth extraction (see Supplementary Material), with 18 different instruments. During the image creation, the instruments are arranged on a surgical cloth on a tray, avoiding inter-instrument occlusions (Fig. 1a), resembling a pre-operative setup. The lighting conditions of the OR and the instrument arrangement are frequently modified. The data are captured using an RGB-D camera (Intel® RealSense™D435) at a resolution of 640 × 480 px.

2.2 Real Multi-instrument Data for Validation and Testing

Both our validation and test sets are composed entirely of real MI images, manually annotated using the tool Hasty [22]. Our validation set includes 141 images, containing 60 instances per instrument class, while our test set considers a total 158 images with 67 instances per class. The datasets are perfectly balanced.

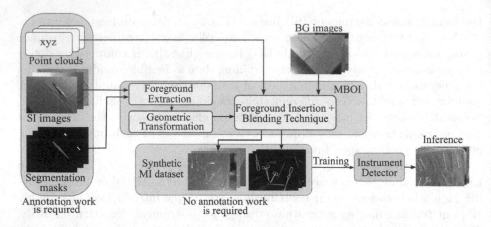

Fig. 2. Graphic representation of our dataset generation strategy. The SI images, together with their corresponding segmentation masks and point clouds, are used for the generation of synthetic MI datasets. The synthetic data are then used for training an instrument detector to enable inference on real images.

2.3   Real Single-Instrument Images for Advanced MBOI

Annotated SI images can be used in combination with BG images to create synthetic MI datasets, as shown in Fig. 2. Thus, we create collections of 90 annotated SI images for each instrument, for a total of 1620 images, with their corresponding point clouds. 220 BG images, depicting the empty surgical tray, are captured as well. While not mandatory, the use of point clouds allows for the preservation of the relative size of the instruments, which enhances the performance of a trained model, as explained in [15]. We estimate an average annotation time per instrument of 35.7 s, for a total of 16.1 h invested for the annotation associated with our training data.

3   Experiments

In this section, we describe our training dataset generation strategy, our experiments and general aspects of our training and evaluation processes.

3.1   Model and Hyperparameters

We select a traditional instance segmentation method, i.e., Mask R-CNN [23], as our instrument detector and rely on stochastic gradient descent as optimizer. Our models are pretrained on the COCO dataset [24] and utilize the same hyperparameters, i.e., learning rate of 0.001 and a batch size of 6. As regularization methods, we rely on weight decay (0.001) and early stopping with patience of 25 epochs. The training images are resized to a resolution of 512×512 px. Information regarding our computing infrastructure is provided in the Supplementary Material.

3.2 Synthetic Training Data from MBOI

For training, we create synthetic MI images using the strategy presented in Fig. 2. The synthetic data is generated by extracting the instrument foregrounds of the SI images, transforming them via a geometric transformation (described in [15]) and inserting them into the BG images. This insertion is performed with the use of blending techniques (see Sect. 3.3), which improve upon the original MBOI method. The gathered point clouds are used to preserve the scale among the inserted instrument foregrounds. The generated MI data are, thus, collages of instrument foregrounds on BG images (Fig. 1b).

We consider collections of SI images with equal size for all instrument classes. All generated datasets are balanced, including a virtually equal number of instances per instrument, with a tolerance of $\pm 1\%$. Each of the synthetic datasets is described using two hyperparametes: 1) the number of employed annotated SI images and corresponding point clouds, α, and 2) the amount of instances per instrument class included in the dataset, β. As an example, a training set corresponding to $\alpha = 30$ and $\beta = 2k$ is created using collections of 30 annotated SI images per class and includes $2k \pm 1\%$ instances of each instrument.

3.3 Advancing Copy-Paste in MBOI

The MBOI method uses *naive insertion* as pasting operation, implying a direct substitution of the pixel values in the BG images. This introduces artifacts in the synthetic data and can reduce the performance of a trained model [17]. Blending techniques, e.g., Gaussian blur and Poisson blending [25], can be incorporated to produce more realistic-looking images (Fig. 3a). With this, we aim to enhance the quality of the synthetic data. We compare these methods by generating two groups of synthetic training sets, each for a different value of $\beta \in \{1k, 3k\}$ and a constant value of $\alpha = 60$. Each group contains three datasets, whose corresponding images differ only in the employed insertion technique and are otherwise identical (Fig. 3a). This comparison corresponds to our first experiment (Fig. 3b).

3.4 Effciency: Performance vs. Invested Resources

The hyperparameter α is proportional to the invested annotation time for a synthetic dataset, while β is an indicator of the associated training time. Higher values of α and β should lead to better performance in a trained model since more information is included in the training set. Thus, a compromise between invested resources (annotation and training times) and the associated performance should be taken into account. As our second experiment, we consider fixed values of $\beta \in \{1k, 3k\}$ and analyze the effect of the variation of $\alpha \in \{5, 15, 30, 45, 60, 75, 90\}$ on a trained instrument detector. As a third experiment, we study the performance of a detector with the variation of $\beta \in \{0.25k, 0.5k, 1k, 2k, 3k, 4k\}$, for fixed values of $\alpha \in \{60, 90\}$. The results are presented in Fig. 4.

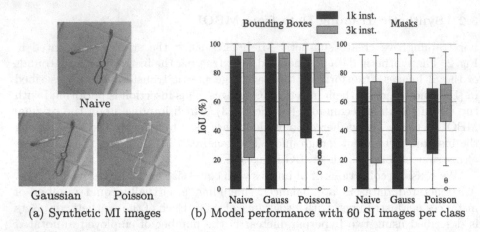

(a) Synthetic MI images   (b) Model performance with 60 SI images per class

Fig. 3. Naive insertion vs. Gaussian blur and Poisson blending (a). The presented box plots (b) suggest the superiority of Poisson blending and larger training sets.

4   Results

As evaluation metrics we rely on Intersection over Union (IoU) and Average Precision (AP), as well as their mean values mIoU and mAP. While IoU measures of the accuracy of the prediction of bounding boxes and masks, AP quantifies the number of correct classifications. We report AP and mAP at IoU = 50% in all cases. The evaluation is always performed on our test set (see Sect. 2.2).

4.1   Naive Insertion vs. Gaussian Blur and Poisson Blending

The results in Fig. 3b clearly show that Poisson blending leads to best performance. With the simple inclusion of Poisson blending we can significantly improve the MBOI method (Student t-tests are in the Supplementary Material), with no overhead in method complexity. We utilize Poisson blending in all further experiments. The superior performance can be explained by the capacity of Poisson blending to adapt the intensities of the complete instrument foreground. This adaptation is suitable for heterogeneous lighting, addressing the challenging illumination conditions of the OR.

4.2   Impact of the Number of SI Images and Training Set Size

Figure 4a and 4b depict the results of our second and third experiments, respectively. The presented curves indicate similar tendencies, portraying a convergent asymptotic growth. This indicates that increasing both α (the amount of annotated data) and β (the number of instances in the training set) lead, in general, to an improvement in a trained model's performance. This is expected since higher values are associated with more information embedded in the training

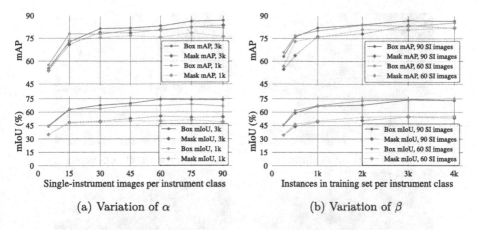

(a) Variation of α (b) Variation of β

Fig. 4. Evaluation metrics vs. the number of a) SI images per class α and b) instances in the training set β. Tendency to saturation is observed in all curves.

data, implying better generalization. Nonetheless, the observed saturation tendency of all curves indicates that, in our case, values of $\alpha \geq 75$ and $\beta \geq 3k$ can be considered inefficient since the additional annotation effort and training time will not translate into a noticeable performance improvement and is, therefore, inadvisable. Our best-performing models are capable of achieving box mAP ≈ 85 and box mIoU $\approx 75\%$. We estimate an average training time of approximately 24.5 h for $\beta = 3k$, which is reasonable considering the achieved performance.

4.3 Evaluation of with Other Detectors Under Optimal Conditions

For an RSN, misclassifications incurred by an instrument detector imply handing the incorrect tool to the surgeon, delaying or compromising the surgical procedure. Thus, we select our best detector on the basis of the mAP metric. With Mask R-CNN, the optimal conditions correspond to $\alpha = 90$ and $\beta = 3k$, leading to 86.9 box mAP and 83.7 mask mAP, with 74.8% box mIoU and 54.0% mask mIoU. An example of the qualitative performance of this model is shown in Fig. 5a and 5b. Class-wise performance is provided in the Supplementary Material.

We use the same datasets and hyperparameters to train different instance segmentation algorithms to evaluate the generalizability of our synthetic data. The training is done with $\alpha = 90$ and $\beta = 3k$. The results are shown in Table 1.

Table 1. Performance with different instance segmentation methods.

	Mask R-CNN	DETR	YOLOv5	YOLOv8
box mAP	86.9	87.5	92.5	91.9
mask mAP	83.7	84.1	85.9	91.6

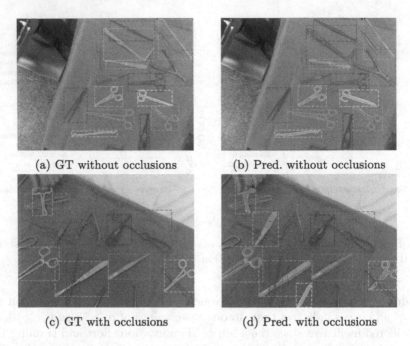

(a) GT without occlusions   (b) Pred. without occlusions

(c) GT with occlusions   (d) Pred. with occlusions

Fig. 5. Qualitative performance of Mask R-CNN detectors with and without the consideration of occlusions. Similarities between ground truth (GT) and predictions (pred.) demonstrate correct performance. Classes are color-encoded. (Color figure online)

The results demonstrate the generalizability of our training data to YOLO [26,27] and DETR [28], achieving even better results than Mask R-CNN. YOLOv8 is considered the best detector with 91.9 box mAP and 91.6 mask mAP. These results are comparable to similar studies [29,30]. Particularly, in [30], their supervised and semi-supervised detectors achieve 88.3 and 91.2 box mAP, respectively, depicting an inferior performance to that of our YOLOv8 model. This is noteworthy since our model handles 50% more classes, allows for the prediction of segmentation masks, does not require additional unlabelled images, and relies exclusively on synthetic data. With annotation and training times of 16.1 h and 24.5 h, respectively, our detector is both powerful and efficient.

5   Conclusion

We show that it is possible to achieve competitive instrument detection performance by training solely on data generated with our proposed strategy. Our approach is efficient in terms of training and annotation times. The models' performances saturate with respect to the amount of annotated and training data, indicating that a trade-off between performance and effort must be considered. We improved the MBOI method with the incorporation of Poisson blending for foreground insertion, without a relevant increase in method complexity.

The applicability of our work is extensive. Preparing custom datasets is simple, allowing an RSN to be compatible with multiple instruments and surgeries. The in situ creation of training data guarantees an accurate representation of the intended working conditions, including both the scene and the employed camera. While the inclusion of a new instrument would require less than an hour of annotation time, allowing for cost-effective modular addition to the dataset, the adaptation of backgrounds costs no annotation effort. Hence, we provide a simple yet effective solution for dataset generation.

We are convinced that our approach can be used to handle inter-instrument occlusions. We trained a model ($\alpha = 90$, $\beta = 3k$) using data with overlapping instruments and obtained qualitatively promising results, as shown in Fig. 5c and 5d. Moreover, using synthetic validation data can further reduce the annotation effort. We trained a Mask R-CNN detector and a YOLOv8 model using synthetic data for both training ($\alpha = 90$, $\beta = 3k$) and validation ($\alpha = 90$, $\beta = 0.5k$). The evaluation led to 84.8 box mAP and 80.8 and mask mAP for Mask R-CNN, and 91.4 box mAP and 90.4 mask mAP for YOLOv8, indicating only a minor sacrifice in performance compared to the results in Table 1. Further experiments regarding the use of data with inter-instrument occlusions and synthetic validation sets will be considered in future work.

Acknowledgements. The authors are deeply thankful for the support provided by the University of Costa Rica, which enabled the creation of this document.

References

1. Marć, M., Bartosiewicz, A., Burzyńska, J., Chmiel, Z., Januszewicz, P.: A nursing shortage-a prospect of global and local policies. Int. Nurs. Rev. **66**(1), 9–16 (2019)
2. Haczyński, J., Skrzypczak, Z., Winter, M.: Nurses in Poland-immediate action needed. Eng. Manag. Prod. Serv. **9**(2), 97–104 (2017)
3. Lowman, G.H., Harms, P.D.: Addressing the nurse workforce crisis: a call for greater integration of the organizational behavior, human resource management and nursing literatures. J. Manag. Psychol. **37**(3), 294–303 (2022)
4. Harms, P.D.: Nursing: a critical profession in a perilous time. Ind. Organ. Psychol. **14**(1–2), 264–266 (2021)
5. Zemmar, A., Lozano, A.M., Nelson, B.J.: The rise of robots in surgical environments during COVID-19. Nat. Mach. Intell. **2**(10), 566–572 (2020)
6. Kyrarini, M., et al.: A survey of robots in healthcare. Technologies **9**(1), 8 (2021)
7. Appendectomy Set, New Med Instruments. https://new-medinstruments.com/appendectomy-set.html. Accessed 26 May 2023
8. Glaucoma Surgical Instrument Set, New Med Instruments. https://new-medinstruments.com/surgery-sets/general-surgery-instruments-sets.html/glaucoma-surgical-instrument-set.html. Accessed 26 May 2023
9. Major General Surgery Set, New Med Instruments. https://new-medinstruments.com/surgery-sets/general-surgery-instruments-sets.html/general-surgery-set.html. Accessed 26 May 2023
10. AlHajj, H., Lamard, M., Conze, P.H., et al.: Challenge on automatic tool annotation for cataract surgery: cataracts. Med. Image Anal. **52**, 24–41 (2019). https://doi.org/10.1016/j.media.2018.11.00

11. Allan, M., Shvets, A., Kurmann, T., et al.: 2017 robotic instrument segmentation challenge. ArXiv arXiv:1902:06426 (2019)
12. Ross, T., Reinke, A., Full, P.M., et al.: Robust medical instrument segmentation challenge. ArXiv preprint (2019)
13. Twinanda, A.P., Shehata, S., Mutter, D., et al.: EndoNet: a deep architecture for recognition tasks on laparoscopic videos. IEEE Trans. Med. Imaging **36**, 86–97 (2017). https://doi.org/10.1109/TMI.2016.2593957
14. Rodrigues, M., Mayo, M., Patros, P.: Evaluation of deep learning techniques on a novel hierarchical surgical tool dataset. In: Long, G., Yu, X., Wang, S. (eds.) AI 2021. LNCS, vol. 13151, pp. 169–180. Springer, Cham (2022). https://doi.org/10.1007/978-3-030-97546-3_14
15. Badilla-Solórzano, J., Spindeldreier, S., Ihler, S., Gellrich, N.C., Spalthoff, S.: Deep-learning-based instrument detection for intra-operative robotic assistance. Int. J. Comput. Assist. Radiol. Surg. **17**(9), 1685–1695 (2022)
16. Peng, H., et al.: Reducing annotating load: active learning with synthetic images in surgical instrument segmentation. arXiv preprint arXiv:2108.03534 (2021)
17. Dwibedi, D., Misra, I., Hebert, M.: Cut, paste and learn: surprisingly easy synthesis for instance detection. In: Proceedings of the IEEE International Conference on Computer Vision, pp. 1301–1310 (2017)
18. Dvornik, N., Mairal, J., Schmid, C.: Modeling visual context is key to augmenting object detection datasets. In: Proceedings of the European Conference on Computer Vision (ECCV), pp. 364–380 (2018)
19. Ghiasi, G., et al.: Simple copy-paste is a strong data augmentation method for instance segmentation. In: Proceedings of the IEEE/CVF Conference on Computer Vision and Pattern Recognition, pp. 2918–2928 (2021)
20. Wang, A., Islam, M., Xu, M., Ren, H.: Rethinking surgical instrument segmentation: a background image can be all you need. In: Wang, L., Dou, Q., Fletcher, P.T., Speidel, S., Li, S. (eds.) MICCAI 2022. LNCS, vol. 13437, pp. 355–364. Springer, Cham (2022). https://doi.org/10.1007/978-3-031-16449-1_34
21. Garcia-Peraza-Herrera, L.C., Fidon, L., D'Ettorre, C., Stoyanov, D., Vercauteren, T., Ourselin, S.: Image compositing for segmentation of surgical tools without manual annotations. IEEE Trans. Med. Imaging **40**(5), 1450–1460 (2021)
22. Hasty: Adaptive Automation for Vision AI. 2023 Hasty GmbH. https://app.hasty.ai. Accessed 28 May 2023
23. He, K., Gkioxari, G., Dollár, P., Girshick, R.: Mask R-CNN. In: Proceedings of the IEEE International Conference on Computer Vision, pp. 2961–2969 (2017)
24. Lin, T.Y., et al.: Microsoft COCO: common objects in context. In: Fleet, D., Pajdla, T., Schiele, B., Tuytelaars, T. (eds.) ECCV 2014. LNCS, vol. 8693, pp. 740–755. Springer, Cham (2014). https://doi.org/10.1007/978-3-319-10602-1_48
25. Pérez, P., Gangnet, M., Blake, A.: Poisson image editing. In: ACM SIGGRAPH 2003 Papers, pp. 313–318 (2003)
26. Jocher, G., et al.: ultralytics/yolov5: v7. 0-YOLOv5 SOTA realtime instance segmentation. Zenodo (2022)
27. Jocher, G., Chaurasia, A., Qiu, J.: YOLO by Ultralytics (version 8.0.0) [computer software]. https://github.com/ultralytics/ultralytics. Accessed 1 June 2023
28. Carion, N., Massa, F., Synnaeve, G., Usunier, N., Kirillov, A., Zagoruyko, S.: End-to-end object detection with transformers. In: Vedaldi, A., Bischof, H., Brox, T., Frahm, J.M. (eds.) ECCV 2020. LNCS, vol. 12346, pp. 213–229. Springer, Cham (2020). https://doi.org/10.1007/978-3-030-58452-8_13

29. Grammatikopoulou, M., et al.: CaDIS: cataract dataset for surgical RGB-image segmentation. Med. Image Anal. **71**, 102053 (2021)
30. Jiang, W., Xia, T., Wang, Z., Jia, F.: Semi-supervised surgical tool detection based on highly confident pseudo labeling and strong augmentation driven consistency. In: Engelhardt, S., et al. (eds.) DGM4MICCAI DALI 2021. LNCS, vol. 13003, pp. 154–162. Springer, Cham (2021). https://doi.org/10.1007/978-3-030-88210-5_14

Adaptive Semi-supervised Segmentation of Brain Vessels with Ambiguous Labels

Fengming Lin[1], Yan Xia[1], Nishant Ravikumar[1], Qiongyao Liu[1], Michael MacRaild[1], and Alejandro F. Frangi[2(✉)]

[1] University of Leeds, Leeds, UK
[2] University of Manchester, Manchester, UK
alejandro.frangi@manchester.ac.uk
https://github.com/fmlinks/domain

Abstract. Accurate segmentation of brain vessels is crucial for cerebrovascular disease diagnosis and treatment. However, existing methods face challenges in capturing small vessels and handling datasets that are partially or ambiguously annotated. In this paper, we propose an adaptive semi-supervised approach to address these challenges. Our approach incorporates innovative techniques including progressive semi-supervised learning, adaptative training strategy, and boundary enhancement. Experimental results on 3DRA datasets demonstrate the superiority of our method in terms of mesh-based segmentation metrics. By leveraging the partially and ambiguously labeled data, which only annotates the main vessels, our method achieves impressive segmentation performance on mislabeled fine vessels, showcasing its potential for clinical applications.

Keywords: Brain vessel segmentation · Semi-supervised learning · Adaptive model

1 Introduction

Accurate segmentation of cerebral vessels is clinically significant as it provides crucial anatomical information for the diagnosis and assessment of cerebrovascular diseases [1]. Furthermore, segmenting small vessels is essential as they play important roles in brain function and pathological processes. Accurate segmentation of small vessels provides comprehensive morphological information about the vascular network, facilitating patient-specific modeling of cerebral hemodynamics, which can be used to better understand pathologies, plan interventions, and design treatment devices [2–5].

However, the task of accurate vessel segmentation is challenging due to several reasons. Firstly, the small proportion of vessels in brain tissue makes segmentation difficult, particularly for small arterioles [6,7]. To address this, convolution-based methods [8] designed for medical imaging are enhanced in segmentation capability through experienced pre-processing and post-processing techniques. Further, transformer-based

Alejandro F. Frangi—AFF is supported by the Royal Academy of Engineering INSILEX Chair (CiET1919/19), UKRI Frontier Research Guarantee INSILICO (EPY0304941), and the EC Sixth Framework Programme @neurIST (FP6-2004-IST-4-027703).

Y. Xue et al. (Eds.): DALI 2023, LNCS 14379, pp. 106–116, 2024.
https://doi.org/10.1007/978-3-031-58171-7_11

methods [9, 10] have been proposed to leverage fully supervised learning to explore the features of small targets in-depth. Secondly, clinical vessel annotations are focused only on regions surrounding pathologies such as aneurysms [11, 12], and only the main vessels are labeled, leaving out fine vessels. This ambiguously-labeled data negatively impacts the performance of fully supervised learning approaches. To overcome this limitation, semi-supervised learning methods with pseudo-labeling techniques [13, 14] have been proposed. Thirdly, clinical images often exhibit high levels of noise [15], and there are significant variations in pixel distribution across different imaging centers. Traditional semi-supervised methods [16–19] using pseudo-labeling [13] tend to overly incentivize the confidence of the model in vessel segmentation, leading to excessive over-segmentation [20].

Therefore, we propose the adaptive semi-supervised model in Fig. 1, aiming to address the challenge of partially annotated intracranial vessel segmentation. The model employs a Teacher-Student structure, with the Swin-UNet [9] serving as the backbone network. We partition the partially annotated data into labeled patches and unlabeled patches, which are fed into the teacher and student networks, respectively. Deviates from the conventional practice of directly supervising the student network in knowledge distillation. The teacher network learns vessel knowledge from the labeled patches and teaches it to the student network. Additionally, the teacher network's output is used as refined pseudo-labels for further learning by the student network. The key innovations are as follows.

- We introduce the adaptive semi-supervised model, utilizing a progressive semi-supervised learning strategy. Ground truth is used to teach the teacher network, and the teacher network in turn instructs the student network, leading to incremental improvements in segmentation performance.
- We propose addressing the challenges associated with semi-supervised learning through unsupervised domain adaptation techniques. This enables the adaptation of knowledge from labeled patches to unlabeled patches without any domain shift.
- We introduce the Fourier high-frequency boundary loss. Except for Dice and Cross-Entropy loss, we extract the high-frequency boundary features using the Fourier transform and calculate their mean squared error.
- We introduced a data augmentation technique called adaptive histogram attention (AHA) to address the variations in pixel distribution within clinical data. AHA enables the model to better focus on discriminating between other brain tissues and vessels, facilitating the extraction of vessel structural features.

2 Methodology

2.1 Preprocessing

The purpose of preprocessing is not only to remove noise but also to facilitate the model in extracting size, structural, and generalization features specific to the vessels.

Resolution standardization: To tackle the resolution inconsistencies in clinical data, all data is standardized to a spacing of 0.35 mm/pixel. This allows the model to learn the size/shape features in cases with initially different resolutions.

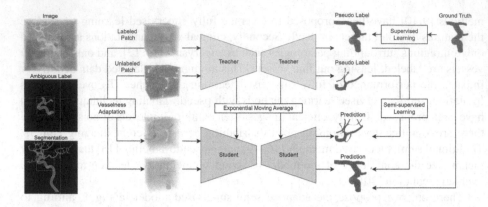

Fig. 1. Schematic of the proposed adaptive semi-supervised model.

Adaptive Histogram Attention: The distribution patterns in 3DRA data histograms show that vessels are typically in the higher pixel value range, brain tissues in the middle, and backgrounds in the lower range. While deep learning models can easily distinguish between the background and vessels, they may struggle with distinguishing between brain tissues and vessels, leading to over-segmentation. AHA tackles this by identifying areas of abrupt shifts in the histogram, using them for normalization, effectively eliminating the background from the histogram, thereby enabling the model to focus on distinguishing between vessels and other brain tissues. This method emphasizes the extraction of structural features rather than mere threshold-based features.

Patch Grouping: We extract overlapped 3D patches from both the annotated and unannotated regions. These two groups of patches are subsequently fed into the teacher and student networks, respectively. This approach enables the model to learn local generalized vessel features rather than specific fitting features of individual cases.

2.2 Problem Formulation

In this paper, we have datasets sampled from two groups. The labeled group contains labeled patch $\mathcal{D}_l = \left\{ (x_i^l, y_i^l) \right\}_{i=1}^{N_l}$, and the unlabeled group contains unlabeled patch $\mathcal{D}_u = \left\{ (x_i^u) \right\}_{i=1}^{N_u}$. We use adaptive histogram attention to get labeled and unlabeled vessel-like patch $\mathcal{D}_{\hat{l}} = \left\{ (\hat{x}_i^l) \right\}_{i=1}^{N_l}$ and $\mathcal{D}_{\hat{u}} = \left\{ (\hat{x}_i^u) \right\}_{i=1}^{N_u}$. Our model consists of teacher and student networks. We update the weights in the student network (encoder F_s, decoder G_s) as an exponential moving average (EMA) of weights in the teacher network (encoder F_t, decoder G_t) to ensemble the information in different training steps. The prediction of teacher network on labeled and unlabeled patch are denoted as $p_i^l = G_t \left(F_t \left(x_i^l \right) \right)$ and $p_i^u = G_t \left(F_t \left(x_i^u \right) \right)$. We also denote the prediction of the student network on labeled and unlabeled vessel-like patch as $\hat{p}_i^l = G_s \left(F_s \left(\hat{x}_i^l \right) \right)$ and $\hat{p}_i^u = G_s \left(F_s \left(\hat{x}_i^u \right) \right)$. Our goal is to learn a task-specific student network using F_s and G_s to accurately predict labels on test data from the unlabeled patches.

2.3 Supervised Learning

In the teacher network, labeled patches $\mathcal{D}_l$ are passed through the CNN-based feature extractor F_t, which are then passed through the task-specific segmentation generator G_t to minimize the supervised loss $\mathcal{L}_{sup}$ which includes cross-entropy $\mathcal{L}_{CE}$, Dice similarity coefficient loss $\mathcal{L}_{DSC}$, and boundary loss $\mathcal{L}_B$.

$$\mathcal{L}_{full\_sup} = \mathcal{L}_{CE} + \mathcal{L}_{DSC} + \mathcal{L}_B \tag{1}$$

$$\mathcal{L}_{CE} = -\frac{1}{N_l} \sum_{i=1}^{N_l} y_i^l \log\left(p_i^l\right) \tag{2}$$

$$\mathcal{L}_{DSC} = \frac{1}{N_l} \sum_{i=1}^{N_l} \left(1 - \frac{2\left|p_i^l \cap y_i^l\right|}{\left|p_i^l\right| + \left|y_i^l\right|}\right) \tag{3}$$

$$\mathcal{L}_B = \frac{1}{N_l} \sum_{i=1}^{N_l} \left(H\left(p_i^l\right) - H\left(y_i^l\right)\right)^2 \tag{4}$$

$$H\left(p_i^l\right) = \mathcal{F}^{-1}\left(\mathcal{F}\left(p_i^l\right) \cdot \mathbb{1}_{mask}\right) \tag{5}$$

where $\mathcal{F}$ and $\mathcal{F}^{-1}$ are the Fourier transform [21] and the Fourier inverse transform respectively. The mask $\mathbb{1}_{mask}$ with value one in the middle and value zero on the edge has the same shape as p_i^l.

2.4 Semi-supervised Learning

To perform alignment at the instance level, the adaptive vessel-like labeled and unlabeled patches are passed through the teacher network to get segmentation prediction p_i^l and p_i^u. Meanwhile, we generate the adaptive vessel-like labeled and unlabeled patches, and they are passed through the student network to get segmentation prediction $\hat{p}_i^l$ and $\hat{p}_i^u$. Next, we employ the mean square error (MSE) [22] and cosine similarity [23] as defined in Eq. 7 and Eq. 8 to reduce the discrepancy between the two predictions and thus increase the vessel invariance of the student model.

$$\mathcal{L}_{semi\_sup} = \mathcal{L}_{mse} + \mathcal{L}_{sim} \tag{6}$$

$$\mathcal{L}_{mse} = \frac{1}{N_l} \sum_{i=1}^{N_l} \left(p_i^l - \hat{p}_i^l\right)^2 + \frac{1}{N_u} \sum_{i=1}^{N_u} \left(\hat{p}_i^u - p_i^u\right)^2 \tag{7}$$

$$\mathcal{L}_{sim} = \frac{1}{N_l} \sum_{i=1}^{N_l} h\left(p_i^l, \hat{p}_i^l\right) + \frac{1}{N_u} \sum_{i=1}^{N_u} h\left(\hat{p}_i^u, p_i^u\right) \tag{8}$$

$$h(u, v) = \exp\left(\frac{u^T v}{\|u\|_2 \|v\|_2}\right) \tag{9}$$

The weight ratio between fully supervised and semi-supervised losses is 4:1. We prioritize the fully supervised loss to ensure training robustness and prevent the network from becoming overly confident and introducing noise during the initialization stage.

3   Experiments and Results

3.1   Datasets

In our experiments, we utilized 3D rotational angiography (3DRA) modality dataset Aneurist [15], which comprises 223 partially annotated 3D brain vessel images. These images were acquired from four different centers using different scanners and imaging protocols. As shown in Fig. 2, there are significant variations in image appearance and resolution across the data from different centers. We trained our models using full-size images and partially and ambiguously annotated labels. Due to the incomplete annotations, quantitative analysis was performed within the bounding box of annotated regions, while qualitative analysis was conducted across the entire image.

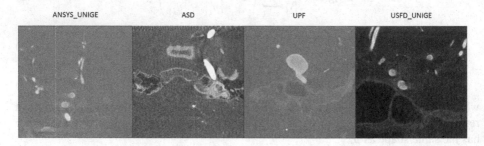

Fig. 2. Examples of 3DRA images in grayscale collected from AneurIST dataset: 2D visualization of data from four different sources showed great differences in pixel distribution and noise levels.

3.2   Experimental Setup

The experiments were conducted using a high-performance computing setup. We utilized an NVIDIA GeForce RTX 3090 GPU with 24 GB of VRAM. The experimental system was equipped with a high-capacity RAM of 128 GB, enabling the handling of large datasets and memory-intensive tasks.

Our proposed adaptive semi-supervised model was implemented based on the Swin-UNet architecture [9], serving as the backbone of both teacher and student networks. During training, we employed a batch size of 1 and utilized patch-based learning with a patch size of [128, 128, 128]. The models were trained for 100 epochs, during which the optimization was performed using the Adam optimizer [24]. We employed data augmentation techniques, such as random rotations and flip, to enhance model generalization. The learning rate was initially set to 0.001, and a learning rate decay strategy was applied, reducing the learning rate by a factor of 0.1 every ten epochs. The parameters of the teacher network are updated normally, and the parameters of the student network are updated according to the exponential moving average (EMA) [25]. To achieve the effect of the EMA during the training process, we employed the no gradient decorator to ensure that gradient calculations are not performed during the EMA process. Prior to optimizing the parameters, we updated the parameters of the teacher network by invoking the EMA function in Eq. 10. In this function, the weight factor *decay* is calculated based on the iteration count and the initial decay rate of 0.999 in Eq. 11. The student network parameters are updated by applying the weight factor *decay*, thereby incorporating the knowledge learned by the teacher network gradually.

$$\mathcal{W}_{\text{stu}} = decay \times \mathcal{W}_{\text{stu}} + (1 - decay) \times \mathcal{W}_{\text{tea}} \tag{10}$$

$$decay = \min\left(1 - \frac{1}{iteration \times 10 + 1}, decay\right) \tag{11}$$

The image data from these databases were split on a patient-wise basis into training, validation, and test sets using a ratio of 7:1:2, respectively. To ensure a thorough evaluation of the segmentation performance, we performed five-fold cross-validation experiments, with the test sets in different cross-validation folds covering the entire dataset.

3.3 Evaluation Metrics

We utilized six evaluation metrics to assess the segmentation performance of our method: Dice similarity coefficient (DSC): Measures the overlap between predicted and ground truth segmentations. Sensitivity: Calculates the proportion of correctly identified positive instances. Precision: Quantifies the accuracy of positive predictions. Specificity: Measures the ability to correctly identify negative instances. Jaccard index (Jac): Evaluates the overall agreement between predicted and ground truth segmentations. Volume similarity (VS): Measures the similarity of segmented volume with the ground truth.

However, due to the ambiguous annotation of the dataset, most of the fine vessels are not labeled. This can lead to situations where segmentation results with higher accuracy actually have lower DSC. To provide a more comprehensive evaluation of segmentation performance, we employed surface-to-surface distance error (Surface Error) metrics to measure segmentation accuracy based on mesh representations. Furthermore, in our qualitative analysis, we employ visualization techniques to further evaluate the segmentation results, including the degree of over-segmentation and the accuracy of fine vessel segmentation.

The surface error metrics estimate the error between the ground-truth surfaces S, and the segmentation prediction surfaces S'. The distance between a point p_i on surface S and the nearest point on surface S' is given by the minimum of the Euclidean norm. And we compare the similarity between the prediction and ground-truth by generating surface mesh-based representations of these structures from their corresponding masks in Eq. 12. Doing this for all N points in the ground-truth surface S gives the average surface-to-surface distance error in Eq. 13. The p-value is calculated based on surface error.

$$d(p_i, S') = \min_{p' \in S'} \|p_i - p'\|_2 \tag{12}$$

$$d(S, S') = \frac{1}{N} \sum_N^i d(p_i, S') \tag{13}$$

3.4 Qualitative Results and Analysis

In Fig. 3, we compared the proposed method with state-of-the-art approaches on four different data sources. Our method demonstrated superior performance in segmenting fine vessels without introducing excessive over-segmentation noise, especially in datasets with high levels of noise, such as ANSYS, ASD, and UPF. Notably, the nnUNet [8] was greatly affected by ambiguous labels and could only segment major vessels. The Swin-UNet [9], utilizing the swin-transformer structure for feature extraction, outperformed convolution in nnUNet by extracting a larger number of vessel branches. VASeg [26], employing majority voting and thresholding techniques, achieved a better recovery of fine vessels. CPS [13], due to the utilization of semi-supervised cross pseudo-supervision, exhibited increased segmentation uncertainty and introduced excessive noise when handling datasets with higher noise levels. Because of our semi-supervised model's emphasis on training robustness, the fully supervised loss is assigned a higher weight compared to the semi-supervised loss. As a result, the network becomes more conservative in its predictions. When dealing with datasets containing lesser noise, the model does not fully unleash its predictive capabilities. Instead, it tends to be more cautious and restrained in making predictions to ensure reliability. In contrast, our method showcased the ability to segment a significant number of fine vessels while maintaining robustness and avoiding the introduction of excessive noise.

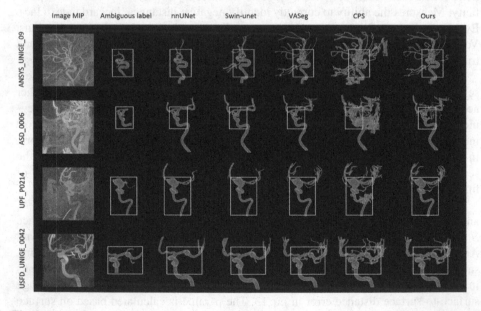

Fig. 3. Comparison with State-of-the-Art Methods on four different data sources. The yellow box is the golden standard area where all quantitative evaluations are carried out. (Color figure online)

3.5 Quantitative Results and Analysis

Due to the uncertain and ambiguous nature of our dataset annotations, where only the main vessels near the aneurysm are labeled, we utilized mesh-based evaluation metrics as our primary performance measure, while pixel-based evaluation metrics such as the DSC were used as supplementary reference metrics.

In Table 1, we compared our method with several approaches, including the convolution-based fully supervised method nnUNet, the transformer-based fully supervised method Swin-UNet, the VASet method that addresses ambiguous label issues through preprocessing and postprocessing, and the traditional semi-supervised method CPS using cross pseudo-supervision. Due to the incomplete annotation, pixel-based metrics such as DSC and VS cannot accurately measure the segmentation accuracy. Segmenting more unannotated vessels may lead to a decrease in DSC and similar metrics. Therefore, we employ mesh-based surface error as a more reliable metric for evaluation. By comparing the surface error, we found that our method achieved the highest accuracy in vessel surface segmentation, with an average mesh error of 0.20 mm (0.35 mm/pixel). Additionally, it is worth noting that our method achieves high sensitivity, second only to CPS. This indicates that our method successfully identifies a larger proportion of positive instances, meaning that it effectively captures the majority of the annotated vessels.

Table 1. Compare with state-of-the-art on whole Aneurist dataset. The mesh-based surface error serves as the primary evaluation metric, while pixel-based metrics such as the DSC are used as supplementary evaluation criteria due to incomplete annotation. Quantitative analysis was performed within the annotated regions instead of the full image.

Methods	nnUNet	Swin-unet	VASeg	CPS	Ours
Sensitivity	0.9196 ± 0.0637	0.8967 ± 0.1219	0.9572 ± 0.0510	0.9872 ± 0.0189	$\mathbf{0.9793 \pm 0.0183}$
Precision	0.9300 ± 0.0345	0.8689 ± 0.0487	0.8792 ± 0.0761	0.6636 ± 0.1238	$\mathbf{0.8018 \pm 0.0877}$
Specificity	0.9956 ± 0.0028	0.9932 ± 0.0032	0.9934 ± 0.0044	0.9740 ± 0.0129	$\mathbf{0.9881 \pm 0.0056}$
Jac	0.8605 ± 0.0680	0.7889 ± 0.1091	0.8440 ± 0.0763	0.6572 ± 0.1209	$\mathbf{0.7873 \pm 0.0817}$
VS	0.9728 ± 0.0263	0.9424 ± 0.0649	0.9450 ± 0.0509	0.7968 ± 0.0996	$\mathbf{0.8977 \pm 0.0602}$
DSC	0.9236 ± 0.0408	0.8772 ± 0.0787	0.9134 ± 0.0479	0.7862 ± 0.0960	$\mathbf{0.8786 \pm 0.0536}$
Surface Error	0.8903 ± 1.2450	0.6801 ± 1.6093	0.2586 ± 0.3066	0.3068 ± 0.1210	$\mathbf{0.2075 \pm 0.0640}$
p-value	<0.05	<0.05	<0.05	<0.05	/

Table 2 presents the results of the ablation study conducted to analyze the impact of different components in our method. We used the fully supervised Swin-UNet as the baseline, trained solely using the teacher network with Dice Cross Entropy loss. In the second set of experiments, we introduced the Fourier boundary loss to the fully supervised loss. The inclusion of this loss led to a noticeable improvement in surface error, indicating enhanced boundary delineation. In the third set of experiments, we employed vessel adaptation by feeding the data into the student network. We also incorporated the semi-supervised loss to train the student network. The results showed a significant increase in the number of predicted vessels, as evidenced by the improved sensitivity. Additionally, the surface error achieved a level of 0.20 mm, indicating precise vessel segmentation at the boundary. After transitioning from fully supervised to semi-supervised learning, the sensitivity increased from 0.92 to 0.97, demonstrating the validity of our hypothesis to utilize the teacher network's predictions to complement ambiguous labels and jointly supervise the student network's output. As a result, the network predicted more segmentation regions that are likely to be vessels.

Table 2. Ablation study.

Modules	Supervised Loss (Dice + CE)	Supervised Loss Boundary Loss	Supervised Loss Boundary Loss Semi-supervised Loss
Sensitivity	0.8967 ± 0.1219	0.9236 ± 0.0600	**0.9793 ±0.0183**
Precision	0.8689 ± 0.0487	0.9116 ± 0.0577	**0.8018 ±0.0877**
Specificity	0.9932 ± 0.0032	0.9954 ± 0.0035	**0.9881 ±0.0056**
Jac	0.7889 ± 0.1091	0.8456 ± 0.0652	**0.7873 ±0.0817**
VS	0.9424 ± 0.0649	0.9636 ± 0.0440	**0.8977 ±0.0602**
DSC	0.8772 ± 0.0787	0.9149 ± 0.0417	**0.8786 ±0.0536**
Surface Error	0.6801 ± 1.6093	0.3483 ± 0.3111	**0.2075 ±0.0640**
p-value	<0.05	<0.05	/

4 Conclusion

In summary, our semi-supervised model brings forward innovative techniques for cerebral vessel segmentation. With semi-supervised learning and domain adaptation-like strategies, Fourier high-frequency boundary loss, and adaptive histogram attention, we achieve better segmentation accuracy and robustness on whole vessels, paving the way for clinical uses such as treatment planning. However, our model might underperform on lower noise datasets due to our focus on robustness. Future research will explore contrastive learning to improve performance on low-noise datasets. We also plan to expand the state-of-the-art (SOTA) comparison to include not only architecture-based comparisons but also models performing similar tasks in the literature [27,28].

References

1. Hennemuth, A., Goubergrits, L., Ivantsits, M., et al.: Cerebral Aneurysm Detection and Analysis. Springer, Cham (2021). https://doi.org/10.1007/978-3-030-72862-5
2. Hilbert, A., Madai, V.I., Akay, E.M., et al.: BRAVE-NET: fully automated arterial brain vessel segmentation in patients with cerebrovascular disease. Front. Artif. Intell. **3**, 552258 (2020)
3. Aydin, O.U., Taha, A.A., Hilbert, A., et al.: An evaluation of performance measures for arterial brain vessel segmentation. BMC Med. Imaging **21**(1), 1–12 (2021)
4. Dai, P., Luo, H., Sheng, H., et al.: A new approach to segment both main and peripheral retinal vessels based on gray-voting and gaussian mixture model. PLoS ONE **10**(6), e0127748 (2015)
5. Ciecholewski, M., Kassjański, M.: Computational methods for liver vessel segmentation in medical imaging: a review. Sensors **21**(6), 2027 (2021)

6. Fu, F., Wei, J., Zhang, M., et al.: Rapid vessel segmentation and reconstruction of head and neck angiograms using 3D convolutional neural network. Nat. Commun. **11**(1), 4829 (2020)

7. Law, M.W.K., Chung, A.C.S.: Vessel and intracranial aneurysm segmentation using multi-range filters and local variances. In: Ayache, N., Ourselin, S., Maeder, A. (eds.) MICCAI 2007. LNCS, vol. 4791, pp. 866–874. Springer, Heidelberg (2007). https://doi.org/10.1007/978-3-540-75757-3_105

8. Isensee, F., Jaeger, P.F., Kohl, S.A.A., et al.: nnU-Net: a self-configuring method for deep learning-based biomedical image segmentation. Nat. Methods **18**(2), 203–211 (2021)

9. Cao, H., et al.: Swin-Unet: Unet-like pure transformer for medical image segmentation. In: Karlinsky, L., Michaeli, T., Nishino, K. (eds.) ECCV 2022. LNCS, vol. 13803, pp. 205–218. Springer, Cham (2022). https://doi.org/10.1007/978-3-031-25066-8_9

10. Chen, J., Lu, Y., Yu, Q., et al.: TransUNet: transformers make strong encoders for medical image segmentation. arXiv preprint arXiv:2102.04306 (2021)

11. Krings, T., Mandell, D.M., Kiehl, T.R., et al.: Intracranial aneurysms: from vessel wall pathology to therapeutic approach. Nat. Rev. Neurol. **7**(10), 547–559 (2011)

12. Samaniego, E.A., Roa, J.A., Hasan, D.: Vessel wall imaging in intracranial aneurysms. J. Neurointerventional Surg. **11**(11), 1105–1112 (2019)

13. Chen, X., Yuan, Y., Zeng, G., et al.: Semi-supervised semantic segmentation with cross pseudo supervision. In: Proceedings of the IEEE/CVF Conference on Computer Vision and Pattern Recognition, pp. 2613–2622 (2021)

14. Chatterjee, S., Prabhu, K., Pattadkal, M., et al.: DS6, deformation-aware semi-supervised learning: application to small vessel segmentation with noisy training data. J. Imaging **8**(10), 259 (2022)

15. Benkner, S., Arbona, A., Berti, G., et al.: @ neurIST: infrastructure for advanced disease management through integration of heterogeneous data, computing, and complex processing services. IEEE Trans. Inf Technol. Biomed. **14**(6), 1365–1377 (2010)

16. Nie, D., Gao, Y., Wang, L., Shen, D.: ASDNet: attention based semi-supervised deep networks for medical image segmentation. In: Frangi, A., Schnabel, J., Davatzikos, C., Alberola-López, C., Fichtinger, G. (eds.) MICCAI 2018. LNCS, vol. 11073, pp. 370–378. Springer, Cham (2018). https://doi.org/10.1007/978-3-030-00937-3_43

17. Chen, S., Bortsova, G., García-Uceda Juárez, A., van Tulder, G., de Bruijne, M.: Multi-task attention-based semi-supervised learning for medical image segmentation. In: Shen, D., et al. (eds.) MICCAI 2019. LNCS, vol. 11766, pp. 457–465. Springer, Cham (2019). https://doi.org/10.1007/978-3-030-32248-9_51

18. Luo, X., Chen, J., Song, T., et al.: Semi-supervised medical image segmentation through dual-task consistency. In: Proceedings of the AAAI Conference on Artificial Intelligence, vol. 35, no. 10, pp. 8801–8809 (2021)

19. Jiao, R., Zhang, Y., Ding, L., et al.: Learning with limited annotations: a survey on deep semi-supervised learning for medical image segmentation. arXiv preprint arXiv:2207.14191 (2022)

20. Rizve, M.N., Duarte, K., Rawat, Y.S., et al.: In defense of pseudo-labeling: an uncertainty-aware pseudo-label selection framework for semi-supervised learning. arXiv preprint arXiv:2101.06329 (2021)

21. Cochran, W.T., Cooley, J.W., Favin, D.L., et al.: What is the fast Fourier transform? Proc. IEEE **55**(10), 1664–1674 (1967)

22. Willmott, C.J., Matsuura, K.: Advantages of the mean absolute error (MAE) over the root mean square error (RMSE) in assessing average model performance. Clim. Res. **30**(1), 79–82 (2005)

23. Lahitani, A.R., Permanasari, A.E., Setiawan, N.A.: Cosine similarity to determine similarity measure: study case in online essay assessment. In: 2016 4th International Conference on Cyber and IT Service Management, pp. 1–6. IEEE (2016)

24. Kingma, D.P., Ba, J.: Adam: a method for stochastic optimization. arXiv preprint arXiv:1412.6980 (2014)
25. Wang, G., Liu, X., Li, C., et al.: A noise-robust framework for automatic segmentation of COVID-19 pneumonia lesions from CT images. IEEE Trans. Med. Imaging **39**(8), 2653–2663 (2020)
26. Lin, F., Xia, Y., Song, S., Ravikumar, N., Frangi, A.F.: High-throughput 3DRA segmentation of brain vasculature and aneurysms using deep learning. Comput. Methods Programs Biomed. **230**, 107355 (2023)
27. Xu, Z., Wang, Y., Lu, D., et al.: Ambiguity-selective consistency regularization for mean-teacher semi-supervised medical image segmentation. Med. Image Anal. **88**, 102880 (2023)
28. Zhao, F., Chen, Y., Chen, F., et al.: Semi-supervised cerebrovascular segmentation by hierarchical convolutional neural network. IEEE Access **6**, 67841–67852 (2018)

Proportion Estimation by Masked Learning from Label Proportion

Takumi Okuo[1(✉)], Kazuya Nishimura[1], Hiroaki Ito[2], Kazuhiro Terada[2], Akihiko Yoshizawa[2], and Ryoma Bise[1]

[1] Kyushu University, Fukuoka, Japan
takumi.okuo@humna.ait.kyushu-u.ac.jp
[2] Kyoto University Hospital, Kyoto, Japan

Abstract. The PD-L1 rate, the number of PD-L1 positive tumor cells over the total number of all tumor cells, is an important metric for immunotherapy. This metric is recorded as diagnostic information with pathological images. In this paper, we propose a proportion estimation method with a small amount of cell-level annotation and proportion annotation, which can be easily collected. Since the PD-L1 rate is calculated from only 'tumor cells' and not using 'non-tumor cells', we first detect tumor cells with a detection model. Then, we estimate the PD-L1 proportion by introducing a masking technique to 'learning from label proportion'. In addition, we propose a weighted focal proportion loss to address data imbalance problems. Experiments using clinical data demonstrate the effectiveness of our method. Our method achieved the best performance in comparisons.

Keywords: Learning from label proportion · Histopathology

1 Introduction

The proportional information of cancer subtypes is recorded as diagnostic information with pathological images in many diagnoses, such as programmed cell death ligand-1 (PD-L1) diagnosis [8,14], chemotherapy, and lung cancer diagnosis [13,15]. For example, the PD-L1 test is conducted to check if cancer immunotherapy will be helpful for a patient. Figure 1 shows an example image (called core image) captured by a whole slide scanner. In the core image, over 10 thousand cells belong to three classes; positive cancer, negative cancer, and non-tumor cells. The PD-L1 rate is calculated by the number of positive tumor cells over all of the tumor cells in a tissue. Note that it does not include non-tumor cells. Counting all cells in the core image is almost impossible; thus, pathologists roughly estimate the PD-L1 rate without counting in clinical. Therefore, there is a demand to develop an automatic proportion estimation method.

A simple solution is to detect positive and negative tumor cells by a deep detection model [10] and calculate the proportion from the detection results.

Supplementary Information The online version contains supplementary material available at https://doi.org/10.1007/978-3-031-58171-7_12.

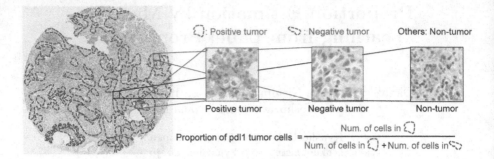

Fig. 1. Illustration of a core image in PD-L1 test. Blue dots regions indicate negative tumors, and red indicates positive tumors. Ideally, the proportion of positive tumor cells is calculated by counting and classifying all cells; however, pathologists roughly estimate the ratio subjective without counting or segmenting. (Color figure online)

However, this approach does not use the useful information, PD-L1 rate, which has already been recorded as diagnosis information and requires a certain amount of cell-level annotation for positive and negative tumor cells. A small amount of annotation can be collected, but the performance of a network trained using insufficient training data is worse. Large datasets with sufficient variability must be collected to address inter-tumor heterogeneity and different staining characteristics, but it is time-consuming and labor-intensive.

Another solution is to estimate the proportion by regression or classification directly. The approach can train a network using proportion information without additional annotation since PD-L1 rates are recorded in clinical settings. However, these methods have two drawbacks. A PD-L1 rate is a 'partial' proportion of all cells, i.e., it is calculated only from tumor cells but ignores non-tumor cells. This ambiguity caused by without using the non-tumor region information makes training difficult to estimate proportion. Another disadvantage is poor interpretability for estimation. When pathologists use the estimated results in clinical, they check the cell distributions of three classes to know how the rate is calculated. A class activation map (CAM)-based approach [16], which visualizes contributed pixels to the output, is unsuitable for this task because class distributions of all tumor regions are required to estimate the proportion.

This paper proposes a proportion estimation method to estimate the proportion of PD-L1 tumor cells and output the distributions of three classes in a core image while keeping annotation costs as low as possible. As discussed above, estimating the proportion without tumor region information is difficult. Thus, we made a small amount of training data to train a cell detection network that detects tumor or non-tumor cells. This enables us to make a tumor region mask, which is used for estimating the proportion (PD-L1 rate). We proposed a masked 'Learning from Label Proportions (LLP)' that estimates the proportion by using the tumor cell region mask predicted by the cell detection network. In addition, we propose a weighted focal proportion loss to address data imbalance problems, where data imbalance often occurs in medical image applications. Experiments using clinical data demonstrate the effectiveness of our method. Our method achieved the best performance in comparison.

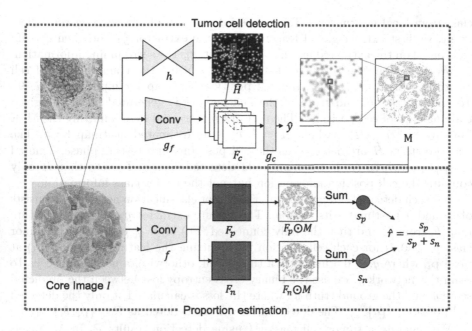

Fig. 2. Overview of proposed method. Top: cell detection network, and Bottom: proportion estimation network.

2   PD-L1 Tumor Proportion Estimation

Our method aims to train a network that estimates the proportion r of PD-L1 tumor cells in core images I. We use three types of annotation for the training. One is a cell position label, the second is a tumor cell region, and the third is the proportion label. For proportion labels, a proportion is often recorded as interval sections in clinical since pathologists roughly estimate the PD-L1 rate subjective without counting. For example, PD-L1 rates are either '0 to 0.01', '0.01 to 0.25', '0.25 to 0.5', '0.5 to 0.75', or '0.75 to 1.00'.

Figure 2 shows an overview of the proposed method. Our method was designed as a two-stage structure to effectively use a small amount of cell-level annotation and a large amount of tissue-level annotation (proportion). We first detect tumor cells in core image I to produce tumor mask M. Then, we estimate the proportion of PD-L1-positive cells of an input image I using mask M.

Tumor Cell Detection: Figure 2 (Top) shows the overview of the tumor cell detection network, which consists of a cell detection model h and a classification model g. For the cell detection model h, we follow the heatmap-based cell detection method [9], which produces a heatmap of all cells, where the coordinates of the peaks in the maps indicate the centroid positions of cells. For the classification model g, we propose a two-stage cell detection method inspired by bounding box-based general object detectors [11]. Since cell shapes are similar between tumor and non-tumor cells, it is difficult to accurately identify their class from local information. To use the information of surrounding cells effectively, we first extract global feature by feature extractor g_f and then classify cells based on the extracted feature, which contains the surrounding information.

We first train the cell detection network h using the training data of cell positions, where h produces the cell position heatmap for input image I [9]. To train h, the ground truth of the heatmap H is generated using the given training data of cell positions. The network h is trained by minimizing the MSE Loss $L_d = \|H - \hat{H}\|^2$, where $\hat{H} = h(I)$ is an estimated heatmap by h. The peak points in $\hat{H}$ are detected as the cell positions in a testing phase, denoted as $\{\hat{\mathbf{p}}_i\}_{i=1}^{N_d}$, where N_d is the number of detected cells in I. Note that $\hat{H}$ only contains the cell position information but not the tumor class information.

For each detected cell position $\hat{\mathbf{p}}_i$, the tumor classification network g (consists of g_f and g_c) estimates its class $\hat{y}_i$. The feature extractor g_f extracts a feature map F_t from I, and then the fully connected (Fc) layer g_c estimates the tumor class $\hat{y}_i \in [0, 1]$ for each cell position by inputting the feature vector $F_t(\hat{\mathbf{p}}_i)$ at pixel $\hat{\mathbf{p}}_i$, where $\hat{y}_i > 0.5$ indicates a tumor cell, otherwise, a non-tumor cell. To train this network g, we use the binary cross-entropy loss between the predicted score $\hat{y}_i$ and the ground truth y_i, where the loss is calculated at only the detected cell positions $\{\hat{\mathbf{p}}_i\}_{i=1}^{N_d}$. The detection results are denoted as $\hat{\mathcal{P}} = \{\hat{\mathbf{p}}_i, \hat{y}_i\}_{i=1}^{N_d}$.

We generate a tumor cell mask M using detection results $\hat{\mathcal{P}}$. In M, pixels around the tumor cell positions $\hat{\mathcal{P}}_c = \{\hat{p}_i | \hat{y}_i > 0.5\}$ takes 1, otherwise 0, where the distance from the detected position to a positive pixel is less than α. This mask is used to estimate the proportions.

PD-L1 Proportion Estimation: The proportion estimation network f estimates the proportion of PD-L1 positive cells among tumor cells. As shown in Fig. 3, the feature extractor of f extracts the positive map F_p and negative map F_n by inputting I. These feature maps are masked to calculate the pixels on only the tumor regions, denoted as $F_p \odot M$ and $F_n \odot M$, respectively, which indicate the maps of the positive/negative 'tumor' cell position maps. Then, the estimated proportion $\hat{r}$ is calculated from these masked maps. The positive score s_p and negative score s_n, which indicate the numbers of positive or negative tumor cells in the image, are defined as the sum of the pixel values in $F_p \odot M$ and $F_n \odot M$. The PD-L1 tumor proportion is calculated by $\hat{r} = \frac{s_p}{s_p + s_n}$. The network is trained using the estimated proportion $\hat{r}$ and the ground truth r. The details of the loss function are proposed below.

As discussed in the introduction, the PD-L1 rate is given as a proportion interval; pathologists give either '0 to 0.01', '0.01 to 0.25', '0.25 to 0.5', '0.5 to 0.75', or '0.75 to 1.00' for a core image. In previous works, the loss for proportion interval [2] outperforms cross-entropy. This loss mitigates the problem of overfitting by sacrificing strictness but at the expense of discriminability. In our problem setting, there are different intervals; the interval in '0 to 0.01' is much smaller than that of others, and there is data imbalance, e.g., the number of core images belonging to '0.5 to 0.75' is much fewer than that of '0 to 0.01'. These issues make training difficult.

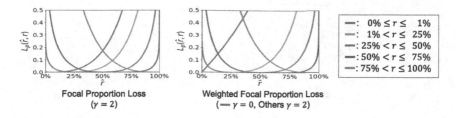

Fig. 3. Left: focal proportion loss. Right: weighted focal proportion loss.

We thus propose a weighted focal proportion loss that can mitigate these issues. This loss is designed inspired by the focal loss [7], which has been widely used for imbalanced data classification. The focal loss is a dynamically scaled cross-entropy loss, where the scaling factor decays to zero as confidence in the correct class increases [7]. We introduce this idea into the proportion loss [1], widely used in LLP. Let us denote r_k, $(k = 1, 2)$ are the proportion of the positive and negative cells. The weighted focal proportion loss is defined as:

$$WFL = -|r - \hat{r}|^\gamma \left(\sum_k r_k \log \frac{r_k}{\hat{r_k}} \right), \qquad (1)$$

where r is the ground truth of the proportion (PD-L1 rate), which takes the mean of the interval; e.g., $r = 0.375$ for '0.25 to 0.5', $\hat{r}$ is the estimated proportion, and γ is a hyper parameter. $\sum_k r_k \log \frac{r_k}{\hat{r_k}}$ indicates the KL-divergence between the truth and estimated proportion (proportion loss), $r_1 = r$ indicates the proportion of the positive cells, and $r_2 = 1 - r_k$ indicates that of the negative one. $|r - \hat{r}|^\gamma$ indicates that the loss decreases when the estimation becomes the correct value.

Figure 3 (Left) shows the plot of the focal proportion loss for each proportion interval when $\gamma = 2$. In this graph, the loss for '0 to 0.01' (blue line) has low gradients, and the loss around 3 % is lower than that of the neighboring interval '0.01 to 0.25'. It makes training difficult to distinguish the proportions from the neighbor intervals. This is because the interval of '0 to 0.01' is much smaller than the others. Therefore, we add the weight for the hyper-parameter γ, where smaller γ gives more significant gradients: we use $\gamma = 0$ for '0 to 0.01' and $\gamma = 2$ for other intervals. Figure 3 (Left) shows the weighted focal proportion loss curves. The blue curve ('0 to 0.01') has larger gradients, and thus this makes training easy to identify the proportion in either '0 to 0.01' or '0.25 to 0.5'.

3   Experiments

Implementation Details: For tumor cell detection, we used U-net structure [12] for the cell detector h, and Resnet-50 [5] for the feature extractor g_f. The Adam optimizer [6] is adopted with learning rates of 0.001 for h and 0.0002 for g, and the batch sizes were 8 and 16 for h and g, respectively. Random rotation and flipping were applied for augmentation during classification training.

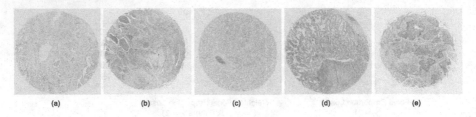

(a)   (b)   (c)   (d)   (e)

Fig. 4. Example of core images in cases of (a) 0 to 1%, (b) 1 to 25%, (c) 25 to 50%, (d) 50 to 75%, (e) 75 to 100%.

For proportion estimation, we used Resnet-18 [5] pre-trained on Imagenet. The Adam optimizer [6] is adopted with a learning rate of 0.0001. The batch size was 16, and the epoch was 100. We used early stopping with a patience of 30 to stop training. We used random rotation and horizontal and vertical flipping for augmentation. We set the hyperparameter γ, which controls the slope of the weighted focal loss function, to 0 for 0 to 1 % and 2 for the other sections.

Dataset: For tumor detection, we used 58 core images of patients with about 10000 × 10000. The tumor or non-tumor regions, pathologists manually annotated, where the average of the labeled region in one core image is 5.71%. For two core images, the cell position is also annotated. The total number of cells is 8000. Note that if we were to train the network using only the supervised data of cell detection, a huge amount of annotation would be required. In contrast, we can train the network using proportion labels and only a small amount of cell-level annotation (5.71% area in a tissue). Proportion labels are available from clinical records, and no public datasets have proportion annotations.

For proportion estimation, we used 606 core images, where the proportion interval is labeled for each core; either '0 to 0.01', '0.01 to 0.25', '0.25 to 0.5', '0.5 to 0.75', or '0.75 to 1.00'. We resized the images to 2048 × 2048 to input the network. Figure 4 shows examples of core images. The images gradually turn brown along with a larger proportion of PD-L1 positive cells. However, it is necessary to observe whether the brown cells are tumors and whether the membranes are dyed. This means that it is not so easy for color-based methods. We performed 4-fold cross-validation and evaluated the average performance metrics.

Evaluation: To confirm the effectiveness of our proportion estimation with mask, we compared our method with ten baseline methods; 1) the detection-based method (Det) modified our cell detection network for 3 classes of cell detection: positive tumor, negative tumor, and non-tumor. The proportion of PD-L1 is calculated from the number of detected positive and negative tumor cells, where the proportion labels were not used to train this method. 2) Classification (Class) [5], which directly classifies the core image into five classes (proportion intervals) with cross-entropy loss. 3) Ordinal regression (O-Reg) [4], which estimates used the proportion using the loss function from [4]. 4)Prop w/o mask [1], which estimates continuous values with proportion loss without using

Table 1. Performance of proportion estimation by comparative methods.

Method	w Mask	0–1 %	1–25 %	25–50 %	50–75 %	75–100 %	mRecall	mPrecision	mF1
Det		0.832	0.587	0.062	0.071	0.568	0.479	0.424	0.429
Class [5]		0.858	0.433	0.312	0.411	0.682	0.539	0.526	0.524
O-Reg [4]		0.811	0.510	0.500	0.411	0.568	0.560	0.541	0.532
Prop w/o mask [1]		0.381	0.779	0.438	0.339	0.750	0.537	0.510	0.451
Ours w/o mask		0.627	0.529	0.125	0.232	0.795	0.462	0.442	0.427
LPI Loss [2]	✓	0.187	**0.808**	0.188	0.429	0.682	0.458	0.519	0.392
Prop	✓	0.474	0.760	0.438	0.464	0.795	0.586	0.561	0.516
WProp	✓	0.795	0.683	0.312	0.393	0.795	0.596	0.552	0.558
WProp + List	✓	0.837	0.692	0.375	0.339	0.705	0.590	0.567	0.565
FocalProp	✓	0.078	0.731	**0.562**	**0.482**	**0.818**	0.534	0.538	0.404
Ours	✓	**0.878**	0.663	0.375	0.393	0.795	**0.621**	**0.606**	**0.603**

the mask. 5) Ours without mask (Ours w/o mask), which uses the weighted focal proportion loss without tumor cell detection. The above 2)-4) methods did not use the tumor region mask M, i.e., the networks were trained to produce the PD-L1 rate directly from the entire image. As an ablation study, the following five methods are introduced into our framework, which uses the mask M and estimates the proportion from the masked maps. 6) LPI Loss [2]. 7) Proportion loss (Prop) [1]. 8) Weighted proportion loss (WProp), where the proportion loss is weighted by the length of the interval. 9) WProp + List, which introduces list-net [3] to the weighted proportion loss. 10) Forcal proportion loss (FocalProp), which introduces the focal loss [7] into the proportion loss. This is proposed by us. 11) Ours, which uses the weighted focal proportion loss.

Table 1 shows the mean of precision, recall, and f1 score for each method. Our method achieved the best performance compared to the other methods. Positive and negative tumor cells have various appearances depending on staining properties and patient variation. Det did not work well for three-class classifications as the positive and negative tumor cells have similar shapes, as shown in Fig. 5. To achieve accurate detection, a large amount of training data is required. Comparing Prop w/o mask and Prop, Prop is better than Prop w/o mask. Since both methods use the same loss function, it shows that the tumor mask contributes to improving performance. The accuracy of '0 to 1 %' in FocalProp is much worse because this loss teats all interval sections the same even though the interval length is different, as discussed in Sect. 2. The proposed method outperformed other mask-based methods because weighted focal loss can handle imbalances (interval and data) while maintaining discriminative ability.

Figure 5 shows examples of estimated intermediate positive and negative feature maps, which can be used for the interpretability of the network; pathologists can understand how the AI classifies the cells to estimate the proportion. The mask (the 3rd column) shows the cell detection results of tumor cells (including both positive and negative). The feature maps show the estimation results of positive (red) or negative (blue) classification, in which the feature map has a low resolution than the original image. A masked feature map is generated by

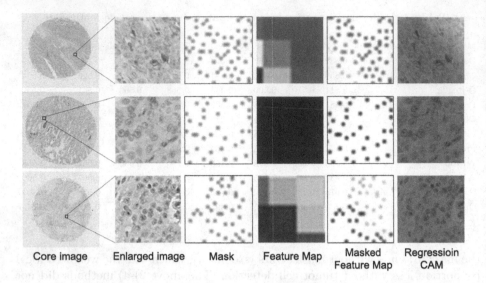

Core image   Enlarged image   Mask   Feature Map   Masked Feature Map   Regressioin CAM

Fig. 5. Visualization by intermediate outputs and CAM-based method [16]. Red indicates a positive, and blue indicates a negative.

combining the mask and feature map. Regression CAM shows the activation map from the regression network, where red indicates the pixels contributing to the network output. The first and second rows are examples of successfully estimated cases, which pathologists confirmed. In these cases, both of them are stained as brown. However, the class of cells is different; positives in the 1st column and negatives in the 2nd one, which is defined by the staining pattern even though they are brown. Our method successfully classified such difficult cases. The third row is an example of a miss-classified case, which is a difficult case. Actually, all of them are positive because their membrane is slightly stained by light brown. However, our method miss-classified them as negative. This is a difficult case, even for medical doctors. The CAM is meaningless in this task because all tumor regions are used to calculate the proportions.

4   Conclusion

We propose a proportion estimation method that can estimate the partial proportion (about only tumor cells) by using a tumor mask and address the imbalanced (interval and data) issues by our weighted focal proportion loss. We first detect tumor cells and generate a tumor mask. Then, we estimate the PD-L1 tumor proportion among tumor cells. By applying the mask, we could represent intermediate output for PD-L1 positive and negative, in which the visualization is useful for pathologists in clinical. In the experiments, our method outperforms other comparisons and achieves state-of-the-art performance.

Acknowledgements. This work was supported by JSPS KAKENHI Grant Number JP23K18509, Japan.

References

1. Ardehaly, E.M., Culotta, A.: Co-training for demographic classification using deep learning from label proportions. In: 2017 IEEE International Conference on Data Mining Workshops (ICDMW), pp. 1017–1024. IEEE (2017)
2. Bortsova, G., et al.: Deep learning from label proportions for emphysema quantification. In: Frangi, A.F., Schnabel, J.A., Davatzikos, C., Alberola-López, C., Fichtinger, G. (eds.) MICCAI 2018. LNCS, vol. 11071, pp. 768–776. Springer, Cham (2018). https://doi.org/10.1007/978-3-030-00934-2_85
3. Cao, Z., Qin, T., Liu, T.Y., Tsai, M.F., Li, H.: Learning to rank: from pairwise approach to listwise approach. In: Proceedings of the 24th International Conference on Machine Learning, pp. 129–136 (2007)
4. Cheng, J., Wang, Z., Pollastri, G.: A neural network approach to ordinal regression. In: 2008 IEEE International Joint Conference on Neural Networks (IEEE World Congress on Computational Intelligence), pp. 1279–1284. IEEE (2008)
5. He, K., Zhang, X., Ren, S., Sun, J.: Deep residual learning for image recognition. In: Proceedings of the IEEE Conference on Computer Vision and Pattern Recognition, pp. 770–778 (2016)
6. Kingma, D.P., Ba, J.: Adam: a method for stochastic optimization. arXiv preprint arXiv:1412.6980 (2014)
7. Lin, T.Y., Goyal, P., Girshick, R., He, K., Dollár, P.: Focal loss for dense object detection. In: Proceedings of the IEEE International Conference on Computer Vision, pp. 2980–2988 (2017)
8. Liu, J., et al.: Automated tumor proportion score analysis for PD-L1 (22C3) expression in lung squamous cell carcinoma. Sci. Rep. **11** (2021). https://doi.org/10.1038/s41598-021-95372-1
9. Nishimura, K., et al.: Weakly supervised cell instance segmentation under various conditions. Med. Image Anal. **73**, 102182 (2021)
10. Redmon, J., Divvala, S., Girshick, R., Farhadi, A.: You only look once: unified, real-time object detection. In: Proceedings of the IEEE Conference on Computer Vision and Pattern Recognition, pp. 779–788 (2016)
11. Ren, S., He, K., Girshick, R., Sun, J.: Faster R-CNN: towards real-time object detection with region proposal networks. In: Advances in Neural Information Processing Systems, vol. 28 (2015)
12. Ronneberger, O., Fischer, P., Brox, T.: U-Net: convolutional networks for biomedical image segmentation. In: Navab, N., Hornegger, J., Wells, W.M., Frangi, A.F. (eds.) MICCAI 2015. LNCS, vol. 9351, pp. 234–241. Springer, Cham (2015). https://doi.org/10.1007/978-3-319-24574-4_28
13. Tokunaga, H., Iwana, B.K., Teramoto, Y., Yoshizawa, A., Bise, R.: Negative pseudo labeling using class proportion for semantic segmentation in pathology. In: Vedaldi, A., Bischof, H., Brox, T., Frahm, J.-M. (eds.) ECCV 2020. LNCS, vol. 12360, pp. 430–446. Springer, Cham (2020). https://doi.org/10.1007/978-3-030-58555-6_26
14. Widmaier, M., et al.: Comparison of continuous measures across diagnostic PD-L1 assays in non-small cell lung cancer using automated image analysis. Modern Pathol. **33** (2020). https://doi.org/10.1038/s41379-019-0349-y

15. Yoshizawa, A., et al.: Impact of proposed IASLC/ATS/ERS classification of lung adenocarcinoma: prognostic subgroups and implications for further revision of staging based on analysis of 514 stage i cases. Mod. Pathol. **24**(5), 653–664 (2011)
16. Zhou, B., Khosla, A., Lapedriza, A., Oliva, A., Torralba, A.: Learning deep features for discriminative localization. In: Proceedings of the IEEE Conference on Computer Vision and Pattern Recognition, pp. 2921–2929 (2016)

Active Learning Strategies on a Real-World Thyroid Ultrasound Dataset

Hari Sreedhar[1,2](✉) (ID), Guillaume P. R. Lajoinie[3] (ID), Charles Raffaelli[2], and Hervé Delingette[1] (ID)

[1] Centre Inria d'Université Côte d'Azur, 06902 Sophia Antipolis Cedex, France
hari.sreedhar@inria.fr
[2] Centre Hospitalier Universitaire de Nice, 06000 Nice, France
[3] Techmed Center for Technical Medicine, University of Twente, 7522 NB Enschede, The Netherlands

Abstract. Machine learning applications in ultrasound imaging are limited by access to ground-truth expert annotations, especially in specialized applications such as thyroid nodule evaluation. Active learning strategies seek to alleviate this concern by making more effective use of expert annotations; however, many proposed techniques do not adapt well to small-scale (i.e. a few hundred images) datasets. In this work, we test active learning strategies including an uncertainty-weighted selection approach with supervised and semi-supervised learning to evaluate the effectiveness of these tools for the prediction of nodule presence on a clinical ultrasound dataset. The results on this as well as two other medical image datasets suggest that even successful active learning strategies have limited clinical significance in terms of reducing annotation burden.

Keywords: Thyroid cancer · Active learning · Ultrasound imaging

1 Background

Thyroid nodules are growths disrupting the normal follicular architecture of the thyroid gland, whose evaluation by ultrasound is essential to facilitate thyroid cancer detection and avoid unnecessary interventions. Ultrasound is ideally suited to this task because it is inexpensive and non-invasive, but this technique is limited by the subjective interpretation of the acquired images by the practitioner.

In response to these limitations, many groups have proposed machine learning algorithms to automate thyroid ultrasound evaluation. These approaches apply neural networks to standard B-mode ultrasound images to perform detection

Supplementary Information The online version contains supplementary material available at https://doi.org/10.1007/978-3-031-58171-7_13.

and segmentation of nodules [4], benign-malignant classification [1], or combined strategies to reproduce the entire clinical evaluation task [8,12,20]. A few groups have even begun to test commercial software for this purpose [3,17].

As these algorithms are tested and validated for clinical use, they must follow training strategies that respect the limitations inherent to ultrasound imaging. Especially when adapting to ultrasound systems in specific hospital centers, high-quality annotations drawn by practitioners specifically experienced in thyroid ultrasound are essential; however, the time of these experts is inherently expensive and annotation tasks have a low priority in the patient-oriented workflow. Clinical implementation of these tools will therefore depend on training strategies that make intelligent use of ground truth labels.

1.1   Active Learning

This is where active learning holds promise, as a means of efficiently utilizing expert annotations. This approach to machine learning is based on the premise that, for a large pool of unlabeled data, there may exist a smaller subset of observations which would be as effective for supervised learning as the entire image pool. In terms of medical image analysis, this means starting with a collection of unlabeled images, with only a small initial subset selected at random to be annotated by an expert radiologist. This subset of labeled images is used for supervised learning, though the unlabeled images may be used for semi-supervised learning of either the task or of feature representations [6,13].

Based on the performance of the algorithm trained on this initial labeled set, additional images are selected for annotation. In the context of radiology, this is typically through a pool-based sampling approach in which some criterion guides selection from among the remaining unlabeled images. Once additional images are selected, the algorithm is retrained, and the cycle is repeated (see Fig. 1) [2].

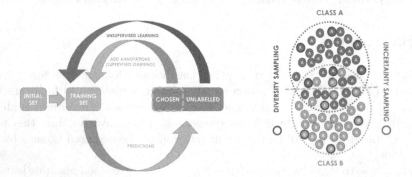

Fig. 1. (Left): The basic cycle of pool-based active learning: an initial set of images is randomly chosen for annotation, and used for training. In subsequent iterations, further images are chosen for annotation from the unlabeled image pool to retrain the algorithm. The unlabeled images can also be used for semi-supervised strategies. (Right): The two main categories of active learning criteria: uncertainty and diversity.

The criteria for selecting images for annotation vary between strategies. The most commonly considered criterion is uncertainty, i.e. selecting cases in which the algorithm's predictions are uncertain in order to improve its performance [2,11]. Relying solely on this measure, however, risks overrepresenting a subset of cases, rather than the entire distribution of images. Therefore, diversity strategies seek to include images dissimilar to each other or to already-labeled images, to prioritize the "representativeness" of the selected instances (see Fig. 1) [14,18].

Whichever specific strategy is chosen, active learning translates logically to the analysis of ultrasound images, because of the cost of manual annotation by expert radiologists. Zhou et al. demonstrated this by combining active learning with transfer learning to fine-tune a convolutional neural network for carotid intima-media thickness interpretation [21]. More recently, Huang et al. proposed a framework for segmentation of breast and knee cartilage ultrasound that combined active learning criteria with semi-supervised learning to better adapt to different ultrasound datasets, along with an uncertainty selection strategy modified to avoid redundant image selection [6].

Despite these advances, many active learning strategies struggle to outperform the baseline of randomly selecting images for annotation [9]. Gaillochet et al., applying active learning to MRI images, addressed this problem with a stochastic batch selection strategy to harness the power of random sampling on small-scale datasets [5]. These examples call into question the feasibility of practical implementation of active learning strategies in a clinical context.

1.2 Active Learning Applied to Thyroid Ultrasound

With this in mind, we have applied active learning on a clinical dataset of ultrasound images. Since clinical thyroid images are not always acquired following standardized protocols (as is often the case for AI studies), we have chosen to assess the potential of active learning techniques on these unmodified, real-life examples. We present therefore an example of binary classification of the presence or absence of thyroid nodules in these images with the following contributions:

1) A novel and simple weighted selection active learning strategy to respect the representative power of random selection with small annotation budgets.
2) A real-world implementation adapted to the difficulties of learning on an actual clinical ultrasound dataset, including using semi-supervised feature extraction to facilitate active learning strategies. The results are assessed with a higher number of repetitions than is typically tested [5,13,19] to ensure statistical relevance.

2 Materials and Methods

2.1 Image Datasets

Ultrasound images for the study were collected from the stored images of thyroid examinations conducted in the course of routine clinical practice by radiologists at the Centre Hospitalier Universitaire de Nice from August 2021 to

June 2022. All scans had been acquired on a Siemens S3000 ultrasound system (Siemens Healthineers, Erlangen, Germany) in accordance with standard practice for our institution. All images from ultrasound examinations of the thyroid were exported in DICOM format and de-identified. The images were then automatically filtered to include only B-mode images with no Doppler or elastography overlays. Finally, images were filtered to only include those in axial views, with recognizable anatomical landmarks of the trachea or the carotid vessels. The resulting 1048 images from 269 patients were then annotated by a non-expert reader, who manually segmented solid, cystic, and mixed solid and cystic nodules. Spongiform lesions were excluded. These annotations, examples of which can be seen in Supplementary Fig. 1, were then converted into equivalent labels of nodule presence (602 images) or absence (446 images).

External Datasets. Given the non-expert annotations and potential difficulties of learning from our dataset, we conducted equivalent tests on two public medical imaging datasets randomly downsampled to an equivalent size. The PneumoniaMNIST dataset contains pediatric chest X-ray images with labels for pneumonia vs normal binary classification [7]. The BreaKHis dataset contains histopathological images in the context of breast cancer, with labels for benign and malignant diagnoses [15].

2.2   Rigged Draw Strategy

Inspired by Gaillochet et al., we sought to harness the power of random selection to represent a small dataset [5]. In order to do this while controlling the relative contribution of the uncertainty criterion, we proposed a weighted selection strategy called rigged draw. In this strategy, the relative weight w_n for selecting any sample in an active learning round is:

$$w_n(\alpha) = 1 + \alpha \frac{c_n}{c_{90}} \qquad (1)$$

where c_n is the value of the uncertainty-based criterion for the nth sample, c_{90} is the 90th percentile value of the criterion across all unlabeled images, and α is a factor weighting the importance of the uncertainty criterion relative to random selection. The choice to normalize relative to the 90th percentile was to avoid the effects of outlier maximum values with certain selection strategies.

2.3   Supervised and Unsupervised Active Learning Strategies

We tested supervised learning using only labeled images with a ResNet18 pretrained on natural images. We compared random selection, LeastConfidence (an uncertainty strategy), and KMeans (a diversity strategy) as implemented in Zhan et al. [10,16,19]. We also tested rigged draw sampling, defining the uncertainty criterion c_n as the positive entropy contribution of sample n:

$$c_n(p_n) = -p_n \log_2(p_n) \qquad (2)$$

where p_n is the probability of nodule presence as predicted by the network (between 0 and 1). With this choice, we would preferentially weight images with a predicted probability close to 0.5.

As suggested by Huang et al., learning from ultrasound data may be difficult for active learning strategies that begin with few labeled images [6]. We therefore also tested semi-supervised learning using the network architecture proposed by Shui et al. for their two-stage WAAL active learning strategy [13]. This strategy depends on a network which conducts classification upon a feature representation which is in turn trained with a loss function seeking to reduce the distance between labeled and unlabeled images.

Our motivation for using this network was to imitate its approach to learning a useful feature representation from the images that would increase the effectiveness of active learning strategies. In addition to testing the entire WAAL strategy, this network structure was also used separately to test the previously mentioned active learning strategies.

3 Results

The active learning strategies were tested with both the supervised and semi-supervised strategies using the DeepAL+ toolkit from Zhan et al. [19]. For each test, a base set of 50 images was taken from a training set of 850 images and used to train the network for a fixed number of epochs (60), with subsequent batches of 50 being selected from among the unlabeled images, up to the maximum size of 750 images. A balanced test set on our dataset was established using 199 images from patients not represented in the training set (102 with nodules, 97 without); on the other two datasets test sets were slightly larger (624 for PneumoniaMNIST and 364 for BreaKHis, as noted in Supplementary Table 1). In order mitigate the effects of different starting sets and the stochastic nature of certain selection strategies, approximately 20 repetitions were used; as seen in Fig. 3, the starting set can create a high degree of variability in strategy performance.

The rigged draw strategy was tested using weights of $\alpha = 5$, $\alpha = 25$, and $\alpha = 50$ to give different importance to the uncertainty criterion during selection. The results with the most effective weight, $\alpha = 25$, are reported here, with the others given in Supplementary Tables 2 and 3.

3.1 Supervised Strategies

We used AUC under the ROC as a measure of classification performance independent of decision threshold. The median binary classification AUC values as a function of the cumulative active learning budget using the supervised strategy are given in Fig. 2, with the distributions of AUC values at different budgets for our strategy given in Fig. 3. The AUC values achieved with different budgets on ultrasound data also varied greatly with different starting sets (see Fig. 3)

The area under the budget curve (AUBC) values, calculated as the area under the curve of classification AUC value vs normalized cumulative budget (from 0 to 1), serves as a measure of the efficacy of the active learning strategies [19]. A summary of these AUBC values for the supervised strategies is given in Table 1. When the AUBC values from the repeated trials with the rigged draw strategy were compared to random selection, no statistically significant difference was found with the two-sample Kolmogorov-Smirnov test. In addition, the AUCs achieved at all budget sizes for the ultrasound dataset were substantially lower than those achieved on the PneumoniaMNIST and BreaKHis datasets (see Fig. 2).

Table 1. Supervised learning AUBC values. Values closer to 1 indicate a more effective strategy.

Dataset	Test Set Size	Measure	Random	LeastCertain	KMeans	RiggedDraw
US Dataset	199	Mean	0.643	0.642	0.641	0.639
		Median	0.642	0.646	0.641	0.639
		STD	0.010	0.011	0.009	0.012
Pneumonia MNIST	624	Mean	0.918	0.917	0.914	0.919
		Median	0.917	0.917	0.916	0.920
		STD	0.006	0.005	0.005	0.004
BreaKHis	364	Mean	0.832	0.828	0.826	0.832
		Median	0.831	0.829	0.823	0.836
		STD	0.015	0.020	0.017	0.022

3.2   Semi-supervised Strategies

For the semi-supervised strategies using the feature representation learned from all images, the median binary classification AUC values as a function of the cumulative active learning budget for each of the strategies and datasets are given in Fig. 2, with the distributions of AUC values at different budgets for our strategy given in Fig. 3. The AUBC values are reported in Table 2. When the AUBC values from the repeated trials with the rigged draw strategy were compared to random selection, a p-value of 0.0082 was found via the Kolmogorov-Smirnov test.

Performance for the rigged draw strategy improved substantially for the ultrasound images using the semi-supervised approach (see Fig. 3). However, the AUBC values for the rigged draw strategy, while greater than random selection, were not substantially different in terms of magnitude (see Table 2), and once again there was considerable variation in AUC values at each budget size (see Fig. 3). In addition, for the PneumoniaMNIST and BreaKHis datasets, high AUC values were reached with very few images, and thus no meaningful differences could be observed between strategies (see Fig. 2).

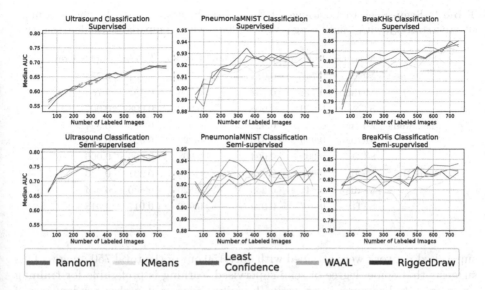

Fig. 2. Median AUC values for different active learning strategies on the three datasets. (Top Row): Supervised strategy. (Bottom Row): Semi-supervised strategy.

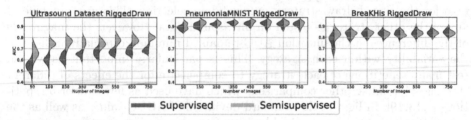

Fig. 3. Violin plots of classification AUC values on the at different label budgets with the rigged draw strategy.

4   Discussion

Overall, the results using supervised learning did not show a significant advantage for any active learning strategy compared to random selection on any of the datasets. In addition, classification performance on the ultrasound dataset was poorer than for the others; AUC improvement on the external datasets began to reach a plateau with budgets of only around 300 out of the total 750 images. This difference could be due to limitations inherent to the non expert annotations or the complexity of the classification task. It could also be related to the differences between our clinical ultrasound images and the public dataset images from different imaging modalities.

Performance on the ultrasound dataset was greatly improved, however, by a semi-supervised approach to learn a feature representation to reduce the distance between labeled and unlabeled images. Better results than were possible with the

Table 2. Semi-supervised learning AUBC values. Values closer to 1 indicate a more effective strategy, with * indicating p-values < 0.05 when compared to random selection

Dataset	Measure	Random	LeastCertain	KMeans	WAAL	RiggedDraw
US Dataset	Mean	0.747	0.751	0.749	0.751	0.754*
	Median	0.748	0.752	0.750	0.751	0.755
	STD	0.009	0.008	0.009	0.008	0.007
Pneumonia MNIST	Mean	0.918	0.923*	0.923	0.923	0.924*
	Median	0.919	0.925	0.922	0.924	0.923
	STD	0.008	0.004	0.008	0.006	0.006
BreaKHis	Mean	0.836	0.828	0.823	0.831	0.833
	Median	0.841	0.830	0.820	0.830	0.834
	STD	0.017	0.026	0.022	0.017	0.018

supervised network were attained with only 150 out of the total 750 images. This suggests that some degree of semi-supervised learning is preferable for training on image sets like ours; in an active learning scenario it makes prudent use of unlabeled data for which annotations are expensive.

The semi-supervised approach also showed a statistically significant advantage for the rigged draw strategy over random selection. This was not true of any of the other strategies tested on ultrasound data. However, the magnitude of the differences in classification AUC remained minimal, especially in light of the variability within each strategy. This is particularly important as we did test many repetitions of each strategy to compensate for the effects of different starting sets, unlike other comparisons which have used as few as 3 or 5 repetitions [5,13,19]. In light of the standard deviation of AUBC values as well as the range of AUC values at individual budget sizes, the impact of active learning on ultrasound data at this scale is unlikely to be clinically relevant.

It should be acknowledged that using non-expert annotations likely contributed to poor performance on our dataset. More specialized networks or pre-training on ultrasound images could also improve overall performance; however, this would not necessarily increase the relative advantage of active learning strategies. Rigorous optimization of the rigged draw strategy (such as the weight or the percentile for normalization) and of the annotation budget per round could have improved active learning results specifically; however, the need to fine-tune strategies to this extent further suggests that they would not be suitable for real clinical thyroid ultrasound applications.

Therefore, at the scale of a thyroid ultrasound dataset from our clinical department, the benefits of existing active learning strategies appear to be limited. Semi-supervised approaches, and strategies like rigged draw that harness the power of random selection increase effectiveness; however, further refinement will be necessary to meaningfully reduce annotation burden. Future practical implementation will only be possible with more robust versions of these active learning tools that work consistently in a real hospital setting.

Acknowledgements. The authors are grateful to the OPAL infrastructure from Université Côte d'Azur for providing resources and support. This project has received funding from the European Union's Horizon 2020 research and innovation program under the Marie Skłodowska-Curie grant agreement No 847581. G.L. acknowledges funding from the 4TU Precision Medicine program supported by High Tech for a Sustainable Future. G.L. also acknowledges funding by the European Union (ERC stg grant, Super-FALCON, project number 101076844).

References

1. Buda, M., et al.: Management of thyroid nodules seen on us images: deep learning may match performance of radiologists. Radiology **292**(3), 695–701 (2019). https://doi.org/10.1148/radiol.2019181343
2. Budd, S., Robinson, E.C., Kainz, B.: A survey on active learning and human-in-the-loop deep learning for medical image analysis. Medi. Image Anal. **71**, 102062 (2021). https://doi.org/10.1016/j.media.2021.102062
3. Chambara, N., Liu, S.Y.W., Lo, X., Ying, M.: Diagnostic performance evaluation of different TI-RADS using ultrasound computer-aided diagnosis of thyroid nodules: an experience with adjusted settings. Plos One **16**(1) (2021). https://doi.org/10.1371/journal.pone.0245617
4. Chen, H., Song, S., Wang, X., Wang, R., Meng, D., Wang, L.: LRTHR-Net: a low-resolution-to-high-resolution framework to iteratively refine the segmentation of thyroid nodule in ultrasound images. In: Shusharina, N., Heinrich, M.P., Huang, R. (eds.) MICCAI 2020. LNCS, vol. 12587, pp. 116–121. Springer, Cham (2021). https://doi.org/10.1007/978-3-030-71827-5_15
5. Gaillochet, M., Desrosiers, C., Lombaert, H.: Active learning for medical image segmentation with stochastic batches. arXiv preprint arXiv:2301.07670 (2023)
6. Huang, K., Huang, J., Wang, W., Xu, M., Liu, F.: A deep active learning framework with information guided label generation for medical image segmentation. In: 2022 IEEE International Conference on Bioinformatics and Biomedicine (BIBM), pp. 1562–1567 (2022). https://doi.org/10.1109/BIBM55620.2022.9995046
7. Kermany, D.S., et al.: Identifying medical diagnoses and treatable diseases by image-based deep learning. Cell **172**(5) (2018). https://doi.org/10.1016/j.cell.2018.02.010
8. Lu, J., Ouyang, X., Liu, T., Shen, D.: Identifying thyroid nodules in ultrasound images through segmentation-guided discriminative localization. In: Shusharina, N., Heinrich, M.P., Huang, R. (eds.) MICCAI 2020. LNCS, vol. 12587, pp. 135–144. Springer, Cham (2021). https://doi.org/10.1007/978-3-030-71827-5_18
9. Munjal, P., Hayat, N., Hayat, M., Sourati, J., Khan, S.: Towards robust and reproducible active learning using neural networks. In: Proceedings of the IEEE/CVF Conference on Computer Vision and Pattern Recognition (CVPR), pp. 223–232 (2022)
10. Pedregosa, F., et al.: Scikit-learn: machine learning in python. J. Mach. Learn. Res. **12**(85), 2825–2830 (2011). http://jmlr.org/papers/v12/pedregosa11a.html
11. Settles, B.: Active learning literature survey. Computer Sciences Technical Report 1648, University of Wisconsin–Madison (2009)
12. Shen, X., Ouyang, X., Liu, T., Shen, D.: Cascaded networks for thyroid nodule diagnosis from ultrasound images. In: Shusharina, N., Heinrich, M.P., Huang, R. (eds.) MICCAI 2020. LNCS, vol. 12587, pp. 145–154. Springer, Cham (2021). https://doi.org/10.1007/978-3-030-71827-5_19

13. Shui, C., Zhou, F., Gagné, C., Wang, B.: Deep active learning: unified and princi-pled method for query and training. In: Chiappa, S., Calandra, R. (eds.) Proceed-ings of the Twenty Third International Conference on Artificial Intelligence and Statistics. Proceedings of Machine Learning Research, vol. 108, pp. 1308–1318. PMLR (2020). https://proceedings.mlr.press/v108/shui20a.html

14. Smailagic, A., et al.: MedAL: accurate and robust deep active learning for medical image analysis. 2018 17th IEEE International Conference on Machine Learning and Applications (ICMLA) (2018). https://doi.org/10.1109/icmla.2018.00078

15. Spanhol, F.A., Oliveira, L.S., Petitjean, C., Heutte, L.: A dataset for breast cancer histopathological image classification. IEEE Trans. Biomed. Eng. **63**(7), 1455–1462 (2016). https://doi.org/10.1109/TBME.2015.2496264

16. Wang, D., Shang, Y.: A new active labeling method for deep learning. In: 2014 International Joint Conference on Neural Networks (IJCNN), pp. 112–119 (2014). https://doi.org/10.1109/IJCNN.2014.6889457

17. Wei, Q., et al.: The value of S-detect in improving the diagnostic performance of radiologists for the differential diagnosis of thyroid nodules. Med. Ultrasonogr. **22**(4), 415–423 (2020). https://doi.org/10.11152/mu-2501

18. Yang, L., Zhang, Y., Chen, J., Zhang, S., Chen, D.Z.: Suggestive annotation: a deep active learning framework for biomedical image segmentation. In: Descoteaux, M., Maier-Hein, L., Franz, A., Jannin, P., Collins, D.L., Duchesne, S. (eds.) MICCAI 2017. LNCS, vol. 10435, pp. 399–407. Springer, Cham (2017). https://doi.org/10.1007/978-3-319-66179-7_46

19. Zhan, X., Wang, Q., Huang, K.H., Xiong, H., Dou, D., Chan, A.B.: A comparative survey of deep active learning. arXiv preprint arXiv:2203.13450 (2022)

20. Zhang, Y., Lai, H., Yang, W.: Cascade UNet and CH-UNet for thyroid nodule segmentation and benign and malignant classification. In: Shusharina, N., Heinrich, M.P., Huang, R. (eds.) MICCAI 2020. LNCS, vol. 12587, pp. 129–134. Springer, Cham (2021). https://doi.org/10.1007/978-3-030-71827-5_17

21. Zhou, Z., Shin, J., Feng, R., Hurst, R.T., Kendall, C.B., Liang, J.: Integrating active learning and transfer learning for carotid intima-media thickness video interpre-tation. J. Digit. Imaging **32**(2), 290–299 (2019). https://doi.org/10.1007/s10278-018-0143-2

A Realistic Collimated X-Ray Image Simulation Pipeline

Benjamin El-Zein[1](✉), Dominik Eckert[2], Thomas Weber[2],
Maximilian Rohleder[1], Ludwig Ritschl[2], Steffen Kappler[2], and Andreas Maier[1]

[1] Pattern Recognition Lab, Friedrich-Alexander University, Erlangen-Nuremberg,
Erlangen, Germany
benjamin.el-zein@fau.de
[2] Siemens Healthineers, Forchheim, Germany

Abstract. Collimator detection remains a challenging task in X-ray systems with unreliable or non-available information about the detectors position relative to the source. This paper presents a physically motivated image processing pipeline for simulating the characteristics of collimator shadows in X-ray images. By generating randomized labels for collimator shapes and locations, incorporating scattered radiation simulation, and including Poisson noise, the pipeline enables the expansion of limited datasets for training deep neural networks. We validate the proposed pipeline by a qualitative and quantitative comparison against real collimator shadows. Furthermore, it is demonstrated that utilizing simulated data within our deep learning framework not only serves as a suitable substitute for actual collimators but also enhances the generalization performance when applied to real-world data.

Keywords: Data Augmentation · Collimation · Medical Physics · Digital Radiography

1 Introduction

In digital radiography, the detection of collimator-covered areas is essential to present diagnostically relevant regions to radiologists. Geometric alignment algorithms, as described in [9], can be employed in X-ray systems with known extrinsic projection parameters. However, despite their availability, these often suffer from inaccuracies sabotaging effectiveness in practice. Due to the inherent geometrical variability in conventional X-ray systems, particularly with mobile flat panel detectors, precise information of the relative position to the detector is unavailable. Moreover, imprecise collimator movement further complicates the detection process, necessitating analysis within image domain. Contrary to a simplistic threshold-based approach, the identification of relevant areas is challenging due to the presence of physical effects like edge-blurring, noise, and scattered radiation. Even human visual perception faces difficulties due to these complexities, as depicted in Fig. 1.

Deep neural networks (DNNs) show promise for collimator detection, but the limited availability of pre-processed raw data poses a challenge for training

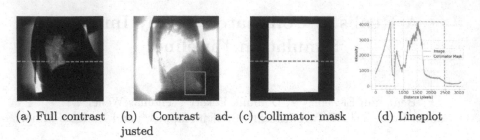

(a) Full contrast   (b)   Contrast   ad- (c) Collimator mask   (d) Lineplot
                          justed

Fig. 1. Illustrative case for collimator detection depicted in two contrast settings. (a) Contrast adjusted to full image. (b) Contrast adjusted to the orange box. The collimated area (c) is shown as a binary mask. In (d), the intensity profile along the dashed line is compared to the collimated area to visualize the complexity of image-based collimator detection. (Color figure online)

robust networks in medical applications. So far, machine learning approaches for collimator detection have not significantly outperformed classic analytical methods in the literature. For instance, comparing the plane detection Hough transform proposed by Kawashita et al. [6] with Mao et al.'s [11] approach that combines random forest learning with a landmark detector in a multi-view learning approach, both methods demonstrate similar performance on unseen data. According to Mao et al. [11], each classifier was trained using only 200 training images.

To enhance the performance of machine learning algorithms, it is reasonable to assume that the implementation of robust data augmentation techniques is beneficial. These techniques aim to increase the quantity and variety of datasets. In this context, suitable augmentation techniques can be categorized into deep learning-based methods, such as generative adversarial networks (GANs) [5], and physically motivated approaches. Although GANs have shown promising potential for post-processed X-ray image augmentation (without collimators) in studies like Bowles et al. [1], Madani et al. [10], Kora et al. [7], and Ng et al. [12], they require sophisticated techniques and lack comprehensibility when aiming to serve as reliable training data.

Unlike this concept, physically motivated approaches offer a robust alternative for augmentation. These methods leverage an understanding of the underlying physics involved in imaging processes. By incorporating physical principles, these approaches ensure reproducibility and reliability, as demonstrated by Eckert et al. [4] and Xu et al. [15].

In this paper a physically motivated image processing pipeline is presented that simulates the characteristics of real collimators enabling the expansion of limited datasets of X-ray images without collimators. The data augmentation method enables the generation of unlimited pre-processed image data e.g. for training DNNs.

2 Methods

2.1 Randomized Collimator Simulation Pipeline

The process of simulating collimator shadows involves three distinct stages. In the first stage random labels are generated to define the shape and position of the collimated area. The second stage introduces scattered radiation, whereas the final stage adds a simulation of noise.

Binary Mask Sampling Strategy: The first part of the pipeline generates a binary mask of the same shape as the X-ray image to be investigated. Thus, all image pixels are classified according to their property of lying inside or outside the assumed collimator shadow. To determine random position, shape and size of the collimator, a centroid location along with width and height are sampled from a truncated normal distribution, yielding a rectangle as shown in Fig. 2a. Due to practical constraints in clinical settings, e.g. with bedridden patients, the resulting images may exhibit rotations or distortions that deviate from the desired orientation. To accommodate these cases, a randomized rotation and distortion transformation are applied to the binary image's rectangle, as shown in Fig. 2b and Fig. 2c.

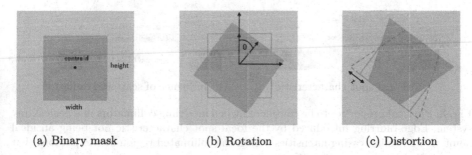

| (a) Binary mask | (b) Rotation | (c) Distortion |

Fig. 2. Example of a rectangular binary mask being transformed afterwards by rotation and shape distortion to cover the range of essential deviations in clinical practice.

Collimator Physics: To account for collimator attenuation, the binary mask is adjusted by assigning its zeros to a damping factor, resulting in the mask M_d. The non-infinitesimal size of the focal spot causes blurring of the collimator edges at the detector as shown in Fig. 3a. As the intensity profile of the radiated X-rays is Gaussian distributed in space, this effect can be approximated by convolving the mask M_d with a Gaussian kernel G_b. Hence, the damping operation can be applied to the input image I_{input} as follows:

$$L(I_{input}) = (M_d * G_b) \cdot I_{input} \tag{1}$$

Scattered Radation Simulation: Incoherent scattering describes the process of an high energetic photon colliding with matter, resulting in a deflection from the initial pathway as shown in Fig. 3b [8]. Due to this fact it predominantly affects X-ray imaging depending on the matter the photon interacts with. A collimator influences the number of photons that pass through the patient, altering the scatter characteristics. This change must be accounted for in the simulation. According to comprehensive Monte Carlo simulation studies [14], it was shown that intensities created by scattered photons are in a range from 1.2%-2% of the primary intensity, e.g. for thorax images of c-arm systems without anti scatter grids. In relation to the dampened intensities by the collimator, contributing 2%-4% of the primary intensity based on empirical analysis, scatter has a significant influence.

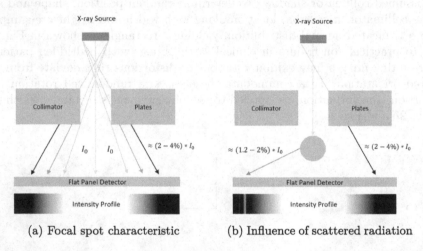

(a) Focal spot characteristic   (b) Influence of scattered radiation

Fig. 3. Physical properties to be considered when modeling collimators in a basic X-ray system. Edge-blurring introduced by the focal spot characteristic not being an ideal point, as well as increasing intensities within the collimated region due to photons that get scattered by the Compton effect.

Scatter Estimation: The intended pipeline requires a methodology capable of modeling the distribution of scattered photons in a collimated X-ray image. Ohnesorge et al. [13] present a convolution kernel based scatter estimation that can be utilized for our application. At first, they define a scatter potential S_p which is defined as follows:

$$S_p(I|I_0) = c \cdot \left(\frac{I}{I_0}\right)^{\alpha} \cdot \ln\left(\frac{I_0}{I}\right)^{\beta} \tag{2}$$

The input image I and the primary intensity I_0 are modified by three hyper parameters α, β and c. Finally, the estimated scatter S_e is obtained by convolving the scatter potential with a Gaussian kernel G_s as demonstrated in this equation:

$$S_e(I) = (S_p(I|I_0) * G_s) \cdot I_0 \tag{3}$$

Scatter Correction: Given the presented framework, this part of the pipeline follows a two-step process. First, the scatter present in I_{input} is removed, as it does not match the scatter of a real collimator specified by $L(I_{input})$. To achieve this, we employ the scatter estimation method proposed by Ohnesorge et al., as depicted by the following equation, in order to obtain a scatter-free image, I_{sc}.

$$I_{sc} = I_{input} - S_e(I_{input}) \tag{4}$$

In the second step, the collimated image I_s with the corresponding scatter is simulated. Equation 1 is applied to collimate the scatter free image. The corresponding scatter map is generated and added to the image as following:

$$I_s = L(I_{sc}) + S_e(L(I_{sc})) \tag{5}$$

Poisson Noise Simulation: Due to the quantum properties of light, photons exhibit random arrival times. Hence, there exists a level of uncertainty regarding the received signal. The probability for z photons arriving at one pixel at the detector can be modeled by the Poisson distribution, which is defined as

$$P(z|\lambda) = \frac{\lambda^z e^{-z}}{z!}. \tag{6}$$

It is dependent on the parameter λ that represents the average rate at which an event occurs, thus the mean arrival rate of the photons.

The damping of real collimators by a factor $\alpha = [0,1]$ causes a reduction of the mean photon arrival rate λ to $\alpha\lambda$ and hence, an increase in noise in the image. Since for a Poisson distribution $\lambda = \sigma = \mu$ holds true, the altered SNR is defined with a new mean μ_n and variance σ_n respectively as

$$\text{SNR} = \frac{\mu_n}{\sigma_n} = \frac{\alpha\lambda}{\sqrt{\alpha\lambda}} = \sqrt{\alpha}. \tag{7}$$

Therefore, besides scaling the intensities in the region of the simulated collimator, the noise level has to be increased to account for the increased uncertainty in the number of arrived photons. So far, applying our collimator mask did change μ to $\alpha\mu$ and σ to $\alpha\sigma$, remaining the SNR unchanged. To compensate for this, we add a normal distribution $N(0, \sigma_x)$ to the signal, to get the right SNR [3] [4]:

$$\sqrt{\alpha} = \frac{\alpha\mu}{\sqrt{\sigma_x^2 + \alpha^2\lambda}} \tag{8}$$

Rearranging the equation yields $\sigma_x = \sqrt{\lambda \cdot (1 - \alpha)}$.

2.2   Experiments

Real Vs. Simulated: For the purpose of evaluation, the pipeline's output is examined by acquiring X-ray images of an anthropomorphic thorax phantom. The acquisitions include both open field and a collimated image, approximately to the lungs. We use our pipeline to simulate a matching collimator on the open field X-ray image and compare that image to the physically collimated image. To perform a detailed analysis, various image patches are extracted and quantitatively analyzed.

Application Case DNN: Using the augmentation method described, we evaluate its effectiveness in simulating collimators within a simple deep learning framework. We generate samples and random labels on-the-fly for 1500 real in-house X-ray images with collimators being manually cropped out. This is called SimNet. In addition, we trained a second DDN, referred to as RealNet, with the uncropped images containing the real collimators and hand-labeled masks. This allows to inspect if it is possible to replace real collimated images with simulated images of our pipeline.

Both DNNs are based on the DeepLabV3 architecture [2], classifying pixels as collimated or non-collimated, utilizing the Dice metric as a loss function and the ADAM optimizer during 500 epochs of training. Evaluation is performed on three datasets calculating the Dice score: a subset of 80 randomly extracted training images, 30 challenging cases with dark attenuating line-shaped implants, and 20 images showing detector line artifacts. RealNet is evaluated with the real collimator version. Furthermore, we check SimNets performance on real and simulated versions of the test sets data in order to reveal the pipelines authenticity and generalization on authentic data.

3   Results

3.1   Framework Validation

Fundamentally, the goal of the simulation pipeline is to generate real collimator intensity distributions. On the one hand, the Figures below show that the desired image impression can be achieved.

On the other hand, uncertainties arising from the inherent approximations made within the pipeline can be identified. The scatter's Gaussian distribution, attributable to the simulation methodology, is distinctly discernible and exhibits a discrepancy from the actual scatter behavior. To obtain a more detailed representation of this observation, we proceed with showing the intensity distribution along the dashed line indicated in Fig. 6. Leveraging the understanding of the impact of a real collimator on images is achieved by showing the real collimator image together with the open field image in Fig. 5a. Subsequently, Fig. 5b presents the same for the real collimator and the simulated collimator, confirming high resemblance from qualitative point of view (Fig. 4).

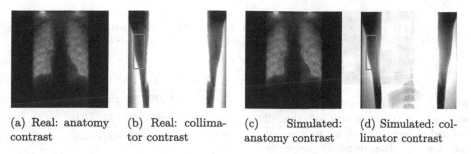

(a) Real: anatomy contrast   (b) Real: collimator contrast   (c)   Simulated: anatomy contrast   (d) Simulated: collimator contrast

Fig. 4. Comparison of a real collimated image with the ouput of the pipeline based on an open field image acquired by the same setup. Both of the images are shown in two different contrast ranges. Besides being in the complete value range, intensities are limited to the indicated box regions.

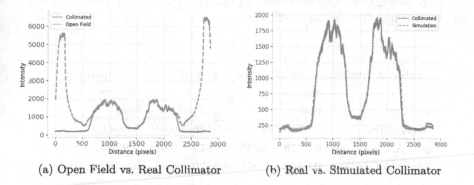

(a) Open Field vs. Real Collimator   (b) Real vs. Simulated Collimator

Fig. 5. Line plots comparing real collimator damping on a real X-ray image as well as presenting the differences between the real and simulated collimator.

Furthermore, real and simulated collimator are quantitatively examined by the normalized mean-squared-error (nMSE), the structural similarity index (SSIM) and the Peak SNR (PSNR) of the image patches depicted in Fig. 5. Table 1 shows that the non-collimated region specifically exhibits an almost identical characteristic. The patches within collimator region however demonstrate that slight diverging behaviour exists, but does not exceed the requirement of being very similar. In particular this is proven by still showing a very high score for the SSIM.

3.2   Network Evaluation

The performance of the DNN based on pipeline augmentation (SimNet), as presented in Table 2, demonstrates that it achieves slightly better results on simulated data, which can be attributed to its training on such data. However, the network's ability to perform very well on real-world data validates the concept and affirms that the images processed by simulation maintain a high level of

Fig. 6. Orientational scheme showcasing the location of the defined image patches as well as the line for the intensity value distributions.

Table 1. Statistical Measures of Image Patches comparing real and simulated collimator images.

Patch	nMSE	SSIM	PSNR
1	0.0001	0.9998	33.2286 [dB]
2	0.0676	0.9962	31.7112 [dB]
3	0.0192	0.9997	32.8377 [dB]

realism. We can further prove this by showing that SimNet even exceeds the performance of RealNet. Future research will focus on exploring network architectures possessing explicit constraints for collimator detection, thereby enabling them to distinguish edges more efficiently.

Table 2. RealNet vs. SimNet Dice score performance comparison.

	SimNet		RealNet
Test sets	Real	Simulated	Real
General Test	**0.9718** ± 0.027	**0.9749** ± 0.041	**0.9641** ± 0.048
Line Artifacts Test	**0.9778** ± 0.025	**0.9873** ± 0.014	**0.9652** ± 0.038
Implants Test	**0.9494** ± 0.071	**0.9820** ± 0.027	**0.9780** ± 0.015

4 Discussion

The presented X-ray image processing pipeline effectively simulates the properties of real collimators by incorporating key physical effects such as scattered radiation and quantum noise, adapting them to the randomly generated labels that define the synthetic collimators shape and location. This approach enables the generation of an unlimited amount of collimator training data. The realism of the generated characteristics is both qualitatively and quantitatively validated. When applied to a dataset of real X-ray images within a DNN environment, the pipeline demonstrates a significantly close performance on real test collimators compared to the simulated ones. Furthermore, it outperforms the corresponding DNN based on training with real collimators and hence no augmentation, affirming the effectiveness of the proposed approach.

Disclaimer. The concepts and information presented in this paper are based on research and are not commercially available.

References

1. Bowles, C., et al.: Gan augmentation: augmenting training data using generative adversarial networks. arXiv preprint arXiv:1810.10863 (2018)
2. Chen, L.C., Papandreou, G., Schroff, F., Adam, H.: Rethinking atrous convolution for semantic image segmentation. ArXiv abs/1706.05587 (2017)
3. Eckert, D., et al.: Deep learning based denoising of mammographic x-ray images: an investigation of loss functions and their detail-preserving properties. In: Medical Imaging 2022: Physics of Medical Imaging, vol. 12031, pp. 455–462. SPIE (2022)
4. Eckert, D., Vesal, S., Ritschl, L., Kappler, S., Maier, A.: Deep learning-based denoising of mammographic images using physics-driven data augmentation. In: Bildverarbeitung für die Medizin 2020. I, pp. 94–100. Springer, Wiesbaden (2020). https://doi.org/10.1007/978-3-658-29267-6_21
5. Goodfellow, I., et al.: Generative adversarial networks. Commun. ACM **63**(11), 139–144 (2020). https://doi.org/10.1145/3422622
6. Kawashita, I., Aoyama, M., Kajiyama, T., Asada, N.: Collimation detection in digital radiographs using plane detection Hough transform. In: Palade, V., Howlett, R.J., Jain, L. (eds.) KES 2003. LNCS (LNAI), vol. 2774, pp. 394–401. Springer, Heidelberg (2003). https://doi.org/10.1007/978-3-540-45226-3_54
7. Kora Venu, S., Ravula, S.: Evaluation of deep convolutional generative adversarial networks for data augmentation of chest x-ray images. Future Internet **13**(1), 8 (2020)
8. Krieger, H.: Grundlagen der Strahlungsphysik und des Strahlenschutzes, vol. 2. Springer, Berlin (2007)
9. Luckner, C., Mertelmeier, T., Maier, A., Ritschl, L.: Estimation of the source-detector alignment of cone-beam x-ray systems using collimator edge tracking. In: CT Meeting (2018)
10. Madani, A., Moradi, M., Karargyris, A., Syeda-Mahmood, T.: Chest x-ray generation and data augmentation for cardiovascular abnormality classification. In: Medical Imaging 2018: Image Processing, vol. 10574, pp. 415–420. SPIE (2018)
11. Mao, H., Peng, Z., Dennerlein, F., Shinagawa, Y., Zhan, Y., Zhou, X.S.: Multi-view learning based robust collimation detection in digital radiographs. In: Medical Imaging 2014: Image Processing, vol. 9034, pp. 525–530. SPIE (2014)
12. Ng, M.F., Hargreaves, C.A.: Generative adversarial networks for the synthesis of chest x-ray images. Eng. Proc. **31**(1), 84 (2023)
13. Ohnesorge, B., Flohr, T., Klingenbeck-Regn, K.: Efficient object scatter correction algorithm for third and fourth generation CT scanners. Eur. Radiol. **9**(3), 563–569 (1999)
14. Sisniega, A., et al.: Monte Carlo study of the effects of system geometry and anti-scatter grids on cone-beam CT scatter distributions. Med. Phys. **40**(5), 051915 (2013)
15. Xu, S., Chen, G., Li, W., Xiang, X.: A physics-driven x-ray image data augmentation method for automated threat detection in nuclear facility entrancement. In: International Conference on Nuclear Engineering, vol. 86397, p. V005T05A041. American Society of Mechanical Engineers (2022)

Masked Conditional Diffusion Models for Image Analysis with Application to Radiographic Diagnosis of Infant Abuse

Shaoju Wu[✉], Sila Kurugol, and Andy Tsai

Boston Children's Hospital and Harvard Medical School, Boston, MA, USA
shaoju.wu@childrens.harvard.edu

Abstract. The classic metaphyseal lesion (CML) is a distinct injury that is highly specific for infant abuse. It commonly occurs in the distal tibia. To aid radiologists detect these subtle fractures, we need to develop a model that can flag abnormal distal tibial radiographs (i.e. those with CMLs). Unfortunately, the development of such a model requires a large and diverse training database, which is often not available. To address this limitation, we propose a novel generative model for data augmentation. Unlike previous models that fail to generate data that span the diverse radiographic appearance of the distal tibial CML, our proposed masked conditional diffusion model (MaC-DM) not only generates realistic-appearing and wide-ranging synthetic images of the distal tibial radiographs with and without CMLs, it also generates their associated segmentation labels. To achieve these tasks, MaC-DM combines the weighted segmentation masks of the tibias and the CML fracture sites as additional conditions for classifier guidance. The augmented images from our model improved the performances of ResNet-34 in classifying normal radiographs and those with CMLs. Further, the augmented images and their associated segmentation masks enhanced the performance of the U-Net in labeling areas of the CMLs on distal tibial radiographs.

Keywords: Diffusion Models · Classification · Fracture Detection

1 Introduction

Child abuse constitutes a major public health problem, with 9.2/1000 children abused per year [15]. Infants ($\leq$1-year-old) are particularly vulnerable to abuse, and constitute 42% of children who die from inflicted injuries [15]. One highly specific fracture for infant abuse is the classic metaphyseal lesion (CML) [1,3,14,21]. The CML is a unique injury characterized by a fracture plane that courses along the long bone metaphysis [11–13,24]. These CMLs can occur in

---

Supplementary Information The online version contains supplementary material available at https://doi.org/10.1007/978-3-031-58171-7_15.

Y. Xue et al. (Eds.): DALI 2023, LNCS 14379, pp. 146–156, 2024.
https://doi.org/10.1007/978-3-031-58171-7_15

any of the long bones, but the distal tibia is one of the most common sites. CML poses a diagnostic challenge to radiologists due to its variable and frequently subtle radiographic appearances. We need to develop a computer algorithm that can automatically flag potentially abnormal radiographs (i.e. those with CML fractures) for special attention during customary radiologic assessment. Unfortunately, the development of such a model requires a large and diverse training database, which is not available even at large pediatric centers. To address this limitation, a generative model for data augmentation is required.

To generate synthetic training data, we typically employ traditional deep learning generative models such as generative adversarial networks (GANs) [4,5,9]. However, these models, such as CycleGAN [26], can be difficult to train and may generate low-quality and repetitive images when trained with limited datasets [20]. Recently, a new generative model called denoising diffusion probabilistic model (DDPM) was shown to be more effective in generating realistic synthetic images and has a more straightforward training process [2]. It has demonstrated utility in data augmentation for brain tumor detection [25], MR image denoising [17], and image generation [10]. One major advantage of DDPM is its ability to incorporate conditional information, including class labels, to generate high quality conditional images [2]. However, current DDPM-based methods [10,17,25] are not applicable for our particular problem of CML fracture detection. Inspired by the conditional DDPM that utilizes conditional mask images as additional inputs for image inpainting [18], we propose a novel mask conditional diffusion model (MaC-DM) that incorporates weighted segmentation masks of the tibias and the CML fractures as priors in generating realistic and diverse synthetic radiographic images of distal tibia with and without CMLs.

We aim to perform binary classification to categorize distal tibial radiographs as either normal or abnormal. To improve the performance of the baseline classification model trained with limited clinical data, we used our proposed MaC-DM for data augmentation. To highlight the added value of this methodology as a data augmenter, we compared our methodology to other common generative models. In addition to generating synthetic images, our proposed model produces masks of the CML fracture sites, which can be used as additional augmented dataset to train a segmentation algorithm in labeling areas of the CMLs in the distal tibial radiographs. In essence, our contributions are three-folds. One, we developed a new generative diffusion model which utilizes both class labels and segmentation masks as conditions to generate realistic and diverse normal and abnormal radiographic images. Two, the segmentation mask obtained from our generative model can be used to improve the segmentation of the CML fracture region, which is beneficial for verification of automated classification. Three, this is the first application of generative diffusion models to augment a CML database to improve the diagnosis of infant abuse.

2 Methods

In this paper, we propose a new generative model for data augmentation of radiographic images called MaC-DM. This model consists of two stages: 1) training the denoising network, and 2) sampling or generation of new data by integrating the conditional information (Fig. 1). In the first stage, we train two different diffusion models using radiographic images, their associated conditional information in the form of their binary class labels (CML fracture versus normal), and their segmentation masks (for both the distal tibia and the CML fracture region). We train one diffusion model to classify noisy CML and normal radiographs, which we use for classifier guidance during sampling; and train another diffusion model to remove noise from the noisy images, which we compute after adding noise to the training dataset. In the second stage, we use the trained diffusion model with classifier guidance to generate 1) synthetic radiographs of the distal tibia, and 2) their corresponding tibial and CML segmentation masks.

2.1   Diffusion Model

DDPM is a special type of generative model designed to transform a Gaussian distribution to an empirical one [8,16]. It is embodied by a forward and a reverse process. In particular, given a data sample $x_0 \sim q(x)$, the forward process gradually adds small amounts of noise to the input data from time steps $t = 0$ to T, according to a pre-determined noise schedule, as described by the following:

$$q(x_t|x_{t-1}) = \mathcal{N}(x_t; \sqrt{1 - \beta_t}x_{t-1}, \beta_t \mathbf{I}) \tag{1}$$

where x_t and β_t represent the noisy image and the noise variance at time step t, respectively; with the noisy image x_t described by $x_t = \sqrt{\bar{\alpha}_t}x_0 + \sqrt{1 - \bar{\alpha}_t}\epsilon$ where $\alpha_t = 1 - \beta_t$ and $\bar{\alpha}_t = \prod_{t=1}^{T} \alpha_t$. In contrast, in the reverse process, we generate samples of the denoised image as follows:

$$p_\theta(\mathbf{x}_{t-1}|\mathbf{x}_t) = \mathcal{N}(\mathbf{x}_{t-1}; \mu_\theta(\mathbf{x}_t, t), \sigma_t^2 \mathbf{I}) \tag{2}$$

where $\mu_\theta(\mathbf{x}_t, t)$ is the mean value learned by DDPM, and $\sigma_t^2 \mathbf{I}$ is the fixed variance.

Typically, the sampling process of DDPM is slow due to the large number of time steps required for denoising. To speedup this process, we use the denoising diffusion implicit model (DDIM) for sampling acceleration [22]. To train our model for denoising, we employ the following loss functional [8]:

$$L = \mathbb{E}_{t \sim [1,T], x_0, \epsilon_t}[\|\epsilon - \epsilon_\theta(x_t, t)\|_2^2] \tag{3}$$

where $\epsilon \sim \mathcal{N}(0, I)$, and ϵ_θ is the learned diffusion model.

2.2   Image Generation via Conditional Diffusion Model

Classifier Guidance. It is desirable for a diffusion model to generate synthetic images with specific attributes such as explicit class labels or with certain properties. This can be accomplished by injecting conditional information into the diffusion model. To enable this attractive feature, Dhariwal et al. [2] trained a classifier using noisy images and used the gradient of the classifier to guide the diffusion model. In particular, given the conditional label y for a diffusion

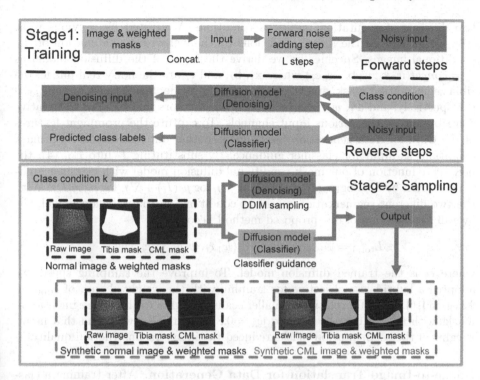

Fig. 1. Algorithmic structure of the MaC-DM, which consists of two stages. In the first stage, noise is gradually added to both training images and masks (forward process). Two separate networks are then trained: one for classification and another for denoising (reverse process). In the second stage, a new synthetic image and its associated masks are sampled from MaC-DM based on the input image from the real dataset and by incorporating mask-based condition along with classifier guidance.

model ϵ_θ, they constructed a modified score function by integrating $p(y|\mathbf{x}_t)$, the posterior distribution for classification. This modified score function is given by

$$\nabla_{x_t} \log(p_\theta(\mathbf{x}_t)p_\phi(y|\mathbf{x}_t)) = \nabla_{x_t} \log p_\theta(\mathbf{x}_t) + \nabla_{x_t} \log p_\phi(y|\mathbf{x}_t) \quad (4)$$

where $\nabla_{x_t} \log p_\theta(\mathbf{x}_t) = -\frac{1}{\sqrt{1-\bar{\alpha}_t}} \epsilon_\theta(x_t)$. Then, the predicted noise obtained from classifier-guided model becomes $\bar{\epsilon}_\theta(x_t) = \epsilon_\theta(x_t) - \sqrt{1-\bar{\alpha}_t}g\nabla_{x_t} \log p_\phi(y|\mathbf{x}_t)$, where $\nabla_{x_t} \log p_\phi(y|\mathbf{x}_t)$ is the gradient of the classifier, and g is a weighting factor to adjust the relative strengths of the gradient for classifier guidance.

Masked Conditional Classifier Guidance. Training a conditional diffusion model with simple class labels (e.g. CML versus normal) may not be sufficient to characterize the geometry of the distal tibia, such as the bone shape and the CML fracture pattern. This stems from the large shape variation of the distal tibia and the CML fracture. To address this deficiency, we explicitly introduce the bone shape and fracture region into the diffusion model by injecting two different segmentation masks as conditions. Motivated by previous work [18], we introduced the image conditions by channel-wise concatenation of the conditional images. Specifically, we derive the input of the diffusion model as $I_t = concat(w_1\mathbf{x}_t, w_2\mathbf{b}_t, w_3\mathbf{c}_t)$ where $\mathbf{x}_t$, $\mathbf{b}_t$, and $\mathbf{c}_t$ are the noisy real image, the tibia segmentation mask, and the CML fracture segmentation mask at time step t, respectively; and w_1, w_2, w_3 are the weighting factors that balance the relative contributions of the various input channels. To capture the prominent features of the CML for data generation, we trained another diffusion model with mask conditions as input for classifier guidance. By substituting I_t into Eq. (4), the new score function of our mask conditional diffusion model with classifier guidance is given by $\nabla_{I_t} \log(p_\theta(I_t)p_\phi(y|I_t)) = \nabla_{I_t} \log p_\theta(I_t) + \nabla_{I_t} \log p_\phi(y|I_t)$. With the two different segmentation masks as conditions to the diffusion model, the overall loss function of our proposed method becomes:

$$L_{\text{total}} = \mathbb{E}_{\epsilon \sim \mathcal{N}(0,\mathbf{I})}[\|\epsilon - \epsilon_\theta(w_1x_t, w_2b_t, w_3c_t, t)\|_2^2] \tag{5}$$

where ϵ_θ is the trained diffusion model. To improve the sampling speed, we adopted a hybrid loss objective for training with the weighted sum of $L_{\text{total}} + \lambda L_{\text{vlb}}$ in [16]. We set a relatively smaller scaling weights to the two segmentation masks with $w_1 = 1.0$, $w_2 = 0.8$ and $w_3 = 0.8$. Empirically, we found that larger weights of the segmentation masks reduced the image reconstruction quality.

Image-to-Image Translation for Data Generation. After training a classifier and a denoising diffusion model with mask conditions, we utilized the proposed MaC-DM for image-to-image translation, when given a class condition K, where $K \in \{0, 1\}$ (i.e., normal or CML). As there are disproportionately more normal radiographs than CML ones in our training datasets, we only used the normal radiographs of the distal tibia as inputs for image translation (i.e. we translated normal-to-CML and normal-to-normal radiographs). This approach generated more augmented CML images to address the class imbalance problem for binary classification. To preserve the overall structure of the tibia during the denoising process, we only used a noisy image x_t from an intermediate time step Z, where $Z < T$ for image generation.

3   Experiments

Datasets. We curated two different datasets of the distal tibial radiograph over two distinct time periods. The primary dataset consisted of 178 normal radiographs and 74 with CMLs (2009–2021). The secondary dataset consisted of 45 normal radiographs and 8 with CMLs (2006–2008 and 2021–2022). Given that these radiographs were obtained over such a long period of time, different X-ray imaging techniques and imaging systems were utilized, resulting in varying image contrast and resolution. This existential image heterogeneity is expected, and underscores the importance of having an algorithm that generalizes to radiographs of differing image qualities. The original 1024×1024 grayscale radiographs were cropped to the distal one-fifth of the tibia to focus over the region of concern (see S.1 in Supplementary Material for details). The resultant images were resized to 256×256 pixels, and normalized to an intensity range of 0 to 1. A radiologist vetted these radiographs in establishing the ground truth (i.e. normal versus CML). Additionally, for each radiograph, the distal tibia and the CML fracture were manually segmented by a radiologist in establishing the ground truth (Fig. 2).

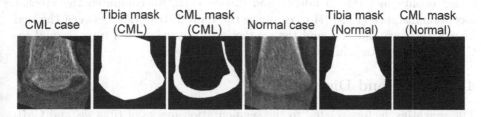

Fig. 2. The distal tibial CML image and its associated tibial and CML segmentation masks are shown in the first three frames. The normal distal tibial image and its associated tibial and CML segmentation masks are shown in the last three frames.

Implementation. We trained the DDPM using an improved version of U-Net architecture [16]. Specifically, we modified this network to have a three-channel input (gray-scale radiograph, and the weighted distal tibial and CML fracture segmentation masks). We trained the conditional diffusion model with a batch size of 5 and 120,000 iterations; and trained the classifier with a batch size of 10 and 150,000 iterations. All the DDPMs were trained using an Adam optimizer, a learning rate of 10^{-4}, and a sampling time step $t = 1000$. The training process took approximately 1.5 days using a Quadro RTX 8000 GPU. All networks were implemented using Pytorch version 1.7.1.

To evaluate the added-value of MaC-DM, we compared the accuracy of five ResNet-34 [6] binary classifiers. We conducted a 5-fold cross validation (CV) experiment to evaluate each classifier. The first classifier was trained with the primary dataset using standard data augmentation (random cropping). To compare our method with other state-of-the-art (SOTA) methods for image-to-image translation, the rest of the four classifiers were trained with augmented data (N = 472, with 188 real and 284 augmented synthetic data) generated from CycleGAN [26], AttentionGAN [23], the baseline diffusion models without mask conditions [2], and our proposed MaC-DM. For MaC-DM and baseline diffusion models, we utilized the DDIM to generate synthetic CML and normal radiographs using normal real radiographs from the primary training dataset as input. To evaluate the generalizability of these classifiers, we employed the trained ResNet that achieved the highest validation performance during the 5-fold CV experiment, and applied it to the secondary dataset (which has a different distribution than the primary dataset used in the 5-fold CV).

We evaluated the utility of the CML segmentation mask generated by MaC-DM in two manners. First, we leveraged MaC-DM to generate synthetic CML radiographs and their corresponding tibial and CML segmentation masks, using 80% of radiographs from the primary dataset as input. We then trained a U-Net model [19] for CML segmentation using a combination of real and synthetic CML images/masks. We evaluated the segmentation performance using the remaining 20% of the primary data for testing. Second, to objectively evaluate the image quality in terms of fidelity and diversity [2], we computed the Fréchet inception distance (FID) [7] to compare the data distribution between the real images (primary dataset) and the synthetic images generated from normal-to-CML translation task in the 5-fold CV.

4   Results and Discussion

The weighting factors related to the segmentation masks of tibia w_2 and CML fractures w_3, as defined in Eq. (5), are important hyperparameters that affect the quality of the synthetic images. To optimize these, we initially set the noise level Z to 600 and the gradient scale for classifier guidance g to 100. Next, we trained our MaC-DM on the primary dataset using various combinations of w_2 and w_3, ranging from 0.2 to 1.0. We then applied the normal-to-CML image translation task to all normal images in the secondary dataset. A blinded radiologist graded the image quality of the generated images for each combination of weights, assigning a score of 1 for excellent image quality and 0 otherwise. In this parametric study, w_2=0.8 and w_3=0.8 received the highest summation scores. Using a similar approach, we identified the optimal noise level of Z=800 and the scale of g=300 for classifier guidance.

Based on our 5-fold CV experiment, our proposed data augmentation method outperformed the other four methods in classifying CML radiographs from normal ones, in terms of accuracy, sensitivity, and specificity (Table 1). When trained on the primary dataset, the proposed MaC-DM achieved the highest accuracy and sensitivity when tested on the secondary dataset, indicating improved generalizability. Of note, although the baseline DDPM method had a slightly better specificity on the secondary dataset than ours (93.3% versus 91.1%), its sensitivity (62.5% versus 87.5%) was much lower. Figure 3 shows that the images produced by other generative methods have blurry bony margins and often contained artifacts, whereas the augmented images from MaC-DM showed uncanny realism.

Table 2 (top) summarized the CML segmentation results via U-Net. The augmented images and their corresponding synthetic segmentation masks generated by MaC-DM improved the segmentation performance of U-Net. Surprisingly, even when training solely on the synthetic images and their generated segmentation masks, MaC-DM was able to improve the U-Net's segmentation performance. These findings suggest that the synthetic images and their segmentation labels produced by MaC-DM are valuable in enhancing the performance of CML segmentation, at no additional labeling cost. In the case of normal-to-CML image translation, MaC-DM achieved an FID of 89.87 (Table 2 (bottom)),

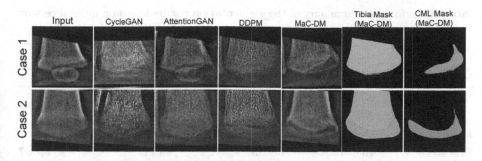

Fig. 3. Example images and segmentation masks generated by MaC-DM, in comparison to images from other generative models. A radiologist checked the quality of the images and concluded that MaC-DM generated more realistic and higher quality CML images than other generative models. In addition, MaC-DM generated tibial and CML segmentation masks without any additional costs.

Table 1. Performance summary of the five classifiers in terms of accuracy, sensitivity, and specificity. The 5-fold CV experiment was conducted using the primary dataset, while independent testing was conducted using the secondary dataset.

	5-fold cross validation				
Method	ResNet	ResNet + CycleGAN [26]	ResNet + AttentionGAN [23]	ResNet + DDPM w/o mask [2]	Ours
Accuracy	93.00%	95.20%	94.00%	96.00%	**96.40%**
Sensitivity	88.00%	90.71%	90.36%	88.90%	**90.73%**
Specificity	96.00%	97.11%	95.48%	98.84%	**98.84%**
	Independent testing				
Method	ResNet	ResNet + CycleGAN [26]	ResNet + AttentionGAN [23]	ResNet + DDPM w/o mask [2]	Ours
Accuracy	84.90%	84.90%	86.80%	88.67%	**90.60%**
Sensitivity	75.00%	62.5%	62.50%	62.50%	**87.50%**
Specificity	86.67%	88.90%	91.10%	**93.33%**	91.10%

outperforming other SOTA methods. Our small training dataset likely hindered other SOTA methods from generating quality synthetic images as it typically requires large datasets for training. These results highlight the importance of our method in synthesizing realistic CML images from a small training dataset.

Table 2. Performance summary of the segmentation results based on mean dice score (top). The image quality evaluation results were based on FID score (bottom).

	Segmentation evaluation		
Method (U-Net)	Real images	Augmented images	Real + augmented images
Dice coefficient	0.74±0.03	0.83±0.05	**0.85±0.04**

	FID score evaluation (lower is better)			
Method	CycleGAN [26]	AttentionGAN [23]	DDPM w/o mask [2]	Ours
FID score	165.33	139.30	99.71	**89.87**

5   Conclusions

We proposed a novel data augmentation method for CML fracture classification and segmentation. Our proposed method overcame the limitations of previous techniques in generating diverse radiographic images of distal tibial CML and produced realistic synthetic images with associated segmentation labels. This method has the potential to improve the accuracy and robustness of machine learning models for the diagnosis of infant abuse.

Acknowledgements. This work was supported in part by the Society for Pediatric Radiology Research and Education Foundation Pilot Grant, National Institute of Child Health and Human Development (No. R21HD108634), National Institute of Diabetic and Digestive and Kidney Diseases (No. R21DK123569 and R01DK125561), and National Institute of Biomedical Imaging and Bioengineering (No. R21EB029627).

References

1. Coley, B.D.: Caffey's Pediatric Diagnostic Imaging E-book. Elsevier, Amsterdam (2013)
2. Dhariwal, P., Nichol, A.: Diffusion models beat GANs on image synthesis. In: Advances in Neural Information Processing Systems, vol. 34, pp. 8780–8794 (2021)
3. Flaherty, E.G., et al.: Evaluating children with fractures for child physical abuse. Pediatrics **133**(2), e477–e489 (2014)
4. Goodfellow, I., et al.: Generative adversarial networks. Commun. ACM **63**(11), 139–144 (2020)
5. Han, C., et al.: MADGAN: unsupervised medical anomaly detection GAN using multiple adjacent brain MRI slice reconstruction. BMC Bioinform. **22**(2), 1–20 (2021)
6. He, K., Zhang, X., Ren, S., Sun, J.: Deep residual learning for image recognition. In: Proceedings of the IEEE Conference on Computer Vision and Pattern Recognition, pp. 770–778 (2016)
7. Heusel, M., Ramsauer, H., Unterthiner, T., Nessler, B., Hochreiter, S.: GANs trained by a two time-scale update rule converge to a local Nash equilibrium. In: Advances in Neural Information Processing Systems, vol. 30 (2017)
8. Ho, J., Jain, A., Abbeel, P.: Denoising diffusion probabilistic models. In: Advances in Neural Information Processing Systems, vol. 33, pp. 6840–6851 (2020)

9. Kearney, V., et al.: Attention-aware discrimination for MR-to-CT image translation using cycle-consistent generative adversarial networks. Radiol.: Artif. Intell. **2**(2), e190027 (2020)

10. Kim, B., Ye, J.C.: Diffusion deformable model for 4D temporal medical image generation. In: Wang, L., Dou, Q., Fletcher, P.T., Speidel, S., Li, S. (eds.) Medical Image Computing and Computer Assisted Intervention - MICCAI 2022. Lecture Notes in Computer Science, vol. 13431, pp. 539–548. Springer, Cham (2022). https://doi.org/10.1007/978-3-031-16431-6_51

11. Kleinman, P.K., Marks, S., Blackbourne, B.: The metaphyseal lesion in abused infants: a radiologic-histopathologic study. Am. J. Roentgenol. **146**(5), 895–905 (1986)

12. Kleinman, P.K., Marks, S.C., Jr.: Relationship of the subperiosteal bone collar to metaphyseal lesions in abused infants. JBJS **77**(10), 1471–1476 (1995)

13. Kleinman, P.K., Marks, S.C., Jr., Richmond, J.M., Blackbourne, B.D.: Inflicted skeletal injury: a postmortem radiologic-histopathologic study in 31 infants. AJR Am. J. Roentgenol. **165**(3), 647–650 (1995)

14. Kleinman, P.K., Perez-Rossello, J.M., Newton, A.W., Feldman, H.A., Kleinman, P.L.: Prevalence of the classic metaphyseal lesion in infants at low versus high risk for abuse. Am. J. Roentgenol. **197**(4), 1005–1008 (2011)

15. Maltreatment, C.: Children's Bureau, Administration on Children, Youth, and Family (2018)

16. Nichol, A.Q., Dhariwal, P.: Improved denoising diffusion probabilistic models. In: International Conference on Machine Learning, pp. 8162–8171. PMLR (2021)

17. Peng, C., Guo, P., Zhou, S.K., Patel, V.M., Chellappa, R.: Towards performant and reliable undersampled MR reconstruction via diffusion model sampling. In: Wang, L., Dou, Q., Fletcher, P.T., Speidel, S., Li, S. (eds.) Medical Image Computing and Computer Assisted Intervention - MICCAI 2022. Lecture Notes in Computer Science, vol. 13436, pp. 623–633. Springer, Cham (2022). https://doi.org/10.1007/978-3-031-16446-0_59

18. Rombach, R., Blattmann, A., Lorenz, D., Esser, P., Ommer, B.: High-resolution image synthesis with latent diffusion models. In: Proceedings of the IEEE/CVF Conference on Computer Vision and Pattern Recognition, pp. 10684–10695 (2022)

19. Ronneberger, O., Fischer, P., Brox, T.: U-Net: convolutional networks for biomedical image segmentation. In: Navab, N., Hornegger, J., Wells, W., Frangi, A. (eds.) Medical Image Computing and Computer-Assisted Intervention - MICCAI 2015. Lecture Notes in Computer Science(), vol. 9351, pp. 234–241. Springer, Cham (2015). https://doi.org/10.1007/978-3-319-24574-4_28

20. Saxena, D., Cao, J.: Generative adversarial networks (GANs) challenges, solutions, and future directions. ACM Comput. Surv. (CSUR) **54**(3), 1–42 (2021)

21. Servaes, S., et al.: The etiology and significance of fractures in infants and young children: a critical multidisciplinary review. Pediatr. Radiol. **46**, 591–600 (2016)

22. Song, J., Meng, C., Ermon, S.: Denoising diffusion implicit models. arXiv preprint: arXiv:2010.02502 (2020)

23. Tang, H., Liu, H., Xu, D., Torr, P.H., Sebe, N.: AttentionGAN: unpaired image-to-image translation using attention-guided generative adversarial networks. IEEE Trans. Neural Netw. Learn. Syst. **34**, 1972–1987 (2021)

24. Tsai, A., McDonald, A.G., Rosenberg, A.E., Gupta, R., Kleinman, P.K.: High-resolution CT with histopathological correlates of the classic metaphyseal lesion of infant abuse. Pediatr. Radiol. **44**, 124–140 (2014)

25. Wolleb, J., Bieder, F., Sandkühler, R., Cattin, P.C.: Diffusion models for medical anomaly detection. In: Wang, L., Dou, Q., Fletcher, P.T., Speidel, S., Li, S. (eds.) Medical Image Computing and Computer Assisted Intervention - MICCAI 2022. Lecture Notes in Computer Science, vol. 13438, pp. 35–45. Springer, Cham (2022). https://doi.org/10.1007/978-3-031-16452-1_4
26. Zhu, J.Y., Park, T., Isola, P., Efros, A.A.: Unpaired image-to-image translation using cycle-consistent adversarial networks. In: Proceedings of the IEEE International Conference on Computer Vision, pp. 2223–2232 (2017)

Self-supervised Single-Image Deconvolution with Siamese Neural Networks

Mikhail Papkov[1](✉), Kaupo Palo[2], and Leopold Parts[1,3]

[1] Institute of Computer Science, University of Tartu, Tartu, Estonia
`mikhail.papkov@ut.ee`
[2] Revvity Inc., Tallinn, Estonia
[3] Wellcome Sanger Institute, Hinxton, UK

Abstract. Inverse problems in image reconstruction are fundamentally complicated by unknown noise properties. Classical iterative deconvolution approaches amplify noise and require careful parameter selection for an optimal trade-off between sharpness and grain. Deep learning methods allow for flexible parametrization of the noise and learning its properties directly from the data. Recently, self-supervised blind-spot neural networks were successfully adopted for image deconvolution by including a known point-spread function in the end-to-end training. However, their practical application has been limited to 2D images in biomedical domain because it implies large kernels, which are poorly optimized. We tackle this problem with Fast Fourier Transform convolutions that provide training speed-up in 3D microscopy deconvolution tasks. Further, we propose to adopt a Siamese invariance loss for deconvolution and empirically identify its optimal position in the neural network between blind-spot and full image branches. The experimental results show that our improved framework outperforms the previous state-of-the-art deconvolution methods with a known point spread function.

Keywords: Deconvolution · Microscopy · Deep learning

1 Introduction and Related Work

Quality enhancement is central for microscopy imaging [26,29]. Its two most important steps are noise removal and blur reduction that improve performance in downstream tasks for both humans and algorithms.

Denoising, approaches to which were developed decades ago [5], was given a boost by recent advances in deep learning methods [1,3,10,11,14,15,18,19,26], which substantially outperform classical algorithms [2,5]. A direct approach to train a denoising neural network is to provide it with pairs of low and high-quality images [26], but such data are rarely available in practice, which raises the need

---

Supplementary Information The online version contains supplementary material available at https://doi.org/10.1007/978-3-031-58171-7_16.

Y. Xue et al. (Eds.): DALI 2023, LNCS 14379, pp. 157–166, 2024.
https://doi.org/10.1007/978-3-031-58171-7_16

for alternative techniques. Lehtinen *et al.* [14] proposed to supervise the training with an independently acquired noisy copy of the input, while Batson and Royer [1] concurrently with Krull *et al.* [10] developed a theory of a J-invariant blind-spot denoising network that operates on a single image in a self-supervised manner. The latter theory is based on the idea that a network cannot learn the noise that is conditionally pixel-wise independent given the signal, so learning to predict the values of masked pixels can improve the performance in restoration. Xie *et al.* [27] further questioned the necessity of blind spots for efficient denoising. They proposed Noise2Same with Siamese invariance loss between outputs of masked and unmasked inputs to prevent the network from learning an identity function. This advance pushed the performance of self-supervised denoising at a cost of doubled training time.

In addition to noise, equipment imperfection imposes blur on the images via a point spread function (PSF) [24]. The blur can be efficiently removed with classical iterative approaches such as Lucy-Richardson [21], but these algorithms tend to amplify the noise with each iteration and require careful regularization and stopping criteria [12]. As supervised methods are not applicable to deconvolution problem due to the ground truth inaccessibility, Lim *et al.* [16] proposed CycleGAN [30] with linear blur kernel, which performed well in both simulation and real microscopy deconvolution. However, the models of this class are notoriously hard to train [17] and tends to converge to a perceptually conceiving solution that does not necessarily reflect the true underlying structure [13]. Besides, it requires clean data examples, albeit unpaired. Deep self-supervised denoising systems were also adopted for deconvolution purposes. Kobayashi *et al.* [9] assumed an intermediate output of the network to be a deconvolved representation and proposed to train Noise2Self [1] as a pseudo-inverse model with a known PSF kernel. This method was only applied to 2D data.

Our contribution is three-fold. Firstly, we adopt the Siamese invariance loss [27] to the deconvolution task and identify the optimal neural network's outputs to apply it. Secondly, we train the first, to our knowledge, 3D self-supervised deconvolutional network without the adversarial component. Lastly, we propose to alleviate the computational costs of training a Siamese network by using the Fast Fourier Transform (FFT) for convolution with the PSF kernel.

2   Methods

We propose a generalized self-supervised deconvolution framework. We follow Kobayashi *et al.* [9] and define the framework as a composition of trainable model $f(\cdot)$ followed by the fixed PSF convolution $g(\cdot)$. The framework (Fig. 1) allows for both one-pass blind-spot training [1,9,10] and two-pass training [27].

For the training, we use two inputs, unmasked $\mathbf{x}$ and masked $\mathbf{x}_{J^c}$ where the pixels at locations J are replaced with Gaussian noise. We optimize the trainable model using the composition loss $\mathcal{L}(f)$ of six terms in Eq. (1).

Blind-Spot Loss. $\mathcal{L}_{bsp}$ is a mean-squared error (MSE) between the network's unmasked input $\mathbf{x}$ and output from the masked forward pass $g(f(\mathbf{x}_{J^c}))_J$ measured at the locations of the masked pixels J [1,10].

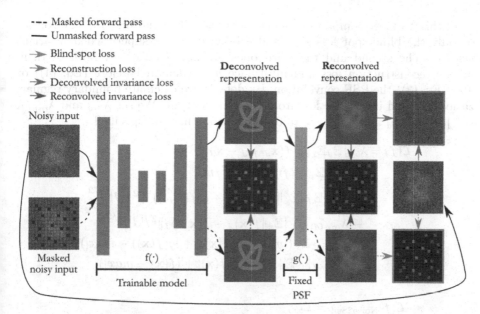

Fig. 1. The self-supervised deconvolution framework. The trainable model $f(\cdot)$ takes noisy input $\mathbf{x}$ in unmasked forward pass (solid) and masked noisy input $\mathbf{x}_{J^c}$ in masked forward pass (dashed). The model produces two intermediate outputs (deconvolved representations). These outputs are convolved with a fixed PSF convolution $g(\cdot)$ to obtain final outputs (reconvolved representations). The deconvolved and reconvolved invariance losses are computed between the respective outputs before and after the PSF. The reconstruction loss is computed between the noisy input and the unmasked forward pass output. The blind-spot loss is computed between the noisy input and masked forward pass output, it does not require an unmasked forward pass.

Reconstruction Loss. $\mathcal{L}_{rec}$ is an MSE between the network's unmasked input $\mathbf{x}$ and output from the unmasked forward pass $g(f(\mathbf{x}))$ [27].

Reconvolved Invariance Loss. $\mathcal{L}_{inv}$ is an MSE between the network's output from the masked forward pass $g(f(\mathbf{x}_{J^c}))_J$ and output from the unmasked forward pass $g(f(\mathbf{x}))_J$.

Deconvolved Invariance Loss. $\mathcal{L}_{inv\,(d)}$ is an MSE between the network's output from the masked forward pass $f(\mathbf{x}_{J^c})_J$ and output from the unmasked forward pass $f(\mathbf{x})_J$ before PSF convolution $g(\cdot)$. Both Siamese invariance losses are computed between the network's outputs from altered (masked and unmasked) inputs at the location of the masked pixels J. They prevent the network from learning an identity function from $\mathcal{L}_{rec}$ minimization, which is especially important in the single-image deconvolution task.

Boundary Losses. $\mathcal{L}_{bound\,(d)}$ and $\mathcal{L}_{bound}$ regularize the outputs to be within $[min, max]$ boundaries before or after the PSF convolution respectively [9]. These losses are measured after destandardization. We use $min = 0$ and $max = 1$.

In this work, we compare three practical cases. The first one, Eq. (2), considers only the blind-spot loss $\mathcal{L}_{bsp}$ and establishes a self-supervised J-invariant baseline. The second and the third ones are not J-invariant, both of them include reconstruction loss and invariance loss calculated before (Eq. (4)) or after (Eq. (3)) the PSF convolution. By default, we calculate boundary regularization loss and invariance loss from the same output. We set λ_{inv} and $\lambda_{inv\,(d)}$ to 2 [27], λ_{bound} and $\lambda_{bound\,(d)}$ to 0.1 [9] unless otherwise specified.

$$
\begin{aligned}
\mathcal{L}(f) = {} & \lambda_{bsp}\, \mathbb{E}_J \mathbb{E}_x \| g(f(\mathbf{x}_{J^c}))_J - \mathbf{x}_J \|^2 \\
& + \lambda_{rec}\, \mathbb{E}_x \| g(f(\mathbf{x})) - \mathbf{x} \|^2 / m \\
& + \lambda_{inv}\, \mathbb{E}_J \left[\mathbb{E}_x \| g(f(\mathbf{x}))_J - g(f(\mathbf{x}_{J^c}))_J \|^2 / |J| \right]^{1/2} \\
& + \lambda_{inv\,(d)}\, \mathbb{E}_J \left[\mathbb{E}_x \| f(\mathbf{x})_J - f(\mathbf{x}_{J^c})_J \|^2 / |J| \right]^{1/2} \\
& + \lambda_{bound}\, \mathbb{E}_x \left(|min - g(f(\mathbf{x}))| + |g(f(\mathbf{x})) - max| \right) \\
& + \lambda_{bound\,(d)}\, \mathbb{E}_x \left(|min - f(\mathbf{x})| + |f(\mathbf{x}) - max| \right)
\end{aligned}
\tag{1}
$$

$$
\mathcal{L}(f)_{\text{Noise2Self}} = \mathcal{L}_{bsp} \tag{2}
$$
$$
\mathcal{L}(f)_{\text{Noise2Same}} = \mathcal{L}_{rec} + \lambda_{inv}\, \mathcal{L}_{inv} + \lambda_{bound}\, \mathcal{L}_{bound} \tag{3}
$$
$$
\mathcal{L}(f)_{\text{Noise2Same (d)}} = \mathcal{L}_{rec} + \lambda_{inv\,(d)}\, \mathcal{L}_{inv\,(d)} + \lambda_{bound\,(d)}\, \mathcal{L}_{bound\,(d)} \tag{4}
$$

Neural Network Architecture. For 2D data, we use the previously proposed [10,27] variation of a U-Net [22] architecture without modifications. The fully-convolutional network of depth 3 consists of an encoder and a decoder with concatenating skip connections at corresponding levels. The first convolutional layer outputs 96 features, and this number doubles with every downsampling step. For 3D data, we modify the network to have 48 output features from the first convolution. We also replace the concatenation operation with an addition in skip connections. Such modification allows for a reduction in training time for 3D convolutional networks without substantial performance sacrifices. We implement the network using PyTorch [20].

Training. During training, we sample a patch (128×128 pixels for 2D images, $64 \times 64 \times 64$ for 3D), randomly rotate and flip it. We use batch sizes of 16 for 2D images and 4 for 3D images. Each image is standardized individually to zero mean and unit variance. For the masked forward pass, we randomly replace 0.5% of pixels from each training image with Gaussian noise ($\sigma = 0.2$) [27]. We use Adam [8] optimizer and multiply its learning rate from $4 \cdot 10^{-4}$ by 0.5 every 500 steps out of 3k total for 2D data [9] and every 2k steps out of 15k total for 3D data. We train and evaluate all models on a single NVIDIA V100 16 GB GPU.

Inference. For inference, we do only unmasked forward pass and discard the PSF convolution during inference [9]. We use the last model checkpoint since we do not possess any reliable validation metric. For large images that do not fit in GPU memory, we predict by overlapping patches and stitch the output together using pyramid weights [7] which allows for avoiding edge artifacts. In 3D data, we predict patches of $128 \times 128 \times 128$ with overlaps of 32 pixels.

Fast Fourier Transform Convolution. We use FFT for the convolution with a fixed PSF during training. Convolution operation $x * k$ is equivalent to element-wise matrix multiplication in Fourier space $F^{-1}(F(x) \odot F(k))$. If image x is $M \times M$ pixels and kernel k is $N \times N$ and both of them have dimensionality of d, the complexity of an ordinary convolution is $O(M^d N^d)$, while the complexity of a Fourier convolution is $O(M^d d \log M)$ and does not depend on N. With large enough N, convolution in Fourier space becomes computationally cheaper, and large kernels (even of the size of the image [24]) are common for PSF. It is recommended to use FFT with 2D kernels for $N > 25$ and with 3D kernels for $N > 9$ [6].

3   Experiments

We validate our approach on 2D and 3D data in a single image deconvolution task. In all the experiments we train one model per image to obtain a lower bound for the extreme self-supervised case. Every image is normalized within $[0, 1]$. We generate blurry images by convolving them with a realistic Richards & Wolf PSF of a 0.8NA 16x microscope objective with 17×17 or $17 \times 17 \times 17$ 0.406-micron pixels. Then we add a mixture of Poisson ($\alpha = 0.001$), Gaussian ($\sigma = 0.1$), and salt-and-pepper (only for 2D images, $p = 0.01$) noise to these images and quantize them with 10 bit precision [9].

We compare the results against classical Lucy-Richardson (LR) deconvolution algorithm [21] and deep learning Self-Supervised Inversion (SSI) [9] algorithm. For LR evaluate the results after 2, 5, 10, and 20 iterations to observe the trade-off between deconvolution quality and noise amplification and report the best ones. We do not include in comparison other classical methods such as Conjugate Gradient optimization [4] and Chambole-Pock primal-dual inversion [4], because they were shown inferior to both LR and SSI [9]. We rerun the baseline experiments ourselves wherever possible.

We evaluate the model performance against clean images using root mean squared error (RMSE), peak signal-to-noise ratio (PSNR) [28], and structural similarity index(SSIM) [25]. For PSNR and SSIM, we explicitly set the data range to the true values $[0, 1]$. Since it was not done in prior work [9], some values in Table 2 are missing to avoid confusion. Additionally, for 2D images, we report mutual information (MI) [23] and spectral mutual information (SMI) [9]. For all metrics except RMSE, higher is better.

3.1   2D Dataset

First, we tested the deconvolution framework performance for the 2D case on a benchmark dataset of 22 single-channeled images [9] with size varying from

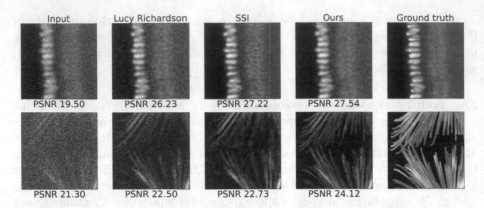

Fig. 2. Example deconvolution results on *Drosophila* 2D image (top), microtubules 3D image, frontal max projection (bottom), magnified. For Lucy Richardson, the result is shown after the best iteration. Our algorithm uses loss from Eq. (4) with $\lambda_{inv\,(d)} = 2$, $\lambda_{bound\,(d)} = 0.1$. PSNR metric is reported for the presented images.

512×512 to 2592×1728 pixels. We compared three different variants of loss function, Eqs. (2)–(4) (Table 1). Loss (4) performed best with $\lambda_{inv\,(d)} = 2$ and $\lambda_{bound\,(d)} = 0.1$, achieving PSNR = 22.79, SSIM = 0.46, and RMSE = 0.078.

We compared our model against the baseline LR and SSI methods (Table 2, Fig. 2). It performed best by PSNR, SMI, and RMSE, and showed similar results by SSIM (0.01 less than LR) and MI (0.01 less than SSI).

3.2   3D Dataset

We evaluated the framework performance for the 3D case on a single synthetic image of microtubules [24] of size $128 \times 256 \times 512$. From the three variants of loss function, Eqs. (2)–(4), loss (3) performed best with $\lambda_{inv} = 2$ and $\lambda_{bound} = 0$ showing the results PSNR = 24.08, SSIM = 0.39, and RMSE = 0.063 (Table 3).

We also compared the best-performing model against the LR and SSI methods (Table 4, Fig. 2). Our model surpassed baselines by a substantial margin (+1.5 PSNR against SSI and +1.7 against LR).

4   Discussion

Our Siamese neural network was superior in single-image deconvolution against both classical and deep learning baselines. The architecture is simple and did not require additional tricks such as masking schedule or adding noise to gradients [9] for training. Training converged to similar performance for all of the several tested random weight initializations.

Loss function performance was inconsistent between the 2D and 3D cases. Invariance loss applied to deconvolved representation proved best for 2D data but failed to give an advantage in 3D: despite the high SSIM, images appear noisy. We

Table 1. Denoising results for the 2D dataset with different coefficients for loss (1) components: λ_{bsp}—coefficient for the blind-spot loss, λ_{rec}—coefficient for the reconstruction loss, $\lambda_{inv\,(d)}$—coefficient for deconvolved invariance loss, λ_{inv}—coefficient for reconvolved invariance loss, λ_{bound} and $\lambda_{bound\,(d)}$—coefficients for boundary regularization loss for reconvolved and deconvolved images. For all metrics except RMSE, higher is better. The best values are highlighted in bold.

	λ_{bsp}	λ_{rec}	$\lambda_{inv\,(d)}$	λ_{inv}	$\lambda_{bound\,(d)}$	λ_{bound}	PSNR ↑	SSIM ↑	RMSE ↓
input							17.77	0.18	0.130
$\mathcal{L}(f)_{\text{Noise2Self}}$	1	0	0	0	0	0	22.49	0.27	0.079
	1	0	0	0	0	0.1	22.51	0.43	0.079
$\mathcal{L}(f)_{\text{Noise2Same}}$	0	1	0	2	0	0	21.49	0.23	0.089
	0	1	0	2	0	0.1	21.81	0.41	0.085
$\mathcal{L}(f)_{\text{Noise2Same (d)}}$	0	1	2	0	0	0	**22.79**	0.46	**0.078**
	0	1	2	0	0.1	0	22.67	**0.46**	0.078

Table 2. Our best-performing method for 2D data compared to Lucy Richardson (LR) [21] and Self-Supervised Inversion (SSI) [9] baselines by denoising metrics (see Sect. 3 for details), training and inference time (measured for *Drosophila* image 1352×532 pixels). For all metrics except RMSE, higher is better. The best values are highlighted in bold. Our algorithm uses loss (4) with $\lambda_{inv\,(d)} = 2$, $\lambda_{bound\,(d)} = 0.1$

	PSNR ↑	SSIM ↑	MI ↑	SMI ↑	RMSE ↓	Train t (s)	Inference t (ms)
input	17.8	0.18	0.07	0.18	0.131	–	–
LR $n = 2$	22.0	**0.47**	0.13	0.25	0.086	–	46
LR $n = 5$	22.2	0.44	0.12	0.25	0.082	–	48
SSI (reported [9])	22.5	–	**0.14**	0.27	–	238	26
SSI (reproduced)	22.0	0.46	0.14	0.26	–	442	26
ours	**22.8**	0.46	0.13	**0.30**	**0.078**	856	53

hypothesize that the optimal solution depends on the data; *e.g.* in microtubules, the 3D dataset signal is very sparse. Boundary loss did not drastically affect the training of Siamese networks.

Despite performance superiority, Siamese networks are twice more expensive in computation because they require two forward passes through the neural network. Additionally, Noise2Same U-Net architecture has 10x more trainable parameters than SSI (5.75M against 0.55M in 2D). This problem is exacerbated by the necessity of convolutions with large PSF kernels which are not optimized in modern GPUs. We propose to alleviate this problem by using FFT for convolution with PSF. It leads to 2.3x speed improvement for 3D deconvolution with PSF of size $17 \times 17 \times 17$, and this advantage will grow for larger kernels. For example, while training with a PSF of $31 \times 31 \times 31$ we observed a 14x speedup.

Table 3. Denoising results for the 3D dataset with different coefficients for loss (1) components: λ_{bsp}—coefficient for the blind-spot loss, λ_{rec}—coefficient for the reconstruction loss, $\lambda_{inv\,(d)}$—coefficient for deconvolved invariance loss, λ_{inv}—coefficient for reconvolved invariance loss, λ_{bound} and $\lambda_{bound\,(d)}$—coefficients for boundary regularization loss for reconvolved and deconvolved images. For all metrics except RMSE, higher is better. The best values are highlighted in bold.

	λ_{bsp}	λ_{rec}	$\lambda_{inv\,(d)}$	λ_{inv}	$\lambda_{bound\,(d)}$	λ_{bound}	PSNR ↑	SSIM ↑	RMSE ↓
input							21.21	0.64	0.087
$\mathcal{L}(f)_{\text{Noise2Self}}$	1	0	0	0	0	0	23.71	0.39	0.065
	1	0	0	0	0	0.1	23.71	0.39	0.065
$\mathcal{L}(f)_{\text{Noise2Same}}$	0	1	0	2	0	0	**24.08**	0.39	**0.063**
	0	1	0	2	0	0.1	24.02	0.39	0.063
$\mathcal{L}(f)_{\text{Noise2Same (d)}}$	0	1	2	0	0	0	21.05	**0.82**	0.089
	0	1	2	0	0.1	0	21.05	**0.82**	0.089

Table 4. Our best performing method for 3D data compared to Lucy Richardson (LR) [21] and Self-Supervised Inversion (SSI) [9] baselines by denoising metrics (see Sect. 3 for details), training and inference time. For all metrics except RMSE, higher is better. The best values are highlighted in bold. Our algorithm uses loss (3) with $\lambda_{inv} = 2$, $\lambda_{bound} = 0$. Training time is reported with and without FFT (in brackets)

	PSNR ↑	SSIM ↑	RMSE ↓	Train t (s)	Inference t (ms)
input	21.2	0.64	0.087	–	–
LR $n = 2$	22.4	0.32	0.076	–	69
SSI	22.6	0.39	0.074	2814 (6580)	578
ours	**24.1**	**0.39**	**0.062**	8160 (18900)	734

5　Conclusion

Blind-spot networks [1,10] were seminal in self-supervised denoising and performed comparably to supervised methods [14,26]. Their success was later translated to image deconvolution [9], a more complicated inverse problem. However, it was shown that J-invariance leads to suboptimal performance in denoising because masked pixels contain useful bits of information [27]. In this work, we presented a novel unified image deconvolution framework, which generalized the accumulated prior advances, and set a new standard for image quality enhancement performance. We investigated the contributions of various self-supervised loss components and empirically identified the optimal usage scenarios for 2D and 3D data. We also proposed using Fast Fourier Transform for the training of deconvolution neural networks, which drastically speeds up the computation, especially for large kernels. This advantage allows one to use our method for non-confocal microscopy with extremely big point spread functions.

Acknowledgements. This work was funded by Revvity Inc. (VLTAT19682) and Wellcome Trust (206194). We thank High Performance Computing Center of the Institute of Computer Science at the University of Tartu for the provided computing power.

References

1. Batson, J., Royer, L.: Noise2Self: blind denoising by self-supervision. In: International Conference on Machine Learning, pp. 524–533. PMLR (2019)
2. Buades, A., Coll, B., Morel, J.M.: Non-local means denoising. Image Process. Line **1**, 208–212 (2011)
3. Buchholz, T.O., Jordan, M., Pigino, G., Jug, F.: Cryo-care: content-aware image restoration for cryo-transmission electron microscopy data. In: 2019 IEEE 16th International Symposium on Biomedical Imaging (ISBI 2019), pp. 502–506. IEEE (2019)
4. Chambolle, A., Pock, T.: A first-order primal-dual algorithm for convex problems with applications to imaging. J. Math. Imaging Vision **40**(1), 120–145 (2011)
5. Dabov, K., Foi, A., Katkovnik, V., Egiazarian, K.: Image denoising by sparse 3-D transform-domain collaborative filtering. IEEE Trans. Image Process. **16**(8), 2080–2095 (2007)
6. Frank Odom, III, F.O.: fkodom/fft-conv-pytorch. https://github.com/fkodom/fft-conv-pytorch
7. Khvedchenya, E.: Pytorch toolbelt (2019). https://github.com/BloodAxe/pytorch-toolbelt
8. Kingma, D.P., Ba, J.: Adam: a method for stochastic optimization (2017)
9. Kobayashi, H., Solak, A.C., Batson, J., Royer, L.A.: Image deconvolution via noise-tolerant self-supervised inversion. arXiv preprint arXiv:2006.06156 (2020)
10. Krull, A., Buchholz, T.O., Jug, F.: Noise2void-learning denoising from single noisy images. In: Proceedings of the IEEE Conference on Computer Vision and Pattern Recognition, pp. 2129–2137 (2019)
11. Krull, A., Vičar, T., Prakash, M., Lalit, M., Jug, F.: Probabilistic noise2void: unsupervised content-aware denoising. Front. Comput. Sci. **2**, 5 (2020)
12. Laasmaa, M., Vendelin, M., Peterson, P.: 3D confocal microscope image enhancement by Richardson-Lucy deconvolution algorithm with total variation regularization: parameters estimation. Biophys. J . **98**(3), 178a (2010)
13. Ledig, C., et al.: Photo-realistic single image super-resolution using a generative adversarial network. In: Proceedings of the IEEE Conference on Computer Vision and Pattern Recognition, pp. 4681–4690 (2017)
14. Lehtinen, J., et al.: Noise2Noise: learning image restoration without clean data. arXiv preprint arXiv:1803.04189 (2018)
15. Lemarchand, F., Montesuma, E.F., Pelcat, M., Nogues, E.: OpenDenoising: an extensible benchmark for building comparative studies of image denoisers. arXiv preprint arXiv:1910.08328 (2019)
16. Lim, S., Park, H., Lee, S.E., Chang, S., Sim, B., Ye, J.C.: CycleGAN with a blur kernel for deconvolution microscopy: optimal transport geometry. IEEE Trans. Comput. Imaging **6**, 1127–1138 (2020)
17. Mescheder, L., Geiger, A., Nowozin, S.: Which training methods for GANs do actually converge? In: International Conference on Machine Learning, pp. 3481–3490. PMLR (2018)

18. Moran, N., Schmidt, D., Zhong, Y., Coady, P.: Noisier2Noise: learning to denoise from unpaired noisy data. In: Proceedings of the IEEE/CVF Conference on Computer Vision and Pattern Recognition, pp. 12064–12072 (2020)
19. Papkov, M., et al.: Noise2Stack: improving image restoration by learning from volumetric data. In: Haq, N., Johnson, P., Maier, A., Würfl, T., Yoo, J. (eds.) MLMIR 2021. LNCS, vol. 12964, pp. 99–108. Springer, Cham (2021). https://doi.org/10.1007/978-3-030-88552-6_10
20. Paszke, A., et al.: PyTorch: an imperative style, high-performance deep learning library. In: Advances in Neural Information Processing Systems, pp. 8026–8037 (2019)
21. Richardson, W.H.: Bayesian-based iterative method of image restoration. JoSA **62**(1), 55–59 (1972)
22. Ronneberger, O., Fischer, P., Brox, T.: U-net: convolutional networks for biomedical image segmentation. In: Navab, N., Hornegger, J., Wells, W.M., Frangi, A.F. (eds.) MICCAI 2015. LNCS, vol. 9351, pp. 234–241. Springer, Cham (2015). https://doi.org/10.1007/978-3-319-24574-4_28
23. Russakoff, D.B., Tomasi, C., Rohlfing, T., Maurer, C.R.: Image similarity using mutual information of regions. In: Pajdla, T., Matas, J. (eds.) ECCV 2004. LNCS, vol. 3023, pp. 596–607. Springer, Heidelberg (2004). https://doi.org/10.1007/978-3-540-24672-5_47
24. Sage, D., et al.: DeconvolutionLab2: an open-source software for deconvolution microscopy. Methods **115**, 28–41 (2017)
25. Wang, Z., Simoncelli, E.P., Bovik, A.C.: Multiscale structural similarity for image quality assessment. In: 2003 the Thrity-Seventh Asilomar Conference on Signals, Systems & Computers, vol. 2, pp. 1398–1402. IEEE (2003)
26. Weigert, M., et al.: Content-aware image restoration: pushing the limits of fluorescence microscopy. Nat. Methods **15**(12), 1090–1097 (2018)
27. Xie, Y., Wang, Z., Ji, S.: Noise2same: Optimizing a self-supervised bound for image denoising. In: Advances in Neural Information Processing Systems, vol. 33, pp. 20320–20330 (2020)
28. Yuanji, W., Jianhua, L., Yi, L., Yao, F., Qinzhong, J.: Image quality evaluation based on image weighted separating block peak signal to noise ratio. In: Proceedings of the 2003 International Conference on Neural Networks and Signal Processing, vol. 2, pp. 994–997. IEEE (2003)
29. Zhang, Y., et al.: A Poisson-Gaussian denoising dataset with real fluorescence microscopy images. In: Proceedings of the IEEE Conference on Computer Vision and Pattern Recognition, pp. 11710–11718 (2019)
30. Zhu, J.Y., Park, T., Isola, P., Efros, A.A.: Unpaired image-to-image translation using cycle-consistent adversarial networks. In: Proceedings of the IEEE International Conference on Computer Vision, pp. 2223–2232 (2017)

Author Index

Y. Xue et al. (Eds.): DALI 2023, LNCS 14379, pp. 167–168, 2024.
https://doi.org/10.1007/978-3-031-58171-7

Printed in the United States
by Baker & Taylor Publisher Services